Victorian Feminists

Emily Davies

Frances Power Cobbe

Josephine Butler

Millicent Garrett Fawcett

Victorian Feminists

BARBARA CAINE

OXFORD UNIVERSITY PRESS

Oxford University Press, Walton Street, Oxford OX2 6DP

Oxford New York Toronto
Delhi Bombay Calcutta Madras Karachi
Kuala Lumpur Singapore Hong Kong Tokyo
Nairobi Dar es Salaam Cape Town
Melbourne Auckland Madrid
and associated companies in
Berlin Ibadan

Oxford is a trade mark of Oxford University Press

Published in the United States
by Oxford University Press Inc., New York

First published 1992
First issued as a Clarendon paperback 1993

British Library Cataloguing in Publication Data
Data available

Library of Congress Cataloging in Publication Data
Caine, Barbara.
Victorian feminists/Barbara Caine.
Includes bibliographical references (p.   ) and index.
1. Feminists—Great Britain—Biography.   2. Feminism—Great
Britain—History—19th Century.   I. Title.
HQ1595A3C34   1992   305.42'0941—dc20   91–24220
ISBN 0–19–820170–2
ISBN 0–19–820433–7 (Pbk.)

1 3 5 7 9 10 8 6 4 2

Printed in Great Britain
on acid-free paper by
Butler and Tanner Ltd,
Frome, Somerset

73600

For Larry, Tessa, and Nicholas

Preface

THIS book on Victorian feminism has had a long period of gestation—some ten years altogether. From the time that I became interested in women's history in the early 1970s, my attention has been focused on feminist ideas and activities. In part, this was a result of the lack of general historical works on Victorian women at the time. Lacking other bibliographical aids, when I decided I wanted to know something about women in Victorian England, I began simply by looking up the catalogue entries under 'Woman' and 'Women' first in the Public Library in Sydney and then in the British Museum. It was a wonderful introduction to the field as I came upon a vast wealth of miscellaneous books, pamphlets, sermons, autobiographies, and essays on a host of different questions. But of course the greatest number was devoted to arguing about the nature and the duties of women and about whether their existing situation was unjust and amenable to change. There were suffrage and anti-suffrage writings, debates about whether or not women could regenerate society, about whether the existing marriage laws were unjust, and about whether or not a man should be allowed to marry his deceased wife's sister. In all it rapidly became clear the 'woman question' was not only a complex and multi-layered one, but that it had been a major preoccupation throughout the nineteenth century.

The great body of this material centred on feminist activity and on the women's movement and it was this question which I took up. Frances Cobbe's autobiography and her collections of essays came to light very early in this process of exploration and, like many recent feminist scholars, I was quite fascinated by Cobbe's attacks on marriage, her advocacy of celibacy, and her adulation of close female friendships, and then by her criticism of the medical profession and her insistence that it played a central role in maintaining women's oppression. But alongside all of this was the need to come to terms with the way in which Cobbe combined staunch support for the Conservative Party with the most outspoken criticism of the position of women and of the various social institutions which perpetuated their oppression.

That Cobbe's approach was not the only one evident amongst Victorian feminists became very obvious when I began reading about Millicent Fawcett and Josephine Butler and after working through their papers on a study leave, I planned a book of essays on Victorian feminism which would look at the three of them and at what I then saw as the appropriate framework for assessing their views. This centred on the need to recognize the connections between liberalism and feminism on the one hand, and on feminism and Victorian domestic ideology on the other. The need to recognize the debt feminism had to both of these currents seemed to me very important, as did the impossibility of simply applying labels like 'liberal' or 'conservative' to feminists or to feminism.

This book never quite saw the light of day. I got as far as the writing of a synopsis for it, but when I began circulating it to publishers, there were no takers. The history of Victorian feminism was of little interest even to feminist scholars in the mid-1970s, most of whom combined a certain impatience and intolerance with the moderation and the sexual reticence of Victorian feminists with an intense interest in exploring the lives and experiences of ordinary or typical women. I put the plan away for a while and went on to other things, but my interest in this question did not abate and I came back to it after writing at length about a group of women who were non- and even anti-feminists.

While I moved away from the study of feminism, many others took it up. The 1980s has seen a huge wave of interest in feminism and its history. Nineteenth- and early twentieth-century English feminism have certainly not been neglected by recent scholars. Many of the blanks in my own research have been filled in by detailed studies of feminist educational, political, and sexual campaigns. The relationship between feminist ideas and other political ideologies, the importance for feminism of particular ideas of womanhood and of close networks of friends and relations have all been discussed, showing, in the process, how diverse and complex a phenomenon feminism both is and was in the past.

My own approach to Victorian feminism has of course changed

enormously as a result of this work. Any individual work is dependent on the research of others in their own and in related fields and the whole subject of Victorian feminism has been largely transformed in the last ten years by the work of Sheila Jeffries, Sandra Holton, Susan Kingsley Kent, Martha Vicinus, Lucy Bland, and many others. Hence this study contains far more discussion about the importance of sexual questions and of the sexual double standard, the extent to which feminism was a form of personal politics and a way of life and not simply an ideology, and far more emphasis on the complex and problematical relationship between feminism and liberalism than I had originally contemplated.

It is not only research on feminism that has been important in changing the ways in which one can write the history of feminism, but also much recent work on political theory, literary theory, cultural history, and autobiography and biography. And while this work is in many ways conventional in its form and approach, it is not an attempt at a definitive study so much as a 'reading' of Victorian feminism in general and of four individual feminists in particular, looking at the ways their ideas developed and were articulated and at the ways in which they constructed both their feminism and their own lives.

The reading that is offered here does not offer any form of psychoanalytic approach to its subjects nor does it deconstruct their texts. I am concerned not so much with individual personalities and conflicts in themselves as with the ways in which individuals experience particular versions of the general situation of women. What the book offers then is contextual readings which seek to explain the nature of particular feminist beliefs and ideas in terms of their place within an individual life lived within a broad social, economic, and political framework. The biographies that are offered concentrate on the question of how these particular women experienced the general situation of Victorian women within their own familial and social settings, how and why they came to see it as oppressive and as wrong, and what they chose to do about it.

My reading of these feminists of course reflects my own feminist beliefs and experiences. It is, on the whole, a sympathetic reading which assumes their analysis of the situation of women to be basically correct and it includes a strong sense of affinity with them and their approach. This affinity does not centre on particular beliefs, values, or moral norms and I do not by any means seek a revival of Victorian values. But it does seem to me that Victorian feminists faced dilemmas which continue to trouble contemporary feminists—and that their articulation and discussion of these dilemmas have a continuing relevance and importance. The need to reconcile the underlying similarities between men and women with their equally fundamental differences with which Victorian feminists were so concerned is a problem which is integral to any form of feminism. In a similar way, all feminists have to reconcile the need to work and to negotiate relationships with men as fathers, husbands, lovers, sons, friends, and supporters with a sense that men, and sometimes these very men, are embodiments of patriarchal power, opponents, and sexual and commercial exploiters of women. The approach to these questions taken by Victorian feminists, while different from ours, none the less offers insights which underlie any feminist analysis. Our specific language and values differ greatly from those of Victorian feminists, but this difference should not preclude recognition of the extent to which we share some of the their basic concerns.

In the late 1970s and early 1980s it was common for both historians and contemporary feminists to castigate the nineteenth-century English women's movement for its sexual prudery, its refusal to acknowledge the existence of women's sexuality and its absolute failure to address the question of women's sexual pleasure. This Victorian approach was contrasted with the recognition by twentieth-century feminists of the importance to women of their own sexuality. But it seems to me that on this question, almost more than on any other, one can see the continuity between Victorian feminism and our own. For both Victorian feminists and twentieth-century ones speak in terms of the dominant sexual values of their time. Mid-twentieth-century feminists did not discover women's sexuality, but rather took their emphasis upon it from a sexual liberation movement which has since ceased to be seen as offering women liberation or fulfilment. Indeed, the critique of the sexual revolution has found its counterpart in a re-evaluation of Victorian feminist attitudes to sexuality and in a new sense of the importance of their ideas about sexual exploitation as a central issue in women's oppression. In my own view, this re-evaluation is not only overdue, but needs to be looked at in terms of all epochs of feminism—not in order to evaluate their merits as against each other, but in order to show how deeply embedded the feminism of any period is in its surrounding culture.

In writing this book I have been greatly helped by many people and have made extensive use of the resources of several libraries. Like anyone interested in English feminism, I have spent a lot of time at the Fawcett Library and I would like to thank David Doughan, Susan Cross, and Veronica Perkins for all their help. For permission to quote from the papers in their possession, I thank the Fawcett Library, City of London Polytechnic for the Butler Papers, the Fawcett Papers and their Autograph Collection of Letters; the Mistress and Fellows of Girton College Cambridge for the Davies Papers and the photographs of Emily Davies; the Manchester Public Library for the National Union of Women's Suffrage Societies Collection and finally, the owners of the Somerville Papers which are deposited in the Bodleian Library for the letters of Frances Power Cobbe. I thank the Fawcett Library and the Mary Evans Picture Library for supplying the pictures of Cobbe and Fawcett for the frontispiece and for the portraits of Philippa Fawcett, of Frances Cobbe as a young woman, of Millicent Fawcett in the 1909 and the picture of the procession to commemorate the 121st birthday of John Stuart Mill.

While I must take full responsibility for all the views and errors in this book, a number of people have been vitally important in the writing of it. My greatest debt is to Sally Alexander and Judith Allen who have shared my enthusiasm for 19th-century feminism for more than a decade. This book was in fact formulated in a series of conversations with each of them in turn over great distances and a long time-span and I thank them both for their wonderful and stimulating friendship and for sharing with me not only their vast knowledge of feminist history and theory, but their critical insights and ideas. But the book was not only discussed in a feminist context. In the course of many conversations over many cups of tea, Deryck Schreuder has shared with me something of his extensive knowledge, understanding, and enthusiasm for Victorian liberalism. I hope that my discussion of it does justice to his ideas. For the expansion of my original trio of Cobbe, Fawcett, and Butler to include Emily Davies, I am indebted to José Harris. It was her

xii PREFACE

invitation to talk about Emily Davies to a 'Special Subject' seminar on nineteenth-century political and social thought which made me re-read Davies and realize how important she was both in the development of Victorian feminism and in twentieth-century ideas about it.

In addition to those who helped in the framing of the book, I would like to thank those who read the earlier versions of it. Carole Adams and Diana Caine worked on the first draft and were ideal readers, managing to convey great enthusiasm alongside careful, detailed, and constructive critical comment which made reworking the book a much easier task. Judith Allen, Robyn Cooper, and Martha Vicinus read later versions and helped greatly with the fine tuning. Stephen Garton exercised his incomparable editorial and critical skills throughout and provided great help in structuring the book. My debt to him is enormous. When it was done, Rhona Ovedoff gave me invaluable help with the proofs and Index.

I would like to thank the staff at Oxford University Press for making the whole process of writing and publishing such a rewarding one. Both Robert Faber and Tony Morris have been wonderful editors, helping to alleviate by their careful and assiduous letters the inevitable isolation involved in writing a book.

Finally I wish to dedicate this book to my family. To Larry Boyd, who continues to provide the supportive framework which makes research not only possible but pleasurable, to my daughter Tessa whose interest in feminism in general and in my feminist research in particular gives the whole endeavour an added purpose, and to Nicholas who eventually came to accept that word processors are not really rocket controls and thereby refrained from obliterating the entire manuscript.

BARBARA CAINE

Sydney 1991

Contents

List of Plates

1

Introduction

THE lives and activities of prominent nineteenth-century English feminists have long been a subject of great interest to historians. Decades before the advent of anything called women's history, there were already biographies of leading feminist activists as well as accounts of some of the more dramatic campaigns undertaken by the women's movement. The suffrage struggle was the most often written about, but there were also books dealing with the campaigns to improve the education of middle-class women and the fight for the repeal of the Contagious Diseases Acts.[1]

In recent years there has been a considerable expansion in the extent of this interest, coupled with a whole series of new approaches to the question of feminism and of the nature and activities of the English women's movement. While biographies of leading feminists continue to appear, these are increasingly accompanied by life histories of less prominent women who serve to illustrate, even to typify, the social origins and outlook of the women's movement or to show the full extent of its geographical

[1] See e.g. Ray Strachey, *The Cause: A Short History of the Women's Movement in Great Britain*, London, 1928 (repr. 1978); Barbara Stephen, *Emily Davies and Girton College*, London, 1927; A. S. G. Butler, *Portrait of Josephine Butler*, London, 1954; Hester Burton, *Barbara Bodichon*, London, 1949; Josephine Kamm, *Rapiers and Battleaxes: The Women's Movement and its Aftermath*, London, 1966, and *Hope Deferred: Girls' Education in English History*, London, 1965; Miriam Ramelson, *The Petticoat Rebellion*, London, 1967; J. A. and Olive Banks, *Feminism and Family Planning*, Liverpool, 1964.

and social range.[2] The membership of the women's suffrage movement has been subject to analysis, as has the relationship between
it and all the various national political parties.[3] Historical research
has now extended to cover the expanding public role of late Victorian women,[4] the connection between the women's movement
and the fictional and journalistic creation of a 'new woman' in
the 1890s, and the whole transformation of political campaigning
which the women's movement wrought.[5]

As a result of this work, there has been a significant change in
our understanding of the nature of Victorian feminism. Where
once feminism was defined as a belief in the need for equal rights
between women and men, there is now a widespread recognition
of the importance Victorian feminists attached to establishing and
maintaining sexual differences between men and women.[6] The idea
that the English women's movement was concerned primarily,
even exclusively, with gaining access for women to the public
sphere, has given way to an ever-increasing recognition of the
extent of Victorian feminist concern with the oppression of women
in domestic life, in marriage, and in all forms of sexual relations.[7]
The assumption that feminism was an offshoot of liberalism has
now been questioned in the light of a growing interest in the
religious, the socialist, and even the conservative roots of feminism

---

[2] Sheila Fletcher, *Maude Royden*, Oxford, 1989; Ann Morley and Liz Stanley, *The Life and Death of Emily Wilding Davison*, London, 1989; Jill Liddington, *The Life and Times of a Respectable Rebel: Selina Cooper*, London, 1984.

[3] See e.g. Jill Liddington and Jill Norris, *One Hand Tied Behind Us: The Rise of the Women's Suffrage Movement*, London, 1978; Andrew Rosen, *Rise Up Women*, London, 1974; Sandra Holton, *Feminism and Democracy: Women's Suffrage and Reform Politics in Britain, 1900–1914*, Cambridge, 1986; Leslie Parker Hume, *The National Union of Women's Suffrage Societies*, New York, 1982; Martha Vicinus, *Independent Women: Work and Community for Single Women, 1850–1920*, London and Chicago, 1985.

[4] Patricia Hollis, *Ladies Elect: Women in English Local Government 1865–1914*, Oxford, 1987; Jane Rendall, *Equal or Different: Women's Politics 1800–1914*, Oxford, 1987, see Pt. II, 'Class, Party and Sexual Politics'.

[5] David Rubinstein, *Before the Suffragettes: Women's Emancipation in the 1890s*, Brighton, 1986; Lisa Tickner, *The Spectacle of Women: Imagery of the Suffrage Campaign, 1907–1914*, London, 1987.

[6] See Banks, *Feminism and Family Planning*, 5–7; cf. Holton, *Feminism and Democracy*, 12–13, and Philippa Levine, *Victorian Feminism, 1850–1900*, London, 1987, 16–23.

[7] See Patricia Hollis, ed., *Women in Public: The English Women's Movement 1850–1900*, London, 1979; cf. Susan Kingsley Kent, *Sex and Suffrage in Britain, 1860–1914*, Princeton, NJ, 1987.

on the one hand, and an increasing awareness of the very problematical relationship between feminism and liberalism on the
other.[8] Inevitably, as the study of feminism has expanded and
developed, historians have become ever more aware of the range
and complexity of feminist activities and of the diversity of
approach and political commitment even amongst the leading
figures of the English women's movement.

In this book I wish to continue this broad discussion of the
diversity and complexity of Victorian feminism by exploring the
intellectual approach and the theoretical framework of four prominent Victorian feminists. This focus is in some ways a narrow one,
but it allows for a detailed analysis of the intricacies of feminist
ideas and beliefs which is not possible if one focuses on whole
movements or on particular campaigns. I am interested in the
interaction between personal experiences, political attitudes,
religious beliefs, social values on the one hand, and feminist ideas
and activities on the other. It is this interaction which seems to me
both to define and to show the full range and complexity of the
feminism of any particular individual.

The four women in this study, Emily Davies, Frances Power
Cobbe, Josephine Butler, and Millicent Garrett Fawcett, were all
very prominent within the nineteenth-century women's
movement. Davies, Butler, and Fawcett each led a major feminist
campaign, respectively the battle for the admission of women to
universities, the fight for the repeal of the Contagious Diseases
Acts, and the suffrage campaign. Cobbe, although not the leader
of a particular campaign, was active in several. These campaigns
do not, however, provide the central focus for this book. It is the
process by which they became feminists, the nature of their analyses
of women's oppression, and the relationship between this analysis
and their other ideas and experiences in which I am particularly
interested. Looking at them from this perspective, one becomes
aware of the wide range of ideas held and developed by Victorian
feminists on many questions about the situation of women, the
nature of femininity, the basis of sexual oppression, while at the

[8] Strachey, *The Cause*; Richard Evans, *The Feminists: Women's Emancipation
Movements in Europe*, London, 1978; cf. Olive Banks, *Faces of Feminism: A Study
of Feminism as a Social Movement*, Oxford, 1986; Zillah Eisenstein, *The Radical
Future of Liberal Feminism*, New York, 1981.

same time seeing the difficulties they faced in translating their theoretical positions into particular activities. One becomes aware also of the complexities and of the many tensions that underlay their whole approach to the situation of women, and of the extent to which they were opposed to, inspired by, and constrained by the prevailing discourse on gender, sexuality, and sexual relations which continued throughout their period.

One difficulty faced by anyone attempting to write the history of feminism is the fact that the word 'feminism' itself was not coined until the end of the nineteenth century.[9] It entered into common usage only in the years immediately preceding the outbreak of the First World War. As a result of this, contemporary historians applying the term 'feminism' to women—or men—in previous centuries do so in a number of different, even contradictory ways. For some, any articulate and active women, particularly any women who wrote about themselves or their lives, become feminists.[10] For others, feminism requires particular beliefs or activities—although there is no agreement as to exactly what these are or how they changed over time.[11]

This broad problem applies very directly to Victorian England. Here too, almost all contemporary historians use the term freely to describe not only those who were active within the women's movement, but also a wide range of female activists and women writers who preceded or who had very little to do with the women's movement. Hence both the meaning of the term and its precise application remain vague and variable. One particular difficulty posed by the Victorian case centres on the widespread recognition that certain aspects of the legal and social position of women were unjust, inequitable, and in need of reform. Thus many writers who would not endorse campaigns to alter the situation of women recognized the need for some reforms in their legal or social situation. In a similar way, certain reforms, in education or in the laws pertaining to the property of married women or in the right to

[9] See Karen Offen, 'Defining Feminism: A Comparative Historical Approach', *Signs*, 14 (1988), 119–57.

[10] See e.g. Moira Ferguson, *First Feminists: British Women Writers*, 1578–1799, Bloomington, Ind., 1975.

[11] Offen, 'Defining Feminism', 119–21. See also Rosalind Delmar, 'What is Feminism?', in *What is Feminism?*, ed. Juliet Mitchell and Ann Oakley, Oxford, 1986, 9–14.

custody, were supported by people who were the determined opponents of women's suffrage or indeed of any idea of the equality of men and women.[12] The range of campaigns to reform the situation of women meant that people could be quite active and outspoken in some, particularly for example those to improve secondary education and extend tertiary education to women, while remaining implacably opposed to others, such as women's suffrage.[13]

Several historians have addressed themselves to this problem in the last few years. Some, such as Olive Banks, have simply accepted that close definition is not possible, using the term in a broad way to refer to 'any groups that have tried to change the position of women, or the ideas about women', and relying on the exploration of the different 'faces' of feminism to show the divergencies between a range of rather varied approaches to the situation of women.[14] Others, such as Philippa Levine, have attempted to assert the feminist consciousness of those most prominent and most closely involved in the English women's movement by stressing 'the conscious woman-centredness of its interests' and insisting on the extent to which Victorian feminism involved the adoption of a set of values different from those dominant within the period. Rejecting the widely-held view of the English women's movement as a series of distinct campaigns which were only loosely connected, Levine has examined the large numbers of women who were prominent in many campaigns and who clearly had a strong sense of the unity underlying all the different campaigns.[15]

Taking a radically different approach in regard to the question of American women, Nancy Cott has recently argued that both of these approaches are misguided. In her view, the term feminism should not be applied to those who lived or worked before it was introduced into the language. Its introduction in the 1910s marked the end of the older 'woman movement' with its central concern about suffrage and women's rights and its belief in the underlying unity of the female sex, and 'signaled a new phase in the debate

[12] See Brian Harrison, *Separate Spheres: The Opposition to Women's Suffrage in Britain*, London, 1978, 55.

[13] See Joyce Senders Pederson, 'Some Victorian Headmistresses: A Conservative Tradition of Social Reform', *Victorian Studies*, 24 (1981), 463–88.

[14] Banks, *Faces of Feminism*, 3.

[15] Levine, *Victorian Feminism*, 19–23.

and agitation about women's rights and freedoms'.[16]

Cott is unquestionably right in her insistence that historians recognize the significance of the introduction of this neologism and of the widespread discussion about its meaning and application which occurred when it was introduced. But this recognition does not necessarily require one to jettison the term when dealing with the nineteenth century. Most political terms—including, for example, liberalism and socialism—are used retrospectively to apply to individuals, groups, or ideas which have some recognized or assumed similarity with those for which the term was originally coined. But the history both of politics and of political theory would be impossible if we did not use these terms. It is hard to think of any broad political or social term or label which has not been problematical or controversial in its meaning or its usage amongst scholars. But to jettison them would leave one without any signposts in a sea of chaos. What needs to be recognized is that there have been significant shifts in the range of ideas, attitudes, and concerns of feminists, as of other political groups and that these shifts are often indicated by changes in the language feminists use. As we shall see, there were significant shifts in the outlook of British, as of American feminists in the early years of the twentieth century, but these were changes within feminism rather than involving a change from something which was pre-feminist or non-feminist to feminism.

I propose then to continue to use the term 'feminist' to describe the women in this study even though none of them used it in reference to themselves, their ideas, or their activities. No other term suggests adequately the extent or the intensity of their concern about the situation of women or their sense of the need to remove the injustices, the obstacles, and the forms of oppression which women faced. Indeed, the definition of feminism offered by Nancy Cott seems to me to apply to all of these women and to state very succinctly their central beliefs. Cott sees three core beliefs as fundamental to feminism: an opposition to sex hierarchy, a belief that women's condition is socially constructed and not ordained either by God or nature, and finally a perception by women that

---

[16] Nancy Cott, *The Grounding of Modern Feminism*, New Haven, Conn., and London, 1987, 3.

they constitute both a biological sex and a social grouping.[17] Davies, Cobbe, Butler, and Fawcett all subscribed to these beliefs, as did many of their contemporaries.

The very generality of this, as of any definition of feminism, means that for Victorians, as for twentieth-century women, designating someone a feminist does not of itself indicate exactly what they thought, even about the nature or the specific causes of women's oppression. The most cursory glance at the ideas and beliefs of the women in this study serves to show their differences from each other on many key issues. All four would obviously have agreed that women were legally, socially, and economically oppressed and that this was an unjust state of affairs which required a remedy. But they disagreed about the basis and the nature of this oppression and about how it should be reformed; about the nature of women and the extent to which the differences between men and women were innate or socially conditioned. They disagreed also about the kind of woman who would and should emerge after women had been emancipated. All of them believed that women and men should have equal political and legal rights, but they differed strongly on the question whether women and men were or could ever be equal intellectually and morally.

These theoretical disagreements were accompanied by differences of opinion regarding feminist strategy. There were sometimes fierce arguments amongst them concerning the targets they should attack, the men they should seek as allies, the relationship between their objectives and other campaigns for political reform, the role which women themselves should take in fighting to end their oppression, and the ways in which the feminist campaigns should be fought. For all of them the emancipation of women was a central goal, but it was a goal open to very different interpretations. They addressed and were preoccupied by many of the same questions and issues, but they analysed and attempted to solve them in very different terms.

As one might expect, from their differences of opinion on these basic questions, Cobbe, Davies, Fawcett, and Butler did not make up a coherent group. They all knew each other and were involved at various times in related or even in the same campaigns. Some of them were allies, or offered mutual support and friendship. But

[17] Ibid. 4.

they were not close friends and each of them expressed strong reservations about or opposition to the ideas and activities of the others on many occasions. What they offer then is not a single feminist network, but rather an insight into the range of ideas, experiences, and beliefs which made up mid-Victorian feminism. Hence the approach will largely be a comparative one as each woman will be treated separately in order to delineate as fully as possible the nature of her own feminism.

The differences amongst these women extend to differences in age and hence in the generations to which they belonged. Davies, Butler, and Cobbe were all born in the period between 1822 and 1830. Fawcett, by contrast, was not born until 1847. Despite this, I wish to look at Fawcett in relation to the others. Despite her youth, her involvement in the women's movement and her engagement in feminist debates were contemporaneous with theirs: like Davies, Cobbe, and Butler, she became deeply involved in the women's movement in the 1860s and continued that involvement until the end of the century. Hence her intellectual roots were struck in the mid-nineteenth century and were very similar to theirs.

The differences in age between Fawcett and the others obviously affected the duration of their involvement in the women's movement and the nature of the questions they had to deal with. Fawcett was only 20 when she first joined the executive Committee of the London National Society for Women's Suffrage in 1867 and she remained a leading figure in the suffrage campaign until 1918. This was more than a decade after the deaths of Cobbe and Butler. Davies was still alive, but she had effectively withdrawn from any involvement in the movement. Fawcett was thus a transitional figure between the mid-nineteenth- and the early twentieth-century women's movements, and it is mostly through her ideas, activities, and conflicts that one can see how and when Victorian feminism was supplanted by its twentieth-century counterpart.

As this suggests, one central theme in this book will involve an exploration of feminism as a personal form of politics, one which centres on the domestic and private sphere. The idea that 'the personal is political' and that women's experiences and perspectives are an integral part of feminist theory was one of the basic insights of the feminist upsurge of the late 1960s and 1970s. Victorian feminists themselves did not argue that personal experience was

the basis of their political conviction. But none the less, this idea
offers a useful insight into the ideas and the activities of Victorian
feminism. Each of the women here experienced a particular version
of girlhood and womanhood and hence was aware in her own life
of at least some of the restrictions and forms of oppression which
all the women of the time faced. The complexity of their own
situations and the solutions they found to their own problems were
often broadened and expanded to make up part of this feminist
framework. Their personal experiences help us to understand the
genesis of their feminist beliefs and hence go some way to explaining the reasons for the various different strands to be found within
Victorian feminism.

Once one begins to look for the personal and experiential dimension of Victorian feminism, one becomes aware, too, that many
feminists did in fact refer either to their own experience or to their
knowledge of the experience of other women and that they often
pointed to these experiences in explaining how and why they took
up the women's cause. In some cases, one can see quite clearly the
importance of particular kinds of deprivation or of a sense of
injustice suffered within a family in developing a feminist consciousness.

This sense of private injustice could even determine the direction
of feminist energies. For Emily Davies, for example, the sense of
personal injustice centred on the fact that she and her sister were
given almost no formal education, while all her brothers were sent
to major public schools and then to Cambridge. For her, as later
for Virginia Woolf, this educational deprivation in gentlemen's
families was one of the most significant aspects of women's
oppression. Her sense of personal suffering helps to explain why,
despite her lack of scholarly interests—or of sympathy with young
women students—she devoted so much of her life to the battle to
gain access for women to higher education. It also underlay her
insistence that women be given exactly the same kind of tertiary
education as men. In other cases, feminists referred to the importance of their knowledge of what women suffered. Cobbe and Butler
in particular stressed the significance of what they had discovered
about the lives of other women in the course of their philanthropic
work in turning their attention to the immediate need for the
emancipation of women. Cobbe's interest in workhouse inmates,

like Butler's months spent amongst the dockland prostitutes of Liverpool, provided the basis for much of their work.

If one takes the question of personal experience in its broadest sense, it also becomes clear that suffering is not the only seed-bed of feminism. Indeed, as the experiences of such notable nineteenth-century women as Caroline Norton, Florence Nightingale, and Beatrice Webb demonstrate, certain kinds of personal suffering often led away from rather than towards feminist involvement. By contrast, experiences of enjoyable female companionship and of domesticity shared with beloved women, and awareness of the talents and abilities which women exhibited in many spheres, could be, as they were for Frances Cobbe, a direct path into the women's movement. For all the women in this study, a vocal feminist commitment in turn brought new relationships, new ideas, and new concerns. Their feminism was not just a set of discrete objectives, but an orientation to the whole world in which they lived. As a result, it contained a celebration of female competence and of female life which was as important as was their criticism of male dominance in the social, legal, and cultural spheres.

To say feminism involves a private dimension is not to deny the importance of public or national politics in the lives or thought of Victorian feminists, many of whom were vitally interested in the national political scene and believed that there was a close connection between their feminist views on the one hand, and their adherence to particular political parties on the other. Frances Cobbe and Emily Davies were staunch Tories. Butler and Fawcett, by contrast, were both strong supporters of the Liberal Party. But for all their sense of this connection, the ties between adherence to a particular political party and feminist politics appear rather complicated. While both Davies and Cobbe attempted to organize their feminist campaigns with the help and support of other Tories, they frequently found that they were rather isolated and that others who shared their party affiliations did not share their sympathy for the plight of women. But, of course, this sense of isolation was not confined to Conservatives. Although Fawcett and Butler knew many Liberals who were sympathetic to their views, they too had to contend with the indifference or even hostility of the Liberal leadership and of the parliamentary Liberal Party as a whole. They also had to come to terms, at various stages, with the realization that few even of the most sympathetic men could understand their real horror at the sexual exploitation of women or their own recognition that the battle which they fought was ultimately a battle of women against men.

While their national political activities were closely related to their feminist agitation, it is not possible to establish or to determine the nature of the feminist beliefs of any of these women simply by referring to their other political ideas. The fact that Davies and Cobbe described themselves as Tories while Fawcett and Butler were Liberals tells us nothing about their overall analysis of women's oppression, nor does it offer any insight into their ideas about the nature or the significance of the differences between men and women. Indeed, as we shall see, if the four women are grouped according to their beliefs on these central feminist questions, they form pairs which cut across their national political affiliations. Butler and Cobbe both tended to emphasize the sexual differences between men and women, basing their demands for the emancipation of women on a particular idea of women's nature. In their view, all women were innately nurturant and compassionate and they sought to have these qualities exercised within the public sphere.

Fawcett and Davies voiced contrasting views. While not wishing to deny that innate differences existed between men and women, both thought that these differences were greatly exaggerated. They both tended to emphasize the intellectual similarities between men and women rather than concentrating on their physical or moral differences. Thus while the question of national politics and party affiliation remains a central one in the study of Victorian feminism, it is one which requires a great deal of careful investigation and analysis.

Within the period covered by this study, the nature of politics and of women's involvement in it changed considerably. Many women became members of party auxiliaries and began to exercise substantial influence over particular political campaigns, while even larger numbers became involved in local government through their participation on School Boards, as Poor Law Guardians and as members of local governments.[18] Although very much aware of these developments, none of the women in this study took a leading

[18] Hollis, *Ladies Elect*, *passim*.

role in them. Davies was a member of the first London School Board and Fawcett joined with others in the National Union of Women's Suffrage Societies in supporting the entry of women into local government. But neither of them devoted the time and energy to these activities that went into their major campaigns. Their energies were directed to national institutions or to politics at a national level. In part this is a reflection of their ages and of their social milieu: Butler's father worked for legislative reform at a national level as did she; Fawcett was married to a Member of Parliament and always saw Parliament as the centre of political life. Davies and Cobbe also mixed with parliamentary circles and chose to work with leading political figures who were demonstrably national leaders. For all of them, the entry of women into local government, while important, meant a smaller-scale endeavour than they were prepared to countenance for themselves.

For Victorian feminists, as for anyone else involved in Victorian public life, religious questions were ones of central importance. For Cobbe and Butler, religion was probably the most important question of all. Their religious beliefs were central to their feminist commitment and provided the framework through which they could articulate their feminist beliefs. Both had suffered profound religious crises in their adolescence or early adulthood. The crises were very different in kind, Butler's centring on the need to recognize herself as called by God to fulfil a special duty in fighting misery and sin, while Cobbe experienced a painful loss of faith in traditional Christianity and had to build a new faith which was less authoritarian and patriarchal than the old. The resolution of Butler's religious crisis laid the foundation which enabled her to undertake the Contagious Diseases agitation, secure in the knowledge of her special relationship with Christ. Cobbe's new religious position centred on her belief in a rational and benevolent Deity, and this in turn was the basis for her insistence on the moral autonomy of women. It allowed her to insist on the equality between men and women without in any way undermining either the significance of sexual difference or the value of women's traditional domestic role.

Neither Davies nor Fawcett experienced the personal religious anguish of the other two, although both rejected the narrow Evangelicalism of their families of origin in favour of the Broad-Church

views of F. D. Maurice. But religion was none the less very important to Davies who rested her own belief in the equality of the sexes
on the existence of one moral law, one catechism, and one set of
social and religious obligations within the Church of England,
which applied equally to women and men. She argued that the
approach evident within religious education should be evident
everywhere. Fawcett, while apparently continuing to be a church-
goer, seems to have had least trouble with religion and was the
one least inclined to include religious discussions in her feminist
activities.

While religion was a central element in the lives of many Victorian feminists, the history of Victorian feminism does not connect
up particularly closely with the history of religion in the nineteenth
century. For feminists, 1858 was a more significant year than 1859
as it saw the start of the Langham Place Circle and of the *English
Woman's Journal*. It was far more significant for them than the
publication of either Darwin's *On the Origin of Species* or *Essays
and Reviews* in 1859. While scientific and religious views played
their role in the development of feminism, they did so in accordance
with the personal story and individual rhythm of particular feminists rather than through the fact that particular religious works
or controversies had any major impact on feminism as a whole.
Cobbe, for example, was concerned about the publication of *On
the Origin of Species*, but this was because she saw it as the harbinger
of a new materialism amongst scientists rather than because it
undermined her own religious position.[19] In a similar way, one can
see that feminists had their own concerns in the later part of the
century. Thus, for example, while others were preoccupied by the
religious doubts and the whole question of the relationship between
religious belief and moral duty, which were raised in Mrs Humphrey Ward's *Robert Elsemere*, for Millicent Garrett Fawcett, Mrs
Humphrey Ward was primarily not a religious writer but one
whose ideas needed to be discussed and combatted because she was
a leading anti-suffragist.

While many feminists, like Fawcett, were grateful both for the
amusement and the renewed energy they derived from enemies
such as Mrs Humphrey Ward, they were obviously more dependent on close friends and relatives. The importance of female

[19] Frances Power Cobbe, *Darwinism in Morals*, London, 1872.

support networks in the lives of Victorian women generally and of prominent women in particular has now been quite extensively demonstrated.[20] Each of the women in this study had a number of close female friends or relatives who formed part of a supportive network of women who shared their feminist concerns. In some cases, their initial engagement in the women's movement was undertaken through such friendships. But while each was part of a network, the four women in this study were not permanent parts of each other's network. On the contrary, the relationships amongst them involved conflict and hostility, much of which was generated by different ideas about and approaches to the women's movement. This conflict in itself illustrates the diversity and complexity of feminist ideas in the mid-nineteenth century. It also offers insights into the vulnerability which many feminists felt about themselves and about their position as women. All of them felt, at various times, that they and other women had only very limited opportunities to influence or to bring about change in their society. Hence the wrong move or the wrong approach would be disastrous, setting back the whole feminist cause irremediably. This sense of vulnerability obviously placed great strain on feminists and helps to explain the intensity of opposition some of them felt to others who were ostensibly engaged in the same general cause.

It is not only female networks, or relationships with other women, which were important in the feminist activities of these women. Some of them were also very greatly dependent on male friendship and male support. The friendships of these Victorian feminists with male colleagues and supporters will be given a close examination. The existence of strong male support for feminist objectives is one of the striking characteristics of Victorian feminist agitation. On the one hand this serves to question the idea that Victorian women lived in a world largely separated from men and to suggest that male–female interaction was much more common than is now often acknowledged.[21] But at the same time, male support was often problematical. Male supporters needed to be negotiated with—as they showed a strong tendency to want to take

---

[20] See Levine, *Victorian Feminism*, 19–21; Judith R. Walkowitz, *Prostitution and Victorian Society: Women, Class and the State*, Cambridge, 1980, 113–35.

[21] For the best-known statement about this separate female world, see Caroll Smith-Rosenberg, 'The Female World of Love and Ritual', *Signs*, 1 (1975), 1–29.

control of the women's movement out of the hands of women. Hence it was particularly in regard to them that Victorian feminists such as Josephine Butler articulated their ideas about the importance of female solidarity and of having women campaign for their own emancipation. Others, such as Emily Davies, took an opposing view, seeking joint action by women and men and rejecting any notion that women should campaign alone.

In view of this diversity, the question whether one can find any distinctive features of Victorian feminism necessarily arises. The answer to this question is yes: alongside all their differences, these women exhibit marked similarities. In part these similarities derive from the social and intellectual context which they shared. The mid-Victorian world in which they lived was characterized not only by a range of social, religious, and political ideas and institutions, but also by an intense concern about marriage and family life, about child-bearing and rearing, and about the physical and mental nature of women. The apparent demographic imbalance between men and women, the disinclination of either sex to marry, the problems faced by single women needing to support themselves, the inequities of the marriage laws, the moral consequences of patriarchal marriages and families, the sexual double standard were all subjects of extensive discussion before a women's movement emerged and hence became part of the framework in which Victorian feminism developed.

This framework gave Victorian feminists a concern about women's social and moral duties, about their need to preserve a moral order and create social harmony, which is certainly not shared by their twentieth-century counterparts, but which gives Victorian feminism its distinctive character.

It is important to recognize this fundamental similarity and to see the connections which underlay the diversity of Victorian feminism. Without this recognition, one runs the risk of misinterpreting their ideas and of emphasizing too greatly their differences. It is already becoming clear, for example, that one could differentiate between Davies on the one hand, and Cobbe and Butler on the other, on the grounds that Davies stressed the similarities between men and women while Cobbe and Butler concentrated more on their differences. Hence using contemporary terminology, one might characterize Davies as an 'equality feminist' while Butler and Cobbe address a 'feminism of difference'. But to do so would be extremely misleading.

In a recent article Joan Scott has warned contemporary historians against this division of feminists into 'equality' versus 'difference' on the grounds that, when paired dichotomously, equality and difference structure an impossible choice. 'If one opts for equality, one is forced to accept the notion that difference is antithetical to it. If one opts for difference, one admits that equality is unattainable.' But feminists cannot give up either the notion of 'difference' which, in Scott's view, 'has been our most creative analytic tool', nor of equality, without which it is impossible 'to speak to the principles and values of our political system'.[22] Scott's views have considerable relevance for an understanding of Victorian feminism, while they in turn provide a further illustration of her contention that feminism cannot be seen in terms of a simple dichotomy between equality and difference. All of these women believed both that women should be equal to men in legal and political terms and that they were fundamentally different from them. Even Emily Davies, while insisting that the differences between men and women were greatly exaggerated in her day, did not ever think of denying the existence or extent of sexual difference. She rejected the idea that women were innately nurturant, but not that they were morally both different from and superior to men. For her, as for all other feminists, it was necessary to address both the similarities between men and women and their differences. The balance which she struck between these two poles was different from that struck by either Butler or Cobbe, but it was none the less the case that she argued both for the equality of the sexes and for a recognition of the differences between them.

Looking back from a late twentieth-century perspective, what is most striking about this is that Davies chose the qualities she attributed to women from precisely the same model of femininity as did Butler, Cobbe, or Fawcett. Davies rejected certain aspects of this model and took it up in a more limited way than the others, but like them, the very articulation of her feminism involved negotiating with and reworking Victorian domestic ideology and hence meant that her feminism was organized around the same

[22] Joan Scott, 'Deconstructing Equality-versus-Difference: Or the Uses of Poststructuralist Theory for Feminism', *Feminist Studies*, 14 (1988), 43.

central set of beliefs and concerns. Several recent historians have bemoaned the conservatism of mid-Victorian feminism, evident particularly in the acceptance by feminists of certain prevailing ideas about the distinctive nature of womanhood. But what this serves really to illustrate is the extent to which feminism is necessarily bound by the preoccupations of the society in which it develops and by the terms in which the situation of women was currently being discussed. Had these mid-Victorian feminists not accepted and addressed the ideal of womanhood articulated in Victorian domestic ideology, they would not have been able to speak to their contemporaries at all. Once they addressed it, it was inevitable that the moral overtones of this ideal would become centrally involved in their feminist discourse. Their example should serve, not to warn us against the Victorians, but rather to sensitize us to the extent to which twentieth-century feminism has accepted and been organized around the agendas which have dominated the societies or the circles from which feminists have come—rather than one which feminists created for themselves. It is these shifts in agenda which allow us to explore and to understand the history of feminism and its relationship to the various societies in which it has developed.

2

Feminism and the Woman Question in Early Victorian England

ALTHOUGH the study of women's history has only been developed as an academic discipline in the last twenty years, it is not the case that the current wave of feminist activity is the first in which interest in women's past was manifest. Almost all feminist movements have had a strong interest in the history and in the activities and contributions of women. From its very beginnings, the nineteenth-century English women's movement sought to expand existing knowledge of the activities and achievements of women in the past. At the same time, like its American counterpart, the English women's movement had a powerful sense of its own historic importance and of its relationship to wider social and political change.

Nowhere is this sense of the historical importance—and of the historical connections between the women's movement and other social and political developments—more evident than in Ray Strachey's classic account of the movement, *The Cause*. 'The true history of the Women's Movement', Strachey argued, 'is the whole history of the nineteenth century.'[1] The women's movement was part of the broad sweep of liberal and progressive reform which was transforming society. Strachey emphasized this connection between the women's movement and the broader sweep of history

---

[1] Ray Strachey, *The Cause: A Short History of the Women's Movement in Great Britain*, London, 1928 (repr. London, 1978), 5.

by highlighting the importance for it of the Enlightenment and the Industrial Revolution.[2] The protest made by the women's movement at the confinement and injustices faced by women were, in Strachey's view, part of the liberal attack on traditional prejudices and injustice which was a central feature of the Enlightenment. This critique of women's confinement was supplemented by the demand for recognition of women's role in the public, particularly the philanthropic, realm. Indeed, it was the criticism of the limitations faced by women on the one hand, and their establishment of a new public role on the other, which provided the core of the movement, determining also its form: its organization around campaigns for legal, political and social reform.[3]

Strachey's analysis was a very illuminating one, nowhere more so than in her insistence that, despite their differences and even antipathy to each other, both the radical Mary Wollstonecraft and the Evangelical Hannah More need to be seen as forerunners of mid-Victorian feminism.[4] At the same time, she omitted some issues which now seem crucial to any discussion of the context of Victorian feminism. Where Strachey pictured a relatively fixed image of domestic women throughout the first half of the nineteenth century, recent historical and literary work suggests that this image was both complex and unstable. The establishment of a separate domestic sphere for women was but one aspect of the enormous changes in sexual and familial relationships which were occurring from the late eighteenth century through to the mid-nineteenth. These changes were accompanied by both anxiety and uncertainty and by the constant articulation of women's duty in a new social world.[5] Recent studies of literary developments at this time have pointed to the widespread discussion of sexual and familial relationships, indeed to the whole question of the nature of manhood and womanhood in both fiction and non-fiction in the late eighteenth and early nineteenth centuries, further emphasizing

[2] Ibid. 6.

[3] For an interesting discussion of *The Cause*, see Rosalind Delmar, 'What is Feminism?' in Juliet Mitchell and Ann Oakley, eds., *What is Feminism?*, Oxford, 1986, 14–24.

[4] Strachey, *The Cause*, 12–13.

[5] Leonore Davidoff and Catherine Hall, *Family Fortunes: Men and Women of the English Middle Class 1780–1850*, London, 1987; Catherine Hall, 'The Early Formation of Victorian Domestic Ideology', in Sandra Burman, ed., *Fit Work for Women*, London and Canberra, 1979.

the possibility that sexual relations and the whole gender order were undergoing a major upheaval.[6]

The recognition amongst contemporary scholars of the complexity of social and sexual changes in the late eighteenth and early nineteenth centuries has been accompanied by a far more critical analysis of the relationship between the Enlightenment and the emancipation of women than Strachey contemplated. Far from accepting the view that women's emancipation was a consequence of the Enlightenment, several recent writers have questioned the extent to which the social and political thought of the Enlightenment can be seen as supporting the movement for women's emancipation at all.[7] While several historians have argued that the Enlightenment critique of absolute government and the insistence on natural rights by the *philosophes* raised questions about the situation of women, others have pointed to the limited interest in the problems of women which they displayed—and to their broad acceptance of women's subordination.[8] Moreover the focus of the debate has shifted away from the political ideas of the Enlightenment and towards the representation of women in the scientific and medical writings of the time. The 'privileged epistemological position' of science and medicine meant that ideas evident within scientific writing had great currency and great sway.[9] One of the major interests of eighteenth-century philosophers and scientists lay in elaborating the physical differences between men and women. In this process, great stress was laid on the differences between male and female anatomy and physiology and on the connection between these differences and their differing intellectual capacities

[6] See also M. le Gates, 'The Cult of Womanhood in Eighteenth Century Thought', *Eighteenth Century Studies*, 10 (1976), 21–39; R. D. Moyniham, 'Clarissa and the Enlightened Woman as Literary Heroine', *Journal of the History of Ideas*, 36 (1975) 159–66; Margaret Kirkham, *Jane Austen: Feminism and Fiction*, Brighton and Princeton, NJ, 1983; Mary Poovey, *Uneven Developments: The Ideology of Gender in Mid-Victorian England*, Chicago, 1988.

[7] See Jane Rendall, *The Origins of Modern Feminism: Women in Britain, France and the United States*, Basingstoke, 1985, 7–32.

[8] See Jane Abray, 'Feminism in the French Revolution', in *American Historical Review*, 80 (1975), 43–62; Abbey R. Kleinbaum, 'Women in the Age of Light', in Renate Bridenthal and Claudia Koonz, eds., *Becoming Visible: Women in European History*, Boston, 1977, 217–35; Samia Spencer, ed., *French Women and the Age of Enlightenment*, Bloomington, Ind., 1984.

[9] Ludmilla Jordanova, *Sexual Visions*, London, 1990, 24.

and social and familial roles.[10] By so doing, eighteenth-century writers provided the framework for conservative Victorian domestic ideology rather than offering any basis on which to challenge the existing balance of sexual power.

Strachey was of course quite unaware of the importance or the implications of eighteenth-century scientific views. For her, the Enlightenment was important primarily because it gave rise to liberalism—and her interpretation of the women's movement centres on its connection with liberal political and economic beliefs. At one level, Victorian feminism was for Strachey the application of liberal ideas to the situation of women. At no point did she recognize the complex and difficult relationship which existed between liberalism and feminism on the one hand, or the importance for feminists of nineteenth-century ideas about femininity on the other. But indeed, Victorian domestic ideology, centring as it did on the notion of separate spheres for women and men, on the intellectual, moral, and emotional differences between men and women, and on the moral superiority of women, was at least as important in the formulation of feminist thought as was liberal political and economic theory.

While Strachey was very aware of the extensive number of pronouncements on women's role and duty made in the early nineteenth century, she is less aware than contemporary historians are of how contentious a question the situation of women actually was. For several decades in the late eighteenth and early nineteenth centuries, there was, on the one hand, a continuous stream of works formulating Victorian domestic ideology while, on the other, there was a contrasting stream criticizing or reformulating this ideology and arguing for an end to women's oppression. The discussion of this domestic ideology alongside comments and criticisms of the actual situation of women and the state of marriage constituted a 'woman question' which was the subject of widespread interest in all areas of society and in all forms of literature.[11] It is impossible to understand the nature of Victorian feminism unless one looks at

---

[10] Ibid. 24–7; see also Londa Scheibinger, 'Skeletons in the Closet: The First Illustrations of the Female Skeleton in Eighteenth Century Anatomy', in *Representations*, 14 (1986), 42–82.

[11] See e.g. Gina Luria, ed., *The Feminist Controversy in England, 1788–1810*, New York, 1974. This edition of facsimile reprints offers some insight into the number of major works addressing these questions in this period.

its connection with this question and hence with the whole range of discussions about the situation of women in the early and mid-nineteenth century.

I

Since the early 1970s, feminist historical and literary scholarship has stressed the importance for women of other women active in their own field of endeavour. The female networks composed of family and friends which offered women support in their daily lives have a counterpart in the female literary traditions which established paths of influence, shared plots, and ideas of female literary style.[12] What has not yet been established or even explored is the extent to which this female tradition operated in regard to feminist theorists and feminist activists.

There is currently considerable debate about both the existence and the importance of a functioning feminist tradition. Some contemporary scholars argue that feminism differs 'from other ideologies like Marxism and Christianity in that it does not feed itself from any founding text'. But many others disagree, arguing that in the English-speaking world, Mary Wollstonecraft's *A Vindication of the Rights of Woman* does in fact constitute such a text.[13] Not only was Wollstonecraft's *Vindication* a key document for both feminists and anti-feminists in the decade it was published, her name was the one most constantly identified with the feminist cause throughout the early nineteenth century.[14] But this position is not accepted by all historians of English feminism. Ray Strachey may have argued that in the *Vindication* 'the whole extent of the feminist ideal is set out, and the whole claim for equal human rights is made; and ... it has remained the text of the movement ever

[12] See e.g. Ellen Moers, *Literary Women*, New York, 1976; Elaine Showalter, *A Literature of Their Own: British Women Novelists from Brontë to Lessing*, Princeton, NJ, 1977; Caroll Smith-Rosenberg, 'The Female World of Love and Ritual: Relations Between Women in Nineteenth-Century America', *Signs*, 1 (1973), 58–72.

[13] For a clear statement of these positions, see Genevieve Fraisse, 'The Form of Historical Feminism', *m/f*, 10 (1985), 6–7, and Sally Alexander's reply in the 'Discussion', Ibid. 11; Cora Kaplan also accepts the *Vindication* as 'the founding text of Anglo-American feminism': 'Wild Nights: Pleasure/Sexuality/Feminism' in her *Sea Changes: Essays on Culture and Feminism*, London, 1986, 34.

[14] Rendall, *Origins of Modern Feminism*, 55–9.

since.'[15] Recently Rosalind Delmar has pointed to the significant differences in intellectual approach evident between Wollstonecraft on the one hand, and most mid-Victorian feminists on the other. Wollstonecraft's philosophical radicalism and her belief in natural rights were both rejected by many later feminists who stressed that it was legal and not natural rights that were at issue. The natural rights argument was not lost entirely, but it became a minority strand in a movement more concerned about property and property rights.[16]

Much of this disagreement arises from the complexities one faces in attempting to assess precisely the nature and extent of Wollstonecraft's influence. That influence was often subtle and operated through a great variety of intermediaries. It could also go in very different directions. Barbara Taylor, for example, rejects the idea of a single link connecting Wollstonecraft with 'modern bourgeois feminism', stressing the radicalism of her political and personal views and her importance for Owenite feminists with their aim of liberating the whole of humanity.[17] Certainly Wollstonecraft's ideas were discussed much more explicitly by Anna Wheeler and William Thompson than they were by many members of the mid-nineteenth-century women's movement—most of whom would neither have known nor desired to know anything about Owenite feminism.

In contrast to the interest in Wollstonecraft evident amongst some of the Owenite feminists, many mid-Victorian feminists seem neither to have read nor to have said anything about her. Few mid-Victorian feminists read Wollstonecraft, and even fewer did so in their early or formative years. Emily Davies's biographer, Barbara Stephen, for example, insists that Davies did not read Wollstonecraft but that her 'feminist views were formed as a result of her own experience and observations'.[18] This would seem to have been the case for Frances Cobbe, Millicent Fawcett, and Josephine Butler as well. None of the women in this book ever claimed to have been influenced by Wollstonecraft. Indeed, for the most part, they refrained from mentioning her at all.

[15] Strachey, *The Cause*, 12.

[16] Delmar, 'What is Feminism?', 18–21.

[17] Barbara Taylor, *Eve and the New Jerusalem: Socialism and Feminism in the Nineteenth Century*, London, 1983, 5–9.

[18] Barbara Stephen, *Emily Davies and Girton College*, London, 1927, 29.

What is clear from all of this is not so much that Wollstonecraft had no influence on mid-Victorian feminism, but rather that mid-Victorian feminists did not seek to connect her name with their activities. Many of them preferred to interpose as large a distance as possible between Wollstonecraft and themselves. This was not because her book was little noticed, but because her conduct was so notorious. Although the *Vindication* was widely and favourably noticed when it first came out in 1792, any praise of it ceased after the publication of Godwin's *Memoir of the Author of a Vindication of the Rights of Woman* in 1798.[19] Whatever his intentions, Godwin's revelation of all the details of Wollstonecraft's private life ensured her posthumous infamy. Lucretia Mott may have kept a copy of a *Vindication of the Rights of Woman* at a centre table in her drawing room for forty years, but few of her English counterparts followed suit.[20] Those who openly admired Wollstonecraft, such as Elizabeth Wolstenholme Elmy, were themselves ostracized because of their sexual radicalism.[21] Even Strachey shows unease in dealing with Wollstonecraft: while acknowledging her importance, Strachey devoted fewer words to Wollstonecraft than she did to much more equivocal figures such as Hannah More or Florence Nightingale—to say nothing of those whom she really lauded like Mary Carpenter or John Stuart Mill.

The question of Wollstonecraft's place in Victorian feminism is then complicated by the fact that one is dealing both with a life-story and with a text—and the two went in strikingly different directions. While her own life was the source of great scandal, the *Vindication* was decidedly restrained in its ideas about sexuality and sexual relations. As Cora Kaplan has recently argued, the *Vindication* is notable for its insistence on sexual restraint and its acceptance of women's sexuality as a destructive force rather than

[19] See R. M. James, 'On the Reception of Mary Wollstonecraft's *A Vindication of the Rights of Woman*', *Journal of the History of Ideas*, 39 (1978), 293–302; cf. Rendall, *Origins of Modern Feminism*, 59–63.

[20] Olive Banks, *Faces of Feminism: A Study of Feminism as a Social Movement*, Oxford, 1986, 29.

[21] Judith Walkowitz, *Prostitution and Victorian Society: Women, Class and the State*, Cambridge, 1980, 123. Elmy was asked by Millicent Garrett Fawcett to resign as secretary of the Married Women's Property Committee because of 'the circumstances connected with your marriage and what took place previous to it'. Millicent Garrett Fawcett to Elizabeth Wolstenholme Elmy, 10 Dec. 1875, Fawcett Library, Autograph Collection, vol. 2C.

for any plea for greater sexual freedom for women. For Kaplan, it is the emphasis on the sexual that is most problematic and most significant in Wollstonecraft. The analysis of sensibility and pleasure as instruments of patriarchal control, the account of how women's sexuality and dependency are constructed both in the existing state of society and in the writings of Rousseau, are evident in the *Vindication*, but rather than attacking them through a demand for women's control of their own sexuality, Wollstonecraft insists on a puritan sexual ethic for women.[22] Written before Wollstonecraft was herself engaged in an unconventional relationship, the *Vindication* in no way foreshadows the sexual radicalism now so widely associated with its author.

The contrast between Wollstonecraft's reprehensible personal conduct and the ideas she put forward in the *Vindication* was the theme of the one lengthy discussion of Wollstonecraft to be found amongst Victorian feminists: that in Fawcett's 'Introduction' to an edition of the *Vindication*, which she edited in the 1890s.[23] It is clear from the start that Fawcett was prepared to offer Wollstonecraft only a limited recognition. She was certainly not prepared to regard her as the author of the founding text for Victorian feminism. On the contrary, she did her best to minimize both Wollstonecraft's originality and the debt owed her by later feminists. Fawcett acknowledged that the *Vindication of the Rights of Woman* was 'almost the first conscious expression' of the need for women's rights in England, but then went on immediately to insist, first, that great movements are not dependent on great individuals, and, secondly, that Wollstonecraft was 'as much the product of the women's rights movement as its earliest confessor'.[24] Fawcett's rather grudging recognition of Wollstonecraft contrasts strongly with her fulsome praise of John Stuart Mill, whom she credits both with the growth of the women's movement and with its 'adaptation to the practical spirit of the nineteenth century'.[25]

The major problem Fawcett had to deal with, and the reason why she sought to limit Wollstonecraft's influence, was of course

---

[22] Kaplan, *Sea Changes*, 34–50. See also Taylor, *Eve and the New Jerusalem*, 47.
[23] See Mary Wollstonecraft, *A Vindication of the Rights of Woman*, ed. Millicent Garrett Fawcett, new edn., London, 1891, 'Introduction', p. 3.
[24] Ibid. 3–5.
[25] Millicent Garrett Fawcett, 'The Women's Suffrage Movement', in *The Woman Question in Europe*, ed. T. Stanton, London, 1888, 1.

to be found in Wollstonecraft's personal conduct. Fawcett rejected entirely Wollstonecraft's life-style, deploring both her 'want of order and system' and the whole tenor of her private life. 'In unravelling the curious tangle of relationships, intrigues, suicides and attempted suicides of the remarkable group of personalities to whom Mary Wollstonecraft belonged one is sickened for ever ... of the subject of irregular relations.'[26] But when it came to the text of the *Vindication*, Fawcett managed to find much that was praiseworthy in Wollstonecraft's condemnation of the frivolity of the women of her time, and in her exaltation of women's duty to their families and especially their children. Wollstonecraft, in her view, was ahead of her time in the demand for female education and occupations—and in her insistence on the importance of chastity for both men and women.[27] She commended the fact that Wollstonecraft stamped the word 'Duty' on the women's rights movement from the outset, thus impressing it with a character it has never lost.

The moderation of Wollstonecraft's sexual views and of the actual demands she made in the *Vindication* help explain one aspect of this whole question which is rarely taken into account: the extent to which her ideas had become almost common currency by the early decades of the nineteenth century—carried in much standard literature, particularly fiction. Several recent studies have shown how important her work was for Jane Austen, for example. Austen may only have provided a 'conservative recuperation' of Wollstonecraft, but her novels are increasingly being pictured as works directly engaged in the feminist controversy of the late eighteenth and early nineteenth centuries, addressing themselves directly to the need for women's equality.[28] Austen's concern with the plight of single women, with women's financial dependence, and with their sufferings through the English system of primogeniture, has long been recognized. But recently more attention has been paid to her discussions of women's education, the sexual double standard, and the whole question of the situation and the abilities of women. Austen does not refer directly to Wollstonecraft and few critics would argue that her heroines were self-conscious feminists. But

[26] See Wollstonecraft, *A Vindication of the Rights of Woman*, ed. Millicent Garrett Fawcett, 22.
[27] Ibid. 24.   [28] See Kaplan, *Sea Changes*, 47.

many of Wollstonecraft's major themes are prominent in her work and her heroines 'are all exemplary of the first claim of Enlightenment feminism: that since women share the same moral nature as men, they ought to share the same moral status, and exercise the same responsibility for their own conduct'.[29]

While Austen shows the importance of Wollstonecraft's ideas in her work without discussing her directly, a number of other prominent nineteenth-century women writers openly acknowledged her importance in their own lives as well as discussing her ideas quite explicitly in their literary work. Elizabeth Barrett Browning, for example, read the *Vindication* at the age of 12 and, as a result, 'through the whole course of my childhood, I had a steady indignation against Nature who made me a woman'.[30] George Eliot, too, both read and wrote about the *Vindication*, anticipating Fawcett in her careful defence of the book, rather than of its creator.[31] While neither of these writers was prepared to endorse the aims and objectives of the women's movement wholeheartedly, both explored feminist themes and problems in their work, suggesting that Wollstonecraft's influence was almost ubiquitous by the mid-nineteenth century—especially for a woman who sought contact with other women or who was looking for ideas and reflections on the 'woman question'.

II

The possibility of coming into contact with Wollstonecraft's ideas through Austen's fiction raises the broader question of the importance of nineteenth-century literature in developing and expanding feminist themes and ideas. The importance of feminist reading and of discussion of feminist issues in nineteenth-century literature has only recently been recognized by twentieth-century literary

[29] Kirkham, *Jane Austen: Feminism and Fiction*, 84; see also L. W. Brown, 'Jane Austen and the Feminist Tradition', *Nineteenth Century Fiction*, 28 (1973), 321–8; M. Lanta, 'Jane Austen's Feminism: An Original Response to Convention', *Critical Quarterly*, 23 (1981), 27–36.

[30] Cited in Nicholas McGuinn, 'George Eliot and Mary Wollstonecraft', in *The Nineteenth Century Woman: Her Cultural and Physical World*, ed. Sara Delamont and Lorna Duffin, London, 1978, 192.

[31] Ibid. 193–200.

scholars,[32] but most of those active in the nineteenth-century women's movement were very well aware of the extent to which their interests and concerns about women were echoed in contemporary literature—particularly in that written by women. Fawcett once remarked that the whole woman question could be found in *Aurora Leigh* and pointed to the importance of that work for later activists.[33] Emily Davies devoured the novels of George Eliot, feeling that *Felix Holt*, for example, 'presents a view of women that we want to have looked at'.[34]

While Davies and Fawcett may have singled out women writers, neither regarded them as the only ones who had an important contribution to make to discussion of their cause. Davies herself was one of the first to point out how extensive was the discussion of women and their nature and role in recent literature. Everywhere she looked, she found works which addressed the very questions with which she was increasingly preoccupied. Tennyson's *The Princess* and the discussion of women's education in Arthur Helps's *Friends in Council* became central texts in the elaboration of her own ideas on the importance for women of gaining access to tertiary education.

I am not wanting to suggest here that it was Tennyson and Helps rather than Wollstonecraft who were formative influences on the development of Davies's feminism. Such a suggestion would contain a pleasing irony, in view of the very limited changes in women's education or in relations between the sexes proposed by these men, but it is highly implausible. Davies's preoccupation with education arose from her own immediate experience: from her deep sense of personal deprivation as a result of the differences between her education and that given to her brothers. The writings of Tennyson and Helps, however, provided a more general discussion of women's education and established the context in which she clarified and articulated her own ideas. Hence while Tennyson proposed a college for women in *The Princess*, only to ridicule and

[32] For an interesting discussion of feminist reading, see e.g. Susan Sheridan, 'Feminist Readings: The Case of Christina Stead', in *Crossing Boundaries: Feminisms and the Critique of Knowledges*, ed. Barbara Caine, E. A. Grosz, Marie de Lepervanche, Sydney, 1988, 82–3.

[33] Millicent Garrett Fawcett, 'In Memoriam. W. T. Stead', *The Common Cause*, 25 Apr. 1912, 37.

[34] Emily Davies to Barbara Bodichon, n.d., Bodichon Papers, B.319.

demolish it, he none the less floated the idea in literature even before the first small steps in improving women's education were being taken by the establishment of Bedford and Queen's Colleges.[35] Tennyson's vision, often transformed into something he would have found unrecognizable, remained an integral part of the discussion about university education for women until the very end of the nineteenth century.[36] Helps, although not suggesting any concrete ways of improving the education of women, apart from insisting that they should be taught to be courageous, at least raised the possibility that men and women could be given the same education and thus served to place this on the agenda.[37]

Davies's use of the ideas of both Tennyson and Helps demonstrates that it was not necessary for books to be explicitly feminist in their orientation in order for them to be either influential or helpful in the formulating of feminist ideas. It was as important for her to have arguments to work against, to mock and to ridicule, as it was to have ones which endorsed or extended her own ideas.[38] At one and the same time, Tennyson raised the possibility of a college for women—and showed the preconceptions, fears, and prejudices which would have to be overcome by anyone who sought to take up this idea and turn it into a reality. He thus offered a very clear example of the kinds of arguments which would have to be dealt with and refuted in any campaign to open higher education to women. In a similar way, by articulating so clearly the idea that women needed to be made courageous, but refusing to make any suggestions as to how this should be done, Helps simultaneously acknowledged the deficiencies in women's education, the pressing need for reform, and the obstacles which would have to be overcome by anyone who attempted to tackle this question.

[35] See Bernard Bergonzi, 'Feminism and Femininity in *The Princess*', in *The Major Victorian Poets: Reconsiderations*, ed. Isobel Armstrong, London, 1969, 35–50; Carol Christ, 'Victorian Masculinity and the Angel in the House', in *A Widening Sphere: Changing Roles of Victorian Women*, ed. Martha Vicinus, Bloomington, Ind., 1977, 146–62; John Kilham, *Tennyson and The Princess: Reflections of an Age*, London, 1958.

[36] See Perry Williams, 'Pioneer Women Students at Cambridge, 1869–81', in Felicity Hunt, ed., *Lessons for Life: The Schooling of Girls and Women, 1850–1950*, Oxford, 1987, 184–5.

[37] Arthur Helps, *Friends in Council: A Series of Readings and Discourses Thereon*, London, 1854, ii. 162–5.

[38] Emily Davies, *The Higher Education of Women*, London, 1866 (repr. London, 1988), 10–31.

The very existence of literary discussions of women's education also served to give Davies's own views legitimacy and to show how widespread was support for some of them. Tennyson's ringing statements of the unity between men and women came constantly to her help.

> The woman's cause is man's: they rise or sink
> Together, dwarf'd or godlike, bond or free:
> For she that out of Lethe scales with man
> The shining steps of Nature, shares with man
> His nights, his days, moves with him to one goal,
> Stays all the fair young planet in her hands—
> If she be small, slight-natured, miserable,
> How shall men grow?[39]

> (*The Princess*, VII. 243–50)

Davies was not the only feminist to look to literature in articulating her views. Working in a quite different area, Josephine Butler recalled the reading of Mrs Gaskell's *Ruth* as a key event in her evolution as a feminist activist.[40] Gaskell's novel (which she did not actually name) was important, despite the fact that it neither mirrored her ideas nor offered her suggestions or insights which she had not had before. None the less, it publicized concerns she had felt for some time and made the whole subject of the sexual double standard a matter for widespread debate. Published in 1852, nearly two decades before Butler became involved in the Contagious Diseases agitation, *Ruth* explored the dire sufferings of a young woman who, bereft of family and lacking caring friends or a responsible employer, succumbed to the advances of a weak, irresponsible, and wealthy young man. Ultimately, of course, he returned to his family, leaving Ruth to cope not only with loneliness and shame, but also with an illegitimate son. She is helped and supported by a Nonconformist preacher who takes her into his home.

The novel is quite uncompromising in its insistence that it was the man who was morally culpable. Ruth's essential purity and goodness are not in any way diminished by her liaison, whereas

[39] Emily Davies, 'Letter Addressed to a Daily paper at Newcastle-upon-Tyne, 1860', reprinted in her *Questions Relating to Women*, London, 1910, 6.

[40] Josephine E. Butler, *An Autobiographical Memoir*, ed. George and Lucy Johnson, London, 1909, 31.

her seducer continues to show himself in all the situations in which we meet him as weak, self-indulgent, irresponsible, and even dishonest. *Ruth* was a powerful attack on the sexual double standard, showing how the whole burden of it fell on hapless women, and demonstrating the cruelty of existing moral and social beliefs. It offered a picture of unrelieved gloom as far as women were concerned: despite her youth and innocence, rehabilitation for Ruth was not possible. Ruth herself, while recognizing that she was led astray, none the less shares fully the sense of her guilt and sin voiced by others. She is forever tarnished. Ruth has to expiate her sin again and again, being recognized fully for her goodness only after an early death, brought on by her selfless nursing of many people—including her former lover—through an epidemic.[41]

Josephine Butler was not immune from the sentimentality with which *Ruth* abounds—as her own description of the first young prostitutes whom she brought into her home to die amply illustrates.[42] Butler thought that *Ruth* had a 'wholesome tendency', but its view of fallen women was rather different from her own.[43] On the one hand, Butler rejected absolutely the view that fallen women were irredeemable, focusing her attack on the notion of rampant male sexuality and on the ways in which prostitution was organized and condoned by military and civilian authorities. Hence her approach to the question of the sexual double standard was quite different from Gaskell's. *Ruth* was essentially a plea for tolerance, sympathy, and understanding from the community and for the recognition by parents, employers, and all responsible adults of the need for them properly to guide and protect the young in their care. Butler, by contrast, argued that the sexual double standard and the very existence of prostitution affected all women, indeed that it underlay the situation of all women in society. But at the same time, Butler accepted absolutely the moral terms of Gaskell's discussion and its insistence that sexual questions were ultimately ones of life and death for women. She could never accept a discussion of prostitution based simply on economic considerations or ones which left out of account questions of sin and atonement.

[41] Elizabeth Gaskell, *Ruth*, London, 1852 (repr. London, 1978).
[42] Butler, *Autobiographical Memoir*, 32.
[43] Ibid. 34.

But for Butler, as earlier for Davies, it was not only the actual terms in which the particular part of the 'woman question' was discussed that mattered, but rather the fact that it was discussed at all in the public arena. Part of the reason why Butler noted the publication of *Ruth* was the fact that it discussed openly a question with which she was preoccupied, but which she had rarely mentioned to anyone else. It was not the content of the book which she emphasized, but rather the fact that it was 'much discussed' and that this discussion 'led to expressions of judgement which seemed to me false—fatally false'.[44] The university men who were her husband's colleagues heaped scorn upon it and declared it unsuitable reading for women. All of this made her aware of how entrenched the double standard was and how great a battle would have to be fought to overcome it.

What is particularly notable in all this is the importance for Victorian feminists of a number of well-known authors who, while addressing the woman question, were not themselves feminists. It was the location and the interests of the readers, rather than the ostensible intentions of the authors, which made the various works they selected ones which fed into a feminist analysis. This is true even in regard to *Ruth*. By making the central character of her novel a 'fallen woman', Mrs Gaskell challenged existing views both of sexual morality and of feminine propriety and made the whole question of the sexual double standard one for ongoing debate. But it was Josephine Butler's personal situation and her reading of the book, rather than Gaskell's own stance, which makes this an important work in the history of Victorian feminism.

III

While mid-Victorian feminists were unhappy about acknowledging a debt to Mary Wollstonecraft, they were in no doubt at all about the importance for their views of the Enlightenment and of the liberal political and economic ideas to which it gave rise. Millicent Garrett Fawcett expressed her own sense of the connection between the Enlightenment and the rise of the women's movement on several occasions.

[44] Butler, *Autobiographical Memoir*, 32.

The fermentation in men's minds which had already produced new thoughts about the rights of man, which was destined presently to over-throw unrestrained despotism wherever it existed in Western Europe, did not pass by without producing its effects on the greatest despotism of all: that of men over women. The idea that women are created simply to minister to the amusement, enjoyment and gratification of men was closely allied to the idea that peasants and workmen exist solely for the satisfaction of the wants and pleasures of the aristocratic classes.[45]

She also insisted on the very close connection between feminist demands and liberal economic theory, arguing, for example, that the demand for the removal of the barrier that excluded women from higher education was only a 'phase of the free trade argument'.[46] Liberal economic arguments were continually used to argue against the barriers women faced in employment and against any attempt to restrict their hours or conditions in ways which were not deemed suitable for men, as well as to demand the vote. Liberal political beliefs, especially those centring on the importance of representative government as a way to ensure good government for all on the one hand, and to raise the educational level of the governed on the other, were constantly repeated by those demanding women's suffrage. Fawcett was only one amongst many feminists who saw all the arguments put forward to support the extensions of manhood suffrage in 1867 and 1884 as applying equally to women.

While Fawcett accepted the general importance of liberalism in establishing the framework for feminist demands, she placed a particularly high value on the contribution of John Stuart Mill in creating the nineteenth-century English women's movement.

There can be no dispute that Mr Mill's influence marks an epoch in the women's movement. He was a master and formed a school of thought. Just as in art, a master forms a school and influences his successors for generations, so the present leaders and champions of the women's movement have been influenced and to a great extent formed by Mr Mill.[47]

Fawcett was not the only Victorian feminist to insist on the

[45] Wollstonecraft, *A Vindication of the Rights of Woman*, ed. Fawcett, 3.

[46] Millicent Garrett Fawcett, 'The Future of Englishwomen', *Nineteenth Century*, 4 (1878), 352.

[47] Millicent Garrett Fawcett, 'The Women's Suffrage Movement', in T. Stanton, ed., *The Woman Question in Europe*, London, 1888, 4.

importance of Mill for the women's movement. There were a number of others, such as Kate Amberley, for whom his *Subjection of Women* became the central text for the movement, and one which she planned to study well so 'that I may get all the arguments into my head and have them ready for any scoffers'.[48] But not all Victorian feminists accepted this evaluation of Mill. It is significant that Fawcett was the youngest of the women in this study and the one whose entry to the women's movement came through the liberal political circles most heavily influenced by Mill. The others, who did not stand towards him in the direct relation of pupil to teacher, were considerably less adulatory than was Fawcett.

The most striking contrast to Fawcett's view is provided by Josephine Butler. Where Fawcett saw Mill as creating a school of thought, Butler argued that his views on women—especially those expressed in *The Subjection*—were not particularly advanced. 'On the contrary they are but the somewhat tardy expression of a conviction which has been gaining strength in society for the last twenty years.'[49] The tardiness of Mill's explicit commitment to the women's cause was noted also by Barbara Bodichon. Having read *The Principles of Political Economy*, shortly after it was published in 1848, Bodichon criticized Mill for omitting any discussion of the marriage contract or of the laws pertaining to married women.[50] Mill's procrastination over publishing *The Subjection of Women* meant that, although written in the 1850s, it did not appear until 1869. This was two years after Emily Davies had published her major work, *The Higher Education of Women*, and hence precluded the possibility that it exercised a major influence on her. By this time, too, Frances Cobbe was a very well-known journalist who had well and truly established her own feminist position.

All of these women acknowledged Mill's importance for the women's movement, but none of them regarded him as their leader. Davies made it quite clear that, in her view, Mill's importance for the women's movement derived from the fact that he was the most eminent man publicly to identify himself with the cause, rather than from the strength or novelty of his ideas. For her, as for

[48] Kate Amberley to John Stuart Mill, 9 June 1869, Mill–Taylor Collection, vol. i, fo. 311.

[49] Josephine Butler to the Rt. Hon. H. A. Bruce, 8 June 1869, Butler Papers.

[50] Candida Lacey, ed., *Barbara Bodichon and the Langham Place Circle*, London, 1987, 4.

Bodichon, it was 'the political purchase of Mill as a publicist' rather than any faith in him as a philosopher which prompted them to campaign for his election to Parliament and then to ask him to present their petition for women's suffrage.[51] Once Mill was in Parliament, however, Davies went so far as to question whether his name did in fact assist the women's cause.

> The newspapers have got into a way of treating the question as an individual crotchet of Mr Mill's ... what we must show is that it is not a personal crotchet of anybody's. If Mr Mill had made it his first concern, it would have been a different case. As it is, we get mixed up in the public mind with Jamaica and the Reform League which does us no good.[52]

Mill is so often seen both as the most important and as the most representative Victorian feminist that little attention has been paid to the very significant differences between his approach to the woman question and that of many of his female contemporaries. But these differences are important. They are most noticeable in their discussions of women's domestic life, of the nature of womanhood, and of the contributions women can actually make to society.

In *The Subjection of Women*, Mill made it clear that in his view, marriage was the normal lot of women. Perhaps it was as a consequence of this belief that his entire discussion of the domestic problems of women focused on the situation of wives. Mill had a long-standing interest in marital problems. As a very young man, he was an advocate of birth control—indeed, he was arrested for distributing birth-control pamphlets when he was only 17.[53] For much of his life, he was concerned about the question of domestic violence and about the ways in which the law even prevented police from intervening when it occurred.[54] When *The Subjection* was published in 1869, it offered one of the most searing and critical

---

[51] Ibid.

[52] Emily Davies to Barbara Bodichon, n.d., Bodichon papers B316(2). As it was, Mill was extremely reticent on the woman question during his term in Parliament. See Evelyn L. Pugh, 'John Stuart Mill and the Women's Question in Parliament, 1865–1868', *Historian*, 42 (1980), 399–418.

[53] Michael St John Packe, *The Life of John Stuart Mill*, London, 1954, 56–9.

[54] See e.g. letters from John Stuart Mill to Sir Robert Collier and to Frank Harrison Hill, both dated 11 Jan. 1870 in *The Later Letters of John Stuart Mill, 1849–1873*, ed. Frances Mineka and Dwight Lindley, London, 1972, iv. 167–9.

pictures of marriage to emerge in the nineteenth century.[55] Mill's insistence that marriage was a form of slavery for women and that it resulted frequently in their neglect and ill-treatment was counterpointed by his argument that the family itself, as presently constituted, exercised a deleterious moral effect on all its members.[56] Mill's view provided a dramatic contrast to the widespread Victorian idealization of marriage and of family life. But while Mill discussed marriage in great detail, he devoted minimal attention to women in any capacity other than that of wife. The situation of daughters and sisters, of single women living either alone or under a paternal roof, were matters which Mill totally ignored.

Mill's omission of these questions immediately separates him from most of the women involved in the women's movement. For them, the plight of single women was of the utmost importance. They concentrated considerable attention on the problems of daughters in particular—thereby addressing the one situation and relationship which all women shared, and the one which was of pre-eminent concern in a society which did not accord daughters much independence. The centrality of the role of daughters for Victorian feminists is evident in the lengthy discussion which the Kensington Discussion Society held on the question, 'What is the true basis, and what are the limits of parental authority?' Many Victorian feminists were unable to undertake their activity in the women's movement without going against parental wishes.[57] For some, like Frances Cobbe, this question occupied a pre-eminent place in all moral and social discussion. Focusing on daughters also had a strategic importance. For Cobbe, in particular, an emphasis on the primacy of the relationship between daughter and parents made marriage into a secondary relationship. Husbands, in her view, had to recognize that their claims on their wives had to give way to the prior claims of parents. Focusing on daughters also gave feminists the appropriate framework for discussing the power of fathers and for delineating the basis of patriarchy.

[55] John Stuart Mill, *The Subjection of Women*, London, 1869, repr. in John Stuart Mill and Harriet Taylor Mill, *Essays on Sex Equality*, ed. Alice S. Rossi, Chicago, 1970.

[56] Ibid. 159–73.

[57] The papers for the Kensington Discussion Society are in the Emily Davies Papers, see ED IX/KEN 5.

The inadequacy of Mill's analysis of the subjection of women has recently been the subject of much discussion. His ready accept-ance of very conventional Victorian beliefs about male and female nature and capacities has attracted particular attention, as has his insistence that men embody the universal standard of human excel-lence.[58] Zillah Eisenstein has commented on the way in which Mill, despite his powerful critique of the subordination of women, none the less perpetuates the patriarchal division of male and female sexual spheres in his insistence that it is both likely and desirable that most women will continue in their domestic role, leaving income-earning activity and involvement in the public sphere to men or to exceptional single women.[59] This is not to suggest that other Victorian feminists challenged in any direct way the pre-vailing ideas in their society about the sexual division of labour or about the appropriate spheres for men and women. But many of them subjected the domestic sphere to a considerably more exten-sive analysis than was offered by Mill. This gave them the basis for asserting a larger and more positive social role for women, based on their domestic experience. Mill, by contrast, was unhappy about the extent of women's social and political influence at the present time. He argued that it was this influence which helped to explain 'two of the most marked features of modern European life—its aversion to war and its addiction to philanthropy'.

While many feminists argued that the very qualities which women exercised in the home rendered them the appropriate people to undertake major public roles, Mill remained steadfast in his belief that it was only exposure to and immersion in the existing public world which would render women competent to participate in that world. Although he believed that women had certain intel-lectual characteristics denied to men, and that their 'insight into present fact' and capacity for intuition would be of great benefit in the public domain, where it would complement the male tendency to think only in terms of general principles, he did not see that women's domestic experience could of itself contribute either to their education or to their understanding of political and social

[58] See Julia Annas, 'Mill and the Subjection of Women', *Philosophy*, 5 (1977), 179–94; Susan Moller Okin, *Women in Western Political Thought*, London, 1980, 197–232.

[59] Mill, *The Subjection of Women*, 178; see also Zillah Eisenstein, *The Radical Future of Liberal Feminism*, New York, 1981, 140–3.

questions. He expressed great reservations about the expanding role of women in philanthropy. While accepting that educated and experienced women might be able to administer charities competently, he feared that most women simply gave money in a charitable spirit, with no idea of the consequences of their actions. Being unfree themselves, women did not understand the importance of independence for the poor and hence contributed to their demoralization.[60] In his view, the distinctive sphere of womanhood had no positive consequences for women. It merely served to isolate women from education and from any form of public activity. As a result, it led only to a selfish concern with the welfare and well-being of those closest to them. It prevented women from developing what was for Mill a major moral attribute: public-spiritedness.

Mill's insistence that women who were immersed in domesticity were quite unsuited for any public or philanthropic work is deeply revealing of his own underlying assumptions about the masculine nature of public life. His approach demonstrates some of the fundamental problems involved in any attempt to graft feminism on to an unreconstructed liberalism. For liberalism, as both Carole Pateman and Zillah Eisenstein have shown, has always accepted the existing European sexual division of labour and the basically patriarchal family structure that this entails. Historically, liberalism has taken for granted and regarded as unproblematical the differences in the legal, political, and social status of women and men. Since the seventeenth century, liberalism has privileged not just the individual, but the male head of a household. It was he whose rationality, autonomy, and need for unrestricted freedom of action it demanded.[61] The role of women within this framework was assumed to be the one dictated by nature: that of wife and mother. Her legal existence was subsumed within that of her husband and was not therefore a question of any particular importance. She was not an original party to the social contract and where she did enter into contractual arrangements, on marriage for example, she relinquished her freedom totally.[62] This acceptance of women's subordination means that liberalism is implicitly for-

[60] Mill, *The Subjection of Women*, 226–7.
[61] Carole Pateman and Teresa Brennan, '"Mere Auxiliaries to the Commonwealth": Women and the Origins of Liberalism', *Political Studies*, 27 (1979); and Carole Pateman, *The Sexual Contract*, Oxford, 1988, see esp. ch. 4.
[62] Pateman, *The Sexual Contract, passim*.

mulated around the idea of a specifically sexed male subject.

Within the nineteenth century, liberalism continued to be for-mulated within this basically patriarchal framework. But to its theoretical endorsement of patriarchy was added a particular mas-culine culture and a specific set of ideas about the sexual division of labour and about the relationship between women and the public sphere. It is very widely known that many prominent Victorian liberals, including both Gladstone and John Bright, held very strongly to an ideal of the family as a private realm beyond the reach of politics and to the view of women as needing the protection of domestic seclusion.[63] But this had as its counterpart an ideal of public life which came from and endorsed the continuation of a particularly masculine cultural tradition. The classical education which was the exclusive preserve of boys' public schools imbued those subject to it with an ideal of public life drawn from that of Athenian democracy, one that placed even greater emphasis on the contrast between the male public realm and the domestic seclusion of women than was evident in Victorian domestic ideology, and which made this seclusion of women an integral part of the survival both of the family and of morality. This education in and adulation of the classical world was accompanied by a knowledge of Latin and Greek languages and literature, freely used in political discussion—and rendering it sometimes unintelligible to women who were denied this education. The reference to this classical model of public life validated its Victorian counterpart and made it easier for those who sought to exclude women from it to see their exclusion as morally correct and as being in accordance with the whole tradition of Western civilization.

This classically based and privileged notion of the masculinity of the public world provided a rationale for excluding working-class men from the political sphere alongside the one it provided for excluding all women. The centrality of its masculine identity has been noted by other students of Victorian liberalism. John Vincent, in his influential study of the British Liberal Party, has

---

[63] See John Bright, 'Speech on the Women's Disabilities Removal Bill 26 April 1876', and W. E. Gladstone, 'Female Suffrage: A Letter to Samuel Smith', both reprinted in *Before the Vote Was Won: Arguments For and Against Women's Suffrage*, ed. Jane Lewis, London, 1987; and Ann P. Robson, 'A Birds' Eye View of Glad-stone', in Bruce Kinzer, ed., *The Gladstonian Turn of Mind: Essays Presented to J. B. Conacher*, Toronto, 1985, 63–96.

argued that 'the great moral idea of liberalism was manliness'. Exhibiting in a rather splendid way the phallocentricism of this whole political tradition, Vincent is oblivious to the gender specificity of this term. He sees it as referring only to questions of social class, defining manliness essentially as a form of middle-class self-assertion—as 'the rejection of the various forms of patronage, from soup and blankets upwards, which had formerly been the normal part of the greatest number'.[64] The sense of full humanity which was central to liberalism, as Vincent explains, entailed that a man 'should provide for his own family, have his own religion and politics, and call no man master'. But while Vincent is unable to see it, the dual exclusion of working men and of all women which is contained in the term seems inescapable. Moreover it is now becoming increasingly evident that every aspect of the ideal of manliness was defined against a female alternative.[65] One cannot but see that the high evaluation of public service and public action so evident in writers such as Mill drew both implicitly and explicitly on the contrast between such public service and its alternatives: the private world of women or the wage-dominated world of labourers.

Victorian feminists were in no doubt about the gendered nature of the public sphere or of the extent to which this gendering made it not only unresponsive to women's needs, but actively hostile to women. They showed this quite easily by introducing a female perspective into the discussion of politics and of the nature of the political order. Once the exclusively masculine culture of the public sphere was looked at from the viewpoint of women, what became evident was not its continuity with ancient Athens, but its insistence on sexual privilege and its misogyny. The fact that any discussion of women in Parliament resulted in obscene jokes, for example, was noted by many feminists, who ventured to hope that the admission of women to the franchise would at the very least improve the manners of male MPs. But feminists also focused attention on the brutality and mindlessness evident in male recreational activities: the self-indulgence and the selfishness of men accustomed to think that the provision of their pleasure was the purpose not only of their own lives, but the lives of many others,

[64] John Vincent, *The Formation of the British Liberal Party, 1857–68*, Harmondsworth, 1972, 14.
[65] Genevieve Lloyd, *The Man of Reason*, Sydney and London, 1986.

and the implications for women of men's sense of their own entitlement to indulge in sexual pleasure as and when they wished.[66] What is evident in all this is a rejection of the view that men embodied the highest human qualities and a recognition that those very qualities deemed most impressive by men often looked quite different when seen from the vantage-point of women.

But while Victorian feminists had no difficulty in offering a critique of the masculinity of the public sphere, or of showing its connection with broader constructions of masculinity, they had much greater difficulty in recognizing that this critique could also be applied to the theoretical foundations of liberalism. For many feminists were powerfully influenced by and felt themselves to be strongly connected both to the liberal tradition and to the Liberal Party. It is unquestionably the case that liberalism offered feminism a language in which to condemn the confinement and restrictions women faced and in which to make their demands for political, legal, and social reform. As we shall see, it also offered some feminists, such as Josephine Butler, a sense of connection with a long-standing reforming tradition. But it did not address adequately the central question of sexual oppression, as distinct from political or social oppression, which lay at the very heart of feminism, nor did it offer a way in which women could enter into or be represented in the political realm. Those feminists most strongly committed to a liberal approach in national politics faced considerable conflict in their attempts to unite their feminism with it, finding themselves forced to turn instead to discussions of sexual difference and of social purity as a way of articulating their fundamental concerns about the sexual oppression of women. At the same time, women sought to articulate an idea of female citizenship which took into account the sexual differences between men and women and the need for women's interests as gendered subjects to be represented in the public world.

In presenting their view of the nature and importance of sexual difference and of the contributions which women could make to society, feminists resorted to Victorian domestic ideology—the frame of mind which is so often seen as the one against which they were protesting. But it was the only language in the nineteenth

---

[66] See esp. Susan Kent, *Sex and Suffrage in Britain, 1860–1914*, Princeton, NJ, 1987, *passim*.

century which offered the basis for asserting the sexual differences between men and women, not in terms of women's inadequacy, but rather in terms of their distinctive merits and virtues. It was this ideology which enabled them to claim a significant place in both the public and the private spheres. Victorian feminists, like their French and American counterparts, asserted the need for female public participation in terms of the particular nature of women and the specific contribution they could make as a consequence of their sex and of their familial duties. But where American and French women asserted the importance of republican motherhood and of having women capable of educating the citizens needed by the new republics, English women drew on the Evangelical tradition and on the religious and moral duties of women in an industrializing society. It was ironic that this should be so because it meant that Victorian feminism was imbued through and through with the values of its conservative opponents.

IV

The religious, economic, and social bases of Victorian domestic ideology, with its new domestic ideal of womanhood and its insistence on the sanctity of the home, have been thoroughly explored recently, as have the changes in this ideology from the late eighteenth through to the late nineteenth centuries.[67] The relationship between feminism and domestic ideology has been less extensively examined.[68] In Ray Strachey's view, the Victorian domestic ideal established a framework for women's lives and an idea of femininity to which feminists were strongly opposed and which they necessarily set out to combat. At the same time, it is becoming more and more evident that many feminists accepted much of this ideology,

[67] See Françoise Basch, *Relative Creatures: Victorian Women in Society and the Novel*, New York, 1984; Walter Houghton, *The Victorian Frame of Mind*, New Haven, Conn., 1957, ch. 13; Davidoff and Hall, *Family Fortunes*, Pt. I; Carol Dyhouse, *Girls Growing up in Late Victorian and Edwardian England*, London, 1981, chs. 1 and 2.

[68] See B. Caine, 'Feminism, Suffrage and the Nineteenth-Century English Women's Movement', *Women's Studies International Forum*, 5 (1982), 537–50; Philippa Levine, *Victorian Feminism, 1850–1900*, London, 1987, 12–14; Sandra Holton, *Feminism and Democracy: Women's Suffrage and Reform Politics in Britain, 1900–1918*, Cambridge, 1986, 1–8.

although they often reformulated it in a way which rejected the idea of women as relative beings who were defined entirely through wifehood and maternity. As my discussion of liberalism suggests, feminists found in early Victorian domestic ideology not only a set of ideas which they had to combat, but also one which helped them to negotiate with liberalism and with the gendered nature of the public sphere. As a result of this, Victorian domestic ideology in some of its many forms occupied a very complex place in Victorian feminist thought.

At first sight, it appears paradoxical to suggest that Victorian domestic ideology was itself one of the formative influences of Victorian feminism, but undoubtedly this was the case. The dominance of a particular notion of submissive, domesticated womanhood throughout the nineteenth century is now widely accepted. What is less recognized, however, is the extent to which the very tracts and manuals intended to establish the nature and the true role of women became in themselves part of the woman question. One might well argue that the very proliferation of discourses on femininity served to undermine the idea that the prevailing role of women was part of the natural order and to render it problematical. Every time the necessary inferiority of women was insisted upon, repressed alternatives were also evident. The Victorians did not have access to Foucault's theory of discourse nor to his ideas about how these could be deconstructed. But the extent of prevailing concern about the social and domestic role, the influence, the education, the sexuality, the proper legal and social status of women is evident from even the most cursory reading of any of the early Victorian works on women.

The disquiet about the situation and the status of women, and the need for constant redefinition of their nature and duties arose in part from the contradictions evident within the best-known religious view of women's role. As Catherine Hall has shown, much of Victorian domestic ideology derived from the Evangelicals. But the need for women to provide the distinctive religious and moral base for middle-class families which was so urgently demanded by the Evangelicals and so rapidly incorporated within the outlook of the commercial middle class involved serious problems. On the one hand, women were seen as naturally subordinate to men and were designed to serve them. On the other hand, the Evangelical disquiet about the increasing irreligion and moral decadence led to an attempt to focus religious and spiritual activities on the home. As the guardians of that home, women were thus charged with the role of leading and guiding those very men whose superiority to themselves they were constantly enjoined to acknowledge.[69]

This particular contradiction is spelled out in much of the literature about women's role and duty which proved to be so popular in the 1830s and 1840s. Writers such as Sarah Lewis, Mrs John Sandford, and, best known of all, Sarah Ellis, expounded at great length on the need for women simultaneously to accept their legal, social, and intellectual inferiority to men, while at the same time forming the moral characters of their children, making their homes the centre of improving discourse, and guiding husbands in their social, familial, and religious duties. Women, they argued, had to recognize their inferiority to men, acknowledging that their lesser mental power was proportional to their inferiority in bodily strength. At the same time, women had to accept that male superiority did not necessarily entail that all men were noble, enlightened and good. Had this been the case, men would themselves have provided perfect models for the weaker sex. But since men usually failed to do this, it was weak women who had to use their influence to ensure that their husbands behaved properly and carried out their familial and social role. The centre of women's influence was their religious strength and their moral purity. This was protected by their domestic seclusion and their isolation from the harsh material world which threatened the piety and the morality of their menfolk. It was because of this moral purity that women could simultaneously be inferior to and guide their menfolk—and the provision of this guidance was their great mission.

The central contradiction in the literature on women's domestic role is quite evident in the way in which discussions of women's domestic activity move imperceptibly on to this question of 'woman's mission'. From a statement of the limitations women face and of their necessary domestic confinement, it thus moves to the demand that women carry first into their homes and then into the wider society something of the religious zeal and fervour which other missionaries were taking to the heathen in foreign lands. Of

[69] Catherine Hall, 'Early Formation of Victorian Domestic Ideology', in Burman, ed., *Fit Work for Women*, 15–32.

course the methods suggested to women had to be entirely different from those of other missionaries: women were to use charm and domestic comfort to make religious values appealing and pleasurable to their menfolk. The idea that women should instruct men was unthinkable. They had rather to use their feminine tact to persuade and to influence them. In some cases, women were instructed almost to seduce their husbands into religion and virtue. Mrs John Sandford, for example, insisted that women of piety should not give rise to the reproach that religious persons are often vulgar or awkward. 'On the contrary, they imbibe more deeply the spirit of their lovely religion, when they carry its charm into the detail of life, when they are fascinating as well as faithful, agreeable as well as good.'[70] But the missionary role is none the less there.

Women's mission began in the home, but it did not end there. Through their domestic role, they were to do no less than bring about the reformation of their entire society. In Mrs Sandford's view, women provided society with its 'balance and tone'. 'She may be a corrective of what is wrong, a moderator of what is unruly, a restraint on what is indecorous. Her presence may be a pledge against impropriety and excess, a check on vice, a protector to virtue.'[71] Sarah Ellis went much further than this, insisting that women, 'have the social morals of their country in their power'.[72] Ruskin went even further, arguing that it was women, through their immense domestic influence, who were responsible for all the evil, disharmony, and even war within society.[73]

The fact that domestic ideology itself could allow women so much influence became a new source of contention. At least from the 1830s, pamphlets and sermons appeared which raged against the excessive influence claimed by or on behalf of women. Clergymen such as James Burgon preached sermons in which they stressed the secondary nature of female creation and hence the fact that woman was intended as man's helper.[74] Woman, as one

[70] Mrs John Sandford, *Woman in Her Social and Domestic Character*, London, 1831, 20.

[71] Ibid. 4.

[72] Sarah Ellis, *The Daughters of England*, London, 1845, 216.

[73] John Ruskin, 'Of Queen's Gardens', in *Sesame and Lilies*, London, 1891, 110–80.

[74] J. W. Burgon, BD, *A Sermon Preached before the University of Oxford, June 8, 1884*, London, 1884.

anonymous author argued, 'has managed to overstep her sphere—she has usurped the dominion of the head, when she should have aimed but at the subjection of the heart; and the hand which ought to be held out to man, only to sustain and cheer him on his journey, now checks his steps and points to the way he is to go!'[75]

It was not only in a theoretical sense that discussions about women's sphere offered alternative possibilities, but also in an immediately practical one; feminists often clarified and developed their ideas in response to those opponents who attempted to lay down the true nature of womanhood in accordance with domestic ideology. Like Mary Wollstonecraft, mid-Victorian feminists were spurred on to elaborate their own ideas by the publication of views on women to which they were totally opposed—especially when they were the views of influential figures. In Wollstonecraft's case, it was Rousseau, the philosopher whose ideas on nature, religion, and society were so important to her, but who regarded women as necessarily the slaves and playthings of men, who became a particular target. By the mid-nineteenth century, it was no longer Rousseau's ideas on women that had to be dealt with by feminists. He had been replaced as the pre-eminent anti-feminist philosopher and social theorist by Auguste Comte, and—for Victorian feminists—by Comte's leading English disciple, Frederick Harrison.[76]

Comte's *System of Positive Polity or Treatise on Sociology* was translated into English in 1851 and was widely read. Although the number of people who regarded themselves as English Positivists was always very small, the influence of Comte's general ideas on social development, the classification of knowledge, and on social order was very considerable. Although not agreeing with all his views, writers as diverse as John Stuart Mill, Harriet Martineau, and George Eliot were profoundly influenced by him, and others, ranging from T. H. Huxley and Herbert Spencer to Beatrice Webb, went to considerable lengths to show how and why they disagreed with him. Feminists, too, singled out Comte for this purpose.

In his theory of how a modern society should be organized, Comte gave women a particular role. It was essentially a moral and religious one. While different groups of men were engaged in

[75] Anon., *Woman as She Is, and as She Should Be*, London, 1835, 2.

[76] Frederick Harrison (1831–1923), author and Positivist. See Martha S. Vogeler, *Frederick Harrison: The Vocations of a Positivist*, Oxford, 1984.

labour or in regulating society, women were to guard the family and the home. In a society which had ceased to recognize any external Deity, but worshipped the spirit of Humanity, women were to be the embodiment of that humanity, worshipped by all and bestowing their care and their beneficence on society through their care of their family and home. In the words of Frederick Harrison,

The true function of woman is to educate, not children only, but men, to train to a higher civilization, not the rising generation, but the actual society. And to do this by diffusing the spirit of affection, of self-restraint, self-sacrifice, fidelity and purity. And this is to be effected, not by writing books about these things in the closet, but by manifesting them hour by hour in each home by the magic of the voice, look, word, and all the incommunicable graces of a woman's tenderness.[77]

The ideas of both Comte and Harrison were fiercely opposed by several feminists. In Frances Cobbe's view, Comte's system 'demands our attentive study ... [because] its action upon the thought of the age, albeit indirect, is already considerable, and may possibly become very extensive'.[78] Cobbe, Butler, and Fawcett all attacked Comtean ideas, either in their original form or in terms of the version offered by Frederick Harrison.

In all cases, it was the denial of autonomy to women which was seen as the central problem in Comtean positivism. Cobbe saw it as one of the philosophies based on the theory 'that the final cause of Woman is the service she can render to Man'. In her role as philosopher to the women's movement, Cobbe protested against the moral consequences of Comte's scheme especially for women themselves. 'While he has been exalting woman into an idol, it seems to me he has utterly forgotten the effect on a human being of the double mischief of deprivation of wholesome work and of such artificial, not to say blasphemous elevation.'[79]

Josephine Butler was even more appalled by Comtean Positivism than was Cobbe, but her attack was concentrated on Frederick Harrison. Harrison was so firmly convinced of the correctness of

---

[77] Harrison, 'The Emancipation of Woman', *Fortnightly Review*, 50 (1891), 445.
[78] Frances Power Cobbe, 'The Final Cause of Woman', in *Woman's Work and Woman's Culture*, ed. Josephine Butler, London, 1869, 15.
[79] Ibid. 16.

his own views that when he heard she was writing a pamphlet on *The Education and Employment of Women*, he wrote to her, stating his belief that women should be excluded from all industrial employment and looked after by their husbands. Butler was quite appalled by his letter. 'I have this morning the most horrible letter from F. Harrison,' she wrote to her good friend Albert Rutson, 'reading it really made me tremble all over.... He says no occupations ought to be open to women, not even light trades, they ought never to work, nor have the means of working. That Trades Unions are founded on wisdom and good sense—that working men do right to drive women out, etc., etc., etc.'[80]

Butler wrote a long letter in reply, also sending Harrison a copy of her pamphlet. In it, she had demonstrated how many women were in fact reliant on their own earnings and how hard it was for them to find work which paid any kind of living wage. She pointed to the role of prejudice, of the exclusion of women from many trades, and of women's own lack of training in limiting their opportunities and keeping down their wages—and she appealed to educated men to use their influence to persuade working men of the justice of women's claims. Butler's main concern in later years, the way in which the lack of other remunerative occupations drove women into prostitution, was not in fact discussed in her pamphlet. It was alluded to in her insistence that 'economics lie at the very root of practical morality',[81] but it was not spelled out in any detail. Moved by her absolute horror at Harrison's views, however, she did spell this out clearly in her letter to him.

According to your theory of shutting them [women] out from all trades, and not suffering them to work at all for subsistence, you have two millions and a half of women for whom there is the alternative of starvation or prostitution.... You say the evils of admitting women to trades etc., are worse than those of exclusion. Have you considered this evil, which is a direct result of shutting women out of every path in which she [*sic*] could honestly win her bread? ... here in Liverpool, there are 9,000 who follow this profession because there is none other open to them. I have gathered up and trained for a better profession some hundreds of fallen women, but such poor little efforts as mine are powerless against the prevalence of such Godless theories as you hold.[82]

---

[80]   Josephine Butler to Albert Rutson, 7 May 1868, Butler Papers.
[81]   Butler, *The Education and Employment of Women*, London, 1868, 14.
[82]   Josephine Butler to Frederick Harrison, 9 May 1868, Butler Papers.

Butler went on to point out that within the working class women who brought in a wage were often more likely to find a husband than those who did not and that marriage by no means guaranteed material support for either a wife or her children.[83]

Millicent Fawcett also took up the question of prostitution in her response to Frederick Harrison but she concentrated on the aspect of the question that had always bothered her, namely the similarity between marriage for money and prostitution. Those women who married only in order to ensure their financial security were, Fawcett insisted, engaging in something 'on a par with what goes on between twelve and two every morning in the Haymarket and Piccadilly Circus'.[84] But Harrison's wish to deny women any form of remunerative work left them no alternative.

All three women castigated the Positivists for their complete ignorance of the real situation and needs of women. Despite the insistence from both Comte and Harrison that they were really concerned to elevate women, feminists insisted that Positivism could do nothing but exacerbate the subordination of women. For all their anger and disdain, it is clear that having a powerful and eloquent adversary was clearly a boon. Butler expressed herself here more strongly than she ever had before—and Fawcett's response to Harrison is one of her most striking essays. As she often acknowledged, without active opponents to spur them on, feminists found it difficult to keep going, and they had nothing to do but to repeat the same basic arguments. The need to respond to those who attacked them was not only energizing, it ensured that their views would not fall into total neglect, but that they would become part of an ongoing debate.

None the less, when one looks at the response of feminists to their opponents, what remains most significant is the extent to which feminists accepted the framework of their opponents and operated within it. Thus Cobbe, Butler, and Fawcett did not

---

[83] Harrison was unconvinced. According to his most recent biographer, he saw the truth in John Morley's 'assertion that upper-class women's harsh treatment of their women servants sometimes drove them into prostitution—but not in the argument of Josephine Butler ... that the solution to the problem lay in better work opportunities for women'. Martha S. Vogeler, *Frederick Harrison: The Vocations of a Positivist*, Oxford, 1984, 108.

[84] Millicent Garrett Fawcett, 'The Emancipation of Women', *Fortnightly Review*, NS, 50 (1891), 679.

entirely reject Harrison's ideas about the domestic and social role of women, but sought rather to demonstrate that his ideas about the moral status of women and about the social implications of this status were misguided and dangerous. In response to the charge that feminists were attempting to unsex women and hence to undermine the sacred role of women within the home, both Butler and Fawcett asserted their own beliefs in the importance of motherhood and the sanctity of women's domestic role. Millicent Fawcett consciously invoked a feminist tradition in defence of this view, arguing that,

From Mary Wollstonecraft and Miss Martineau, the spokeswomen for women's freedom have always held in the highest esteem the value of women's work in the home. The fact that to the mother in nearly all classes is consigned the training of children in their most impressionable years in itself is one of the strongest claims that has ever been made for the emancipation of women.[85]

Elsewhere, Fawcett even went so far as to argue that the women's movement had been accompanied by a new emphasis on women's domestic role and by the establishment of higher standards in all areas of women's work.[86]

It is not only on the question of women's domestic role that one can see a similarity of approach between feminists and their opponents. This is also the case in discussions of marriage. Despite their attacks on the problems women faced in marriage, few feminists painted a more dismal picture of the lot of married women generally than was evident in the writings of Sarah Ellis. Emily Davies expressed strong views about the boredom, the unrelieved drudgery, and the loneliness and isolation of many married women. The presence of their spouse was not even a help. 'There are many wives who have very little to talk to their husbands about, except the virtues or crimes of servants and the little gossip of the neighbourhood. If their husbands will not listen to what they have to say on these subjects, they are obliged to take refuge in silence.'[87] But her view is mild compared to that of Sarah Ellis. What, Ellis asks, does a woman expect from marriage?

[85] Fawcett, 'The Emancipation of Women', 677–8.
[86] Millicent Garrett Fawcett, 'The Future of Englishwomen: a Reply', *Nineteenth Century*, IV. 1878, 354.
[87] Davies, *The Higher Education of Women*, 114.

Depend upon it, if your faults were never brought to light before, they will be so now. Are you expecting to be always indulged? Depend upon it, if your temper was never tried before, it will be so now. Are you expecting to be always admired? Depend upon it, if you were never humble and insignificant before, you will have to be so now. Yes, you had better make up your mind to be uninteresting as long as you live ... You had better settle it in your calculation, that you will have to be crossed oftener than the day; and the part of wisdom will dictate, that if you persist in your determination to be married, you shall not only be satisfied, but cheerful to have these things so.[88]

Ellis's direful warning to young brides about what to expect in marriage leaves one asking how she could have expected any young woman to enter into it. Ellis does, at least, have the grace to regret that women cannot, 'consistently with female delicacy', cultivate, before an engagement, a sufficient knowledge of their future husbands to ensure that their choice is wise. She suggests that, if a woman cannot open her heart to her fiancé, and finds him excessively distant or authoritative, that she end the engagement rather than finding herself enslaved to a fearful husband. But even those women who made a good choice are warned about what awaits them.

For all the similarities evident both in the range of questions addressed by feminists and their opponents and in the fact that both accepted aspects of Victorian domestic ideology, there were none the less significant differences between them. In part these differences centre on what they saw as the causes of women's subordination and hence whether they saw it as remediable. This is clearly the case in regard to the discussions of marriage provided by Davies and by Sarah Ellis where the major difference lies, not in their sense of what marriage is like for many women, but rather in what they think can be done about it. Ellis regarded women's subordination as natural and as a reflection of their intellectual inferiority. Hence she counsels acceptance and resignation—sometimes on the grounds that women are themselves to blame for what they suffer. Davies, by contrast, saw the confinement of wives to the home and lack of communication between women and men as the result of social arrangements and social conventions. Hence she

---

[88] Sarah Ellis, *The Wives of England: Their Relative Duties, Domestic Influence and Social Obligations*, London, 1843, 16.

argued that if women were educated and given access to employment, they could either avoid marriage altogether or turn the marital relationship into a companionate one based on shared interests and ideas and on mutual respect. The condition of women was for Davies socially constructed rather than being divinely or naturally ordained, and hence it was amenable to alteration.

But for all their emphasis on the possibilities of changing the circumstances of women, Victorian feminists adhered strongly to the view that there were fundamental, significant, and unalterable differences between men and women. What is most noticeable about feminist discussions of sexual difference in the nineteenth century is the emphasis placed on women's bodies and on the connection between the physical and the social and moral qualities of women. Like eighteenth- and nineteenth-century scientists, feminists emphasized the reproductive capacities of women and the centrality of potential or actual maternity in the formation of their personalities. Women, as Frances Cobbe once put it, were 'human beings of the mother sex'.[89] Hence their natural characteristics were the ones which were associated with maternity. As we have seen, by concentrating on maternity rather than wifehood, feminists from Wollstonecraft onwards could base their claims for social reforms and for representation, on their duties towards their children. This had the obvious effect of removing from the central point in the discussion the question of marriage and of the sexual relationships between women and men.

This emphasis on the body was also necessary if feminists were to argue that they would undertake a different public and political role from men. To a large extent, the proponents of Victorian domestic ideology equated women's moral purity with their innocence and hence with their confinement in the home. Implicit always was the suggestion that, once outside these domestic confines, women would lose their innocence and subside into sensuality and evil. By emphasizing the connection between the female body and women's moral qualities, feminists were able to argue that in any social situation or in any occupation, women would carry with them their nurturing qualities and their compassion, their moral sense and their chastity. These qualities were expressed most

[89] Frances Power Cobbe, *The Duties of Women*, London, 1881, 26.

clearly in maternity, but they were part and parcel of every woman, whether she had children or not. In making these arguments, feminists took up the construction of femininity evident in domestic ideology, but moulded it to their own purposes by separating it from any notion of sexual hierarchy or domestic servitude. As Carole Pateman has argued, in the process, they established a basis for demanding female political representation and female inclusion within the political world.[90]

The problems and limitations of this version of womanhood have long been lamented, most particularly its close connection with Victorian sexual morality and with a single ideal of womanhood. But one could equally well argue that Victorian feminists had no alternatives to the ones they took: that the only scope available to them lay in inverting and reformulating Victorian domestic ideology, in using it to rethink both the domestic and the public spheres. As we have seen, liberalism offered no alternative since, while it offered a critique of women's unequal treatment in some areas, it served to reinforce the subordination and confinement of women to the domestic sphere. Indeed there is a slightly circular situation here in which liberalism offers a certain capacity to criticize the position of women, but does not address the sexual basis of women's oppression. Domestic ideology, by contrast, offered a way to expand liberalism and to negotiate the patriarchal political world which liberalism accepted. It is their use of both outlooks which defines and characterizes Victorian feminism, and which shows how closely bound feminism was to the mid-nineteenth century formulation of the woman question.

[90] Pateman, *The Sexual Contract*, 231.

3

Emily Davies

As the founder of Girton College and the leader of the fight for the higher education of women, Emily Davies has an assured place in any study of the nineteenth-century English women's movement.[1] Indeed, the growing interest in the history of women's education over the last twenty years has meant that Davies is one of the most frequently discussed of all Victorian feminists. Her role in establishing Girton College has received the most extensive analysis,[2] but there are studies dealing with most of her other educational activities as well. Her leadership of the campaign to have the university local examinations opened to girls, and her insistence that girls' schools be included in the terms of reference of the Taunton Commission have been thoroughly explored, as has her involvement in creating and running the London School-mistresses' Association, her work on the London School Board, and her various battles to have women admitted to Cambridge University degrees.[3]

But while most of Davies's campaigns have been studied, no

[1] Sarah Emily Davies, 1830–1921. Davies has been better served by biographers than the other women in this study. See particularly Barbara Stephen, *Emily Davies and Girton College*, London, 1927. Despite the appearance of Daphne Bennett, *Emily Davies and the Liberation of Women*, London, 1989, Stephen remains the essential book for anyone seriously interested in Davies.

[2] See Stephen, *Emily Davies*; Muriel Bradbrook, '*That Infidel Place*': *A Short History of Girton College*, London, 1969; Margaret Forster, *Significant Sisters: The Grassroots of Active Feminism 1839–1939*, Harmondsworth, 1986, ch. 4, 'Education. Emily Davies'.

[3] See e.g. Sheila Fletcher, *Feminists and Bureaucrats: A Study in the Development of Girls' Education in the Nineteenth Century*, Cambridge, 1980, 17–24; Sarah

attention has yet been paid to her ideas. Indeed it is notable that while no work on the nineteenth-century women's movement is complete without some mention of Davies, there are almost no published analyses of her feminism.[4] Some commentators and historians would almost deny that there is anything in it to discuss. Her major work, *The Higher Education of Women*, has recently been republished. Yet even in the Introduction to this, her most interesting book, she is described as contributing to the cause 'as a "worker" rather than a "thinker"' and her 'doctrinaire qualities' and refusal to compromise on the question of whether women should be given the same education as men or a different one is attributed to her conservatism rather than to any 'coherent feminist theory'.[5]

Davies was a ceaseless and indefatigable worker in all the campaigns she took up. She acknowledged to her friends that she rather enjoyed the routine of committee work which others found so tedious—and it was precisely through her committee work that much of the clarity and sharpness of Davies's intellect becomes most evident. In her habitual capacity as secretary, she provided detailed and illuminating analyses of the issues which she saw the women's movement as facing in its battle to improve educational facilities for women. She used this position to set agendas for debate and to determine the strategy of several different educational campaigns, offering in the process both enormous insight into the outlook of her opponents and a very clear analysis of the reasons

Delamont, 'The Domestic Ideology and Women's Education', in S. Delamont and Lorna Duffin, eds. *The Nineteenth Century Woman: Her Cultural and Physical World*, London, 1978, 134–63; Rita McWilliams-Tullberg, *Women at Cambridge: A Men's University—Though of a Mixed Type*, London, 1975, *passim*; Patricia Hollis, *Ladies Elect: Women in English Local Government 1865–1914*, Oxford, 1987, 71–90; Martha Vicinus, *Independent Women: Work and Community for Single Women, 1850–1920*, Chicago and London, 1985, 125–9.

[4] Davies is not, for example, included either in Dale Spender's *Women of Ideas and What Men Have Done to Them* or in Spender, ed., *Feminist Theorists: Three Centuries of Women's Intellectual Traditions*, London 1983. Jane Rendall's excellent discussion of the *English Woman's Journal* is the only work which addresses Davies's overall ideas about women, their nature and social role, and about the nature of the women's movement. See Jane Rendall, '"A Moral Engine"? Feminism, Liberalism and the *English Woman's Journal*' in J. Rendall, ed., *Equal or Different: Women's Politics 1800–1914*, Oxford, 1987.

[5] Emily Davies, *The Higher Education of Women* (*1866*), ed. and with an Introduction by Janet Howarth, London and Ronceverte, 1988, p. xxv.

why women should insist on having access to the same education as was given to men.

Davies's enjoyment of committee work, and the diligence and attention to detail which made her so effective in this realm, serve to contrast her strongly with Josephine Butler—and perhaps to help to explain the antagonism between these two women. Davies obviously preferred the back-room approach, avoiding the lime-light and rarely giving speeches or even writing articles. When she felt strongly about a question, she was more likely to try to persuade someone else whom she deemed better fitted than herself to write about it than to enter the debate personally.[6] By contrast, Butler eschewed the detailed work of committees and relied on friends and paid organizers to run the Contagious Diseases campaign. Her great forte was the inspirational address which was subsequently published and circulated amongst her followers. Davies had little enthusiasm for this style, but she also felt that Butler was forgetful and unreliable—and there is no question that Butler was quite incapable of keeping the detailed records which Davies auto-matically made of meetings.

Reading Davies, whether it be her correspondence, the record of her life which she provided in her 'Family Chronicle', or her book, *The Higher Education of Women*, is an extraordinary and unexpected pleasure. Her acute sense of humour and lack of sen-timentality, her sharpness of tongue, her frankness, her complete lack of sympathy with any of the Victorian idealization of woman-hood, all combine to make her ideas and comments both unusual and refreshing. Moreover through her voluminous corre-spondence, and her published and unpublished papers, Emily Davies has left an extensive set of comments and reflections on many aspects of the situation of women, the problems which they faced, and the ways in which these should be addressed.

Like most other Victorian feminists, Davies was constantly engaged with the activity and the campaigns of the women's move-ment. She was not, any more than any of the other prominent members of the women's movement, an abstract theorist. Her

---

[6] When, for example, Henry Maudsley published his article, 'Sex in Mind and Education' in the *Fortnightly Review* (1874), while others urged Davies to respond, she left it to the person she deemed appropriate: Elizabeth Garrett Anderson. See Stephen, *Emily Davies*, 290–2.

feminism was often articulated in relation to specific issues and campaigns. But in the course of these campaigns, she expressed not only ideas about strategy and policy, but also a set of views concerning the nature of women's sexual oppression, the differences between women and men, the meaning of women's emancipation. These ideas are sufficiently general, cogent, and coherent to warrant recognition as a feminist theory.

The tendency for historians to dismiss Davies's feminist ideas is increased because of her strongly conservative social and political views. Despite the problems inherent in liberal feminism, the English feminist tradition continues to be seen as a liberal/radical and progressive one, shifting ground in the later nineteenth century to incorporate the concern about the economic basis of women's oppression which was stressed by socialists.[7] The very idea that feminism could come to be associated with some other intellectual framework is thus hard to accept. The difficulty posed by Davies's conservatism is evident in the way that her feminism is seen as something quite distinct from her other social and political ideas. Barbara Stephen first suggested this contrast when she opposed Davies's 'revolutionary ideas' about women to her conservatism on all other questions.[8] Although it has since been echoed by several other historians, it offers a distinction which is impossible to sustain. Davies herself saw her feminism and her conservatism as integrally connected. From her childhood, Davies had seen herself as a Conservative and she automatically applied both the term and the framework to all her interests in women and all her activities in the women's movement.* She used it to explain her ideas about

[7] See e.g. Olive Banks, *Becoming a Feminist: The Social Origins of 'First Wave' Feminism*, Brighton, 1986, 21–3; and her *Faces of Feminism: A Study of Feminism as a Social Movement*, Oxford, 1986, 28–47.

[8] Stephen, *Emily Davies*, 2; see also Ray Strachey, *The Cause: A Short History of the Women's Movement in Great Britain*, London, 1928, 100.

* Davies always used a capital letter when referring to herself as a Conservative, as she did when writing about other women as Liberals or Radicals. For her, as for the other women in this book, there is no clear separation between a general philosophical or political tradition and adherence to a political party. Josephine Butler and Millicent Fawcett both referred to themselves as Liberals, with a capital letter, even when they disagreed with the actions and the policy of the Liberal Party. After the Home-Rule crisis, Fawcett ceased to support the Liberal Party, but still saw herself as an embodiment of Liberalism. I have tended to use a capital letter for political terms when they would have done so, to convey their sense of the connection between party and general principle and their sense that the political

the suffrage, her broad approach to questions of strategy as a way of indicating how she chose some women as colleagues on her committees and rejected others. For Davies, as for Josephine Butler and most other Victorian feminists, ideas about national politics and the whole question of party affiliation were tied up with familial attitudes and beliefs and were a central part of their own sense of identity.

Davies was not, of course, the first English feminist to support the Tory Party. The expanding feminist tradition of which we are now becoming so aware makes it evident that, in seeking antecedents for her, we need to look beyond Mary Wollstonecraft and back to Mary Astell. It is indeed rather curious that while there is now quite extensive discussion of Astell's ideas, often centring on the importance of her conservative religious and political views and the relationship between these ideas on the one hand, and her analysis of the oppression of women on the other, none of the questions raised in this literature has yet been applied to Emily Davies.[9] Davies's literary output was not quite as extensive as Astell's, but there is certainly a body of work to assess. It is hard to avoid the conclusion that Davies's very success as a campaigner has deflected attention away from her writing and towards her activities.

In one way, comparing Davies with Astell can be misleading, for conservatism itself changed quite considerably in the two hundred years that separated them. Where Astell was essentially a seventeenth-century Church-and-King Tory, Davies was a pragmatic mid-Victorian Conservative who accepted a large number of liberal ideas on economic and social questions and who recognized that in certain circumstances, constitutional and broad-scale social changes were both necessary and expedient. Like many other moderate conservatives, her main concern was to ensure that these changes were empirically rather than theoretically necessary, and that they were moderate in extent and implemented with wisdom.

traditions surrounding liberalism and conservatism were as important and as specific as the party organization.

[9] See e.g. Bridget Hill, ed., *The First English Feminist: The Writings of Mary Astell*, London, 1987; Joan Kinnaird, 'Mary Astell and the Conservative Contribution to English Feminism', *Journal of British Studies*, 19/1 (1979), 53–75; Ruth Perry, *The Celebrated Mary Astell: An Early English Feminist*, Chicago and London, 1986.

Davies also differed strongly from Astell in her approach to women. Although they shared an interest in education, Davies did not see this as the only question of importance, regarding it merely as one amongst many. Nor did Davies like Astell's ideal of conventual seclusion for women, wanting rather to encourage the free mixing of men and women on equal terms as companions and colleagues. But ultimately, Davies resembled Astell in the way she combined a clear-sighted analysis of the oppression of women with a strong commitment to the existing social and political order and with a very strong sense of the limits of change which she wished for even in regard to women.

Davies was not the only Conservative in the nineteenth-century English women's movement. Most of the women whom Davies regularly sought as members of her own committees, such as Mrs Russell Gurney or Lady Stanley, shared her outlook, both in regard to the woman question and on other matters of politics. As we shall see, Frances Cobbe shared her enthusiasm for the Conservative Party and her general sense that women had nothing to gain from the Liberals. Looking at the broad picture, Olive Banks may well be correct in insisting that 'first-wave' feminism tended to be associated with the party for political and social reform and hence that it did not have a close tie with the Conservative Party.[10] But it is none the less clear that some very prominent feminists came from Conservative political backgrounds, finding there no hindrance either to their views on women or to their engagement in feminist agitation.

The central question one has to deal with in regard to Emily Davies then is precisely how to combine and connect her adherence to the Conservative Party, her conservativism on many social and political questions, and her feminism. Is it helpful, or even possible, to call her a 'conservative feminist'? The answer to this question is of course complicated. It is perhaps worth remembering that from the composite term, 'conservative feminist', Davies would only have selected the 'conservative' as applying to herself. She always thought and spoke of herself as a Conservative, but she never used the term feminist. Indeed, Davies sometimes even rejected the notion that there was such a thing as the women's movement, stressing always the separation between the various

[10] Banks, *Becoming a Feminist*, 22–3.

campaigns and the disagreements and even hostilities which existed amongst those fighting for particular reforms.[11] She did accept that there had been a suffrage movement of which she was a member— but even here, she stressed the differences in approach and outlook amongst suffragists.[12] For later historians, it is the complex and difficult interaction between Davies's conservatism and her feminism which remain crucial if one is fully to understand either her feminist ideas or her activities in the women's movement.

I

The nineteenth-century English women's movement has often been seen as one which was primarily concerned with the plight of single middle-class women in a society which emphasized women's familial and reproductive role.[13] Emily Davies typifies this kind of woman—and in her own early life, she served well to illustrate their plight. Throughout her twenties, Davies was preoccupied with the question of what to do with herself. Denied a proper education, an outlet for her obvious abilities, or a way of making her own living, the question of how to dispose of her time and of how to make a life for herself lay heavily upon her. Ultimately it was the women's movement which provided an answer as Davies became one of the select group which was engaged in fighting for the cause on a full-time basis.

Emily Davies's social background was fairly typical of that of most mid-Victorian feminists. Born in 1830, she was the fourth of the five children of the Reverend John Davies and his wife, Mary Hopkinson. Her father, as a clergyman and schoolmaster, was a member of the professional upper-middle class. Her mother came from a family which, having made its money in business, hastened to invest it in land. Emily Davies was very conscious of her superi-

[11] When W. Lyon Blease's *Emancipation of English Women*, London 1910, appeared, Davies wrote a detailed criticism of it, stressing the disagreements between different groups of women and insisting that these disagreements 'made it impossible to regard the cause as one and indivisible'. See notes headed 'Emancipation of English Women', Davies Papers, ED XXL 19a.

[12] See Davies's MSS letter to the Editor of *The Times*, n.d., Davies Papers, ED XIX 139.

[13] See Banks, *Feminism and Family Planning*, 27–41; cf. Banks, *Becoming a Feminist*, 34–9.

ority in status to ordinary middle-class shopkeepers and tradesmen. From time to time, she made deliberate—and unsuccessful—attempts to expand her acquaintance amongst what she referred to as 'lower middle class people', by offering her services in local schools where she would meet the children of tradesmen and shop-keepers. But the very terms in which she describes these attempts show her own sense of social distance from her humble neighbours.[14]

Like other women of her class, Davies's childhood was spent mainly in the family home. Her family moved around for the first few years of her life, shifting from Chichester to Southampton and back, before moving permanently to Gateshead near Newcastle in 1840.[15] Her father began his working life in Chichester as a schoolteacher and religious writer. He had some hopes of being offered a Chair in Moral and Political Philosophy at London University, but had to give them up when it became clear that the position was unpaid.[16] Although John Davies apparently had extensive intellectual and philosophical interests, such at least as led him to write an *Estimate of the Human Mind*, he was not a man of notable breadth of vision on religious and social matters. His religious works were mainly Evangelical pamphlets attacking Sabbath-breaking by those of high rank on the one hand, and Popery and Tractarianism on the other.[17] He was apparently a rather argumentative and difficult man who found his few friends only amongst his own faction within the Anglican Church.[18] His work and his intellectual occupations took up all his time so that the entire care of the family—as well as all its financial management—were left to his wife.

The importance of supportive fathers in the development of feminists has recently been stressed and one can certainly see it in regard both to Josephine Butler and Millicent Fawcett.[19] It was not, however, part of the background of Emily Davies. On the

[14] Davies, 'Family Chronicle', fo. 241.

[15] Ibid., fos. 11–14; 61–8.

[16] Ibid., fos. 16–48. With customary thoroughness Davies reproduced the entire correspondence concerning this position in her 'Family Chronicle'.

[17] Ibid., fos. 13–14.

[18] Davies's 'Family Chronicle' includes a long and quarrelsome correspondence with Manning as well as details of her father's falling out with others in the Church. Ibid., fos. 20–5.

[19] Banks, *Becoming a Feminist*, 28.

contrary, she was indebted to her father for her early experience
of the hostility to and prejudices against women which she would
later have to fight against. Although for some time a schoolmaster
himself, John Davies paid little attention to his daughters'
education. When he was installed as rector at Gateshead, he
excluded girls from the school, which was run by one of his curates,
on the grounds that their presence would lower its status![20] In a
general way, John Davies seems to have been a familial burden
rather than a support. He was a man of nervous temperament and
uncertain health, suffering a series of breakdowns. These illnesses
caused the family to leave Chichester in search of a quieter and
more restful location. Emily's 'Family Chronicle' suggests both
that her father's physical and emotional needs absorbed a great
deal of the family's energy and that she personally had little sympathy with him.

In contrast to this, Davies's portrait of her mother suggests a
vital and interesting woman who struggled hard in order to accept
her lot. Mary Davies did her best to behave as the wife of a
clergyman should. Early in their married life, her husband gave
her a diary in which to record her spiritual life. The extracts from
this which Davies quotes show her as a woman constantly battling
to do right in her husband's eyes, against her own vitality and
capacity for enjoyment. When her god-daughter visited her, she
bewailed her inability to undertake the girl's spiritual instruction
and guidance. The possibility of her husband gaining a Chair at
London University filled her 'carnal heart' with pleasure at the
thought of living in London amidst the 'honour and fame which I
anticipated for my dear husband'.[21] She recognized that 'the situation was a very dangerous one to our spiritual interest' and hence
accepted without apparent bitterness its failure to materialize.
Mary Davies was clearly a competent and energetic woman, who
managed her family wherever they were, escaping occasionally to
spend time with her parents and with other relatives and friends.
During her absences, she wrote affectionate letters to her children
and she seems generally to have entered very fully into their lives.

The Davies family was far from wealthy. Their income—supplemented by generous gifts from Mary's parents—was, however,

---

[20] Davies, 'Family Chronicle', fo. 64.
[21] Ibid, fo. 16.

sufficient to purchase a public-school and university education for their sons. All three boys went to well-known public schools, one to Repton and two to Rugby, and then to Trinity College, Cambridge. Whether it was a question of insufficient means or of lack of thought, there was apparently never any question of paying highly for the education of their two daughters. Emily attended a day school briefly but apart from that had to make do with occasional paid lessons in languages and music. For a time, there was also a weekly theme set and corrected by her father. She and her sister Jane were given some help by their mother, but Mary Davies had herself received only a limited education and was quite unable to offer her daughters any guidance in either science or languages, the areas of Emily's interest.

Quite apart from her own incapacities as a teacher, Mary Davies ceased to have time to teach her daughters after the family moved north in 1840. The rectory at Gateshead was quite a large house, with four sitting-rooms and eight bedrooms. The Davies took with them 'one maid of all work to double as a cook'. When they moved into the house, they found already installed a housemaid, a parlourmaid, and a gardener. Within a short time the domestic staff was reduced to a cook and a housemaid, with the result, as Emily said, 'that we were not much waited upon and had to do a great deal for ourselves'. Domestic life was simple and routinized: 'the menus were very simple. At breakfast, coffee, bread and butter, and cold meat; at dinner at 1 o' clock, or 1.30, a joint and two vegetables, and some simple pudding.... tea at 6. p.m. consisted of tea and bread and butter, and dry toast; and after Prayers at 9.p.m., there was a slight supper in the Library, of milk porridge or bread and milk.' Her parents added to this routine the luxury of adjourning to the library for half an hour after dinner to drink wine.[22] Emily and her sister were not, she later recalled, required to cook but they did do the ironing and the mending.

When the Davies moved to Gateshead, it was a very small town— Emily noted that it lacked even a bank—and it offered them little in the way of social life.[23] They made friends in Newcastle, but on a daily basis, the Davies children provided companionship for each other. Emily was particularly close to William, the brother who

[22] Ibid., fo. 62–3.
[23] Ibid., fo. 64.

was nearest to her in age. This closeness made it all the more miserable for Emily when her brothers left home to go to boarding school. She was left behind with her sister Jane as her only companion. Emily Davies's lack of comment about this relationship, in contrast to her discussions of Llewellyn and William, suggest that she and Jane were never close companions. Although Jane was six years older than Emily, they did their lessons together. Jane was more interested in music than Emily and had more tuition in this field. The contrast between the two girls is suggested in the letter of a family friend who wrote to Mary Davies when the girls were staying with her.

You were regretting Jane's want of order and neatness. We think her much improved in both respects—she is never likely to have my sweet Emily's precision, but there is no fear of her not being quite respectable in that department of female excellence, if she goes on to improve for the few following years as she has done for the last. Her treatment of Emily was beautiful.[24]

No alternative to the company of her family was available to Davies until the Crow family moved there in 1848. It was at this time that Emily met Jane Crow who became a lifelong friend. The Crows had moved to Gateshead from London where Jane had attended a school in Blackheath run by the two Miss Brownings. This was also the school attended by the Garretts and while there, Jane had become friendly with Elizabeth Garrett whom Emily met when she visited the Crows in their new home. Elizabeth Garrett and Emily Davies seem to have become close friends very quickly and Davies subsequently visited the Garrett home in Aldeburgh.

It would have been almost unthinkable for Davies directly to criticize either her parents or the tenor of her family's domestic life. But her feelings about her own lack of education are clearly expressed in her 'Family Chronicle'. 'Our education answered to the description of that of clergymen's daughters generally, given by Mark Pattison in his evidence to one of the Education Commissions. "Do they go to school? No. Do they have governesses at home? No. They have lessons and get on as they can." (I write from memory).'[25] In her later years, Davies expressed a series of

[24] Rhoda J. Hack to Mary Davies, n.d., Davies, 'Family Chronicle', fos. 48–9.
[25] Ibid., fo. 65.

very negative views about marriage and family life as options for women, stressing the extent of their responsibilities and their loneliness and isolation. She personally took a strong dislike to any form of domestic work and to the parish work that fell to her lot as the daughter of a clergyman. Her insistence that Girton not be modelled on a family seems further to indicate her desire to avoid any further contact with family life. Perhaps the clearest insight into her experience is offered by the comment she wrote in response to those who counselled her against any suggestion that college life might be preferable for young women to their own domestic world. She could hardly avoid suggesting this, she insisted, for 'I do not believe that our utmost efforts to poison the students' lives at College will make them half so miserable as they are at home.'[26]

The intensity of Davies's commitment to the cause of women's education cannot be understood without recognizing the embittering nature of her own experience. Her educational deprivation, although not uncommon in the nineteenth century, was more extensive than that of many other feminists. In contrast to her complete lack of schooling, Cobbe, Butler, and Fawcett all attended schools as well as receiving regular lessons at home. Davies's educational ambition was greater than theirs, perhaps because her experience of formal education was so much smaller. For Davies, as later for Virginia Woolf, the educational deprivation of women was most clearly symbolized by their exclusion from any understanding of Greek and Latin, the languages which formed the basis of the classical education. Davies began lessons in both languages on several occasions, but these casual lessons proved hard to sustain and could never make up for the continuous instruction her brothers received at their boarding schools.

Davies had two brothers before her, each providing his own ways to underline her deprivation. Her eldest brother Llewellyn had a very distinguished record at Cambridge. After taking his degree, he was elected a fellow of his college. Shortly after, he published a translation of Plato's *Republic* which was extremely well received. By contrast, William did not engage in any serious study at Cambridge. At the very time that Emily was herself so aware of the contrast between the narrow confines of her life and the wide horizons of her brother's, William was indulging in card-playing,

[26] Stephen, *Emily Davies*, 174.

drinking, and falling into debt. His brief period of rebellion against the strictures of his father was short as he subsequently confessed, repented—and became a naval chaplain! Although the family forgave him, this squandering of opportunity really rankled with Emily. Even after his death, she carefully noted his transgressions in her 'Family Chronicle'.

The Davies family always took an interest in public and political matters. Even in the years when John Davies had been unwell or had not been involved in clerical duties, he had participated in public affairs. In the years in Southampton, for example, Emily recalled that he addressed meetings calling for the abolition of slavery.[27] John Davies called himself a 'Liberal' in his early days, but Emily always regarded him as a Conservative. His political outlook, like her own, was defined by his admiration of Burke and by his constant citing of Burke's 'a disposition to preserve, and ability to improve are my standard of a statesman'[28] as his own guide. It is possible that John Davies did in fact change his political allegiances in the 1830s and early 1840s, finding in Peel the balance between preservation and reform which he admired. It was at this time that his children began to articulate their Conservative views. In 1841, when Emily was 11 and William 13, they began writing weekly newspapers. The surviving copies contain their manifesto: 'Our political views are strictly Conservative and we endeavour to support the present ministry by all the means in our power.'[29]

As the daughter of a clergyman, Emily was expected to undertake parish work and she apparently did become involved, helping to run the local school and dispensing charity. She did not provide any details of this work, but seems to have found it extremely uncongenial for she explicitly rejected both teaching and philanthropy when casting around for an occupation for herself. She discussed the question of parish work for women in her first published writings, the series of letters she sent to a Newcastle newspaper in 1860. The main purpose of these letters was to argue the

---

[27] Davies, 'Family Chronicle', fo. 13.
[28] See ibid., fo. 13a.
[29] Ibid., fo. 82. In 1844, Emily wrote another newspaper, the *North of England Record*. She derived the name from the Evangelical paper of that date—and later noted that the contents had consisted entirely of 'denunciations and warnings against Popery and Tractarianism', fo. 84.

need for an expanded range of occupations for upper-middle-class girls. 'I am aware', she wrote,

that I shall here be met with the objection that in a community like our own, and in most large towns, the difficulty is not to find work, but to find labourers; that there is abundant employment for all in visiting the poor, in the management of schools, and in other works of charity. In answer to this, I beg leave to submit, that all women are not made to be phil-anthropists. It would be considered unreasonable to expect that all men should take Holy Orders, or enrol themselves as town missionaries, and it is equally unreasonable to expect that all women should engage in similar work.[30]

Davies's account of her early years suggests that her own sense of the inferior position of women and of the injustices they faced developed early—particularly through the contrast she was so well aware of between her lot and that of her brothers. She found some women friends who shared her intellectual interests in her late adolescence, at a time when she attempted unsuccessfully to fill the gaps in her education through a variety of casual lessons. It is unfortunately not possible to trace the further developments she underwent from her late adolescence until the time, when she was nearly 30, that she found out about the start of the women's movement.[31]

Like most other Victorian women, Davies gained much of her access to the outside world through members of her family. She was unusually fortunate, however, in having one sibling who shared her interests and who introduced her to the world she most wanted to know. Llewellyn Davies settled in London in 1851. Although a clergyman, he was of a very different stamp from his father. Reject-ing his father's narrow Evangelical creed, he chose to move to London, became a follower of F. D. Maurice and was a very promi-nent Broad-Churchman. He also rejected his father's narrow approach to education, devoting his time to the Working Men's College in Great Ormond Street and taking a keen interest in women's education. Where John Davies excluded girls from the schools of his parish, Llewellyn Davies served as the principal of

[30] Emily Davies, 'Letters Addressed to a Daily Paper 1860', repr. in her *Thoughts on Some Questions Relating to Women, 1860–1900*, London, 1910, 4–5.

[31] One hundred pages of Davies's 'Family Chronicle', dealing with the years 1849–61—and hence with the whole of her early adult life—have disappeared from the Davies Papers in Girton College.

Queen's College from 1873–4 and again from 1878–86. When Emily visited him in London, she met many of the men who were associated with educational and religious reform.

When Emily Davies first visited her brother in London in the late 1850s, she attended church with him and was thus exposed to the preaching and the ideas of Maurice. Her own religious position seems to have undergone a change, as she moved away from the strict Evangelicalism of her father to a Broad-Church position akin to Llewellyn's. There is no suggestion that this change was a traumatic one for her. Rather it appears that the approach of Maurice was extremely congenial to her allowing both for her own desire for religious observance and for her broad tolerance of other religious positions. She found here too a combination of religious belief and sympathy for the plight of women which had been quite lacking in her father's Evangelicalism.

While in London, Davies also explored the small world of women's education, visiting and indeed becoming one of the Lady Visitors who chaperoned the students at Bedford College. Although London offered her a new range of activities, Emily Davies was not given time to enjoy them. Within a short time of her arrival, she was called back to undertake family duties. In the late 1850s illness struck the Davies family and Emily was required first of all to nurse Jane, who had tuberculosis, and then to take her youngest brother, Henry, to Algiers in the hope that the warmer climate would assist his health. The timing of this trip was fortunate for Emily, as she arrived in Algiers at the very time that Barbara and Annie Leigh Smith were there, seeking health for Barbara after the breakdown that followed the end of her relationship with John Chapman.

It was when she met the Leigh Smiths in Algiers that Davies first learnt about the existence of an organized English women's movement. Barbara Leigh Smith had been active in the cause of women's emancipation for some years prior to her meeting with Davies, publishing a pamphlet on the legal situation of married women in 1854 and organizing in the following year a petition in support for reform of the laws which deprived married women of their property, their earnings, or their rights to their children.[32] In

[32] For Barbara Bodichon, see Sheila R. Herstein, *A Mid-Victorian Feminist: Barbara Leigh Smith Bodichon*, New Haven, Conn., 1986.

1859 she and her friends extended their efforts with the establishment of the *English Woman's Journal*.

Davies's meeting with these women made one of the few gleams of light in a sorrowful and dismal period. Her sister Jane died of consumption in 1858, and was closely followed by Henry and William. These deaths meant that Emily was required to be the constant companion and support of her parents and, although she now knew about and was very interested in the work of the women's movement, she was forced to be based at Gateshead, making only short visits to London.

When she visited London, Davies met all the women who made up the Langham Place Circle: Isa Craig, Maria Rye, Jessie Boucheret, Adelaide Proctor, and Sarah Lewin.[33] She visited them in the room in Cavendish Square which served as an office before the house at 19 Langham Place was taken in 1859. This was large enough to provide the headquarters of the Society for the Promotion of the Employment of Women, the editorial office for the *English Woman's Journal*, a room in which to hold classes, and the facilities for a ladies' club which offered a library and a dining-room.

Although aware of what was happening in London and deeply interested in it, Emily Davies was not immediately able to take an active role in the women's movement. She attempted to establish her own version of Langham Place work by investigating the conditions of women's work in factories around Gateshead, where she lived. She wrote letters to manufacturers, and was amused when they replied politely to the Reverend E. Davies, assuming that the letters had been written by her father.[34] She wrote reports on the results of her investigations and attempted to expand her education by taking lessons in singing and in Greek. She did manage a couple of brief trips to London. In the course of these, she visited Barbara Leigh Smith Bodichon, saw Elizabeth Garrett, and went to Langham Place. On her return, she established a Northumberland and Durham Branch for the Society for Promoting the Employment of Women, but later wrote that although 'a few rather promi-

[33] For the membership of the group and their activities, see Candida Ann Lacey, ed., *Barbara Leigh Smith Bodichon and the Langham Place Group*, London and New York, 1987.

[34] Davies, 'Family Chronicle', fos. 209–12.

nent people were induced to give their names to supporting it, I do not think any work was done'.[35]

In 1861 Davies managed a longer stay in London, remaining there from June until August. She stayed with her brother Llewellyn and his family for a while, but then found lodgings closer to Langham Place which enabled her to spend much of her time there and to get to know the circle very well. Later in that year, Emily's father died and shortly after that, she and her mother moved to London. The following year, in 1862, Emily Davies finally became one of the regular inhabitants of Langham Place.

From the moment that she arrived in London, Emily Davies was not short of interesting activity. Within a few weeks, she had set up a desk in Langham Place and from there she organized the campaign which was necessary to enable her friend, Elizabeth Garrett, to obtain a medical degree. While doing this, Davies also undertook the broader educational campaigns aimed at altering the Charter of London University so that women might have access to its degrees and at opening the Oxford and Cambridge University Local Examinations to girls. Davies worked closely with Isa Craig, doing the secretarial and administrative work of the National Association for the Promotion of Social Science and ensuring that the meetings of this association addressed all the concerns felt by the Langham Place Circle about the situation of women. Only a few months after she arrived in London, in September of 1862, Davies took over from Bessie Parkes as editor of the *English Woman's Journal* and, when it folded, she edited the *Victoria Magazine*.

In the mid-1860s, when the Langham Place Circle had more or less come to an end, Davies moved the site of operations to her own home, but continued her extensive educational work. In addition, she was the secretary of the Kensington Discussion Society, of the London Association of Schoolmistresses, and of the first women's suffrage committee. One could mount a strong case for arguing that in the early 1860s, Emily Davies was the women's movement. The extent of her labour was enormous and it seems that there was no one else who would have undertaken that load. When she felt unable to continue in her role as secretary to the

[35] Davies, 'Family Chronicle', fo. 219a.

London Association of Schoolmistresses, for example, the association ceased to function.[36]

London thus offered Davies an enormous amount of intellectual stimulation. It also offered a very active social life. She attended parties at the homes of several people who were prominent in the women's movement, including Emily Faithfull, Barbara Leigh Smith Bodichon, and Clementia and Peter Taylor. In the early 1860s Davies also became very friendly with Frances Cobbe. She made many new friends. At these various parties she met writers, political and religious figures, and even foreign *émigrés* and exiles. In July 1862, for example, she noted that she had met Trollope, Louis Blanc, F. D. Maurice, R. H. Hutton, Emily Shaen, Holman Hunt, Russell Gurney, and William Allingham in addition to the regular feminist group.[37] This social world gave her great pleasure, indeed she often commented guiltily on her willingness to leave her work in order to enjoy dissipation. Davies's Evangelical background made it impossible for her to experience pleasure in social life without guilt, especially when she was invited into high society. Visits to Lady Amberley or Lady Stanley, for example, required new clothes and she wondered if it was 'well to spend one's money in bonnets and flys instead of on instructive books?'[38]

Despite her unhappiness at home as a young girl, Davies retained very close ties with her family. She lived in her adult years, as in her childhood ones, surrounded by family and family duties. Until her mother's death in 1886, Emily shared a home with her. After that, she moved to rooms which were very close to the home of Llewellyn and his large family, who were always the focus of her care and attention. Llewellyn Davies participated in all Emily's activities, offering advice and becoming a member of many of the committees she established. Her mother, too, seems to have offered support, accepting Emily's many and extended absences, ensuring her a comfortable home and getting on well with her many friends.

Although Davies had a wide circle of acquaintances and friends, her friendships do not seem to have had quite the intimacy enjoyed

---

[36] Ibid., fo. 455. The only other woman who was involved in as many activities as Davies at this time was Elizabeth Wolstenholme.

[37] Ibid., fo. 262.

[38] Stephen, *Emily Davies*, 110–11.

by Cobbe or by so many other Victorian spinsters. She lived with her mother and thus did not seek a domestic companion, but there seems to have been no one else with whom Emily Davies ever contemplated setting up a home. This is not to suggest that Davies lacked women friends. As we have seen, in her late adolescence, she had already become friendly with Jane Crow and Elizabeth Garrett. Her first visit to the Langham Place office was undertaken with Garrett and both of them went to hear the lecture by Elizabeth Blackwell which set the path for Garrett's medical career. Jane Crow was also interested in the women's movement and supported Davies's efforts throughout her adult life. Thus Davies had the start of a feminist network even before she became involved in the women's movement. That involvement in turn brought a series of new friends.

After meeting Barbara Bodichon in Algiers, Davies visited her in London and the two became lifelong friends. The women's movement even provided her with friends in the provinces. Thus when Davies went to London and visited Langham Place, she read the *English Women's Journal*. On being told that someone in Newcastle subscribed, Davies made a point of contacting the person and met Anna Richardson, a Quaker of independent means with a great interest both in education and in the women's movement, and the woman who became Davies's closest friend.[39]

But while it is clear that Davies had an extensive supportive network, her friendships were none the less limited. Her tendency to comment on and to criticize the behaviour of her friends, while emanating from concern and from a general sense of responsibility for all those women engaged in the cause, was not always endearing. She did not, for example, hesitate to criticize Elizabeth Garrett's conduct on the London School Board after she had just been elected to it. Davies chastised Garrett for her cheekiness in daring to assume that the fact that she received the highest number of votes in the London School Board election of 1870 might entitle her to take the chair.[40] (It was traditional for the man with the highest number of votes to do so.) Elizabeth Garrett commented to her fiancé that she 'did not mind a little north-east wind. . . .

---

[39] Stephen, *Emily Davies*, 54–5. For much of the period after 1861, Davies's 'Family Chronicle' consists of copies of her letters to Anna Richardson.

[40] Hollis, *Ladies Elect*, 80.

Miss Davies is a good deal my senior, and if I live to be 100 she will still be so and will feel it as much as she did in girlhood.' [41] But it does not seem to have made their friendship closer! While the two women continued to be friends, the closeness between them evident in Elizabeth Garrett's student days and in the early years of her career does not really seem to have survived Garrett's marriage.

An interesting contrast is provided by the relationship between Emily Davies and Anna Richardson. Richardson was slightly older and very much more highly educated than was Davies. Shortly after they met, Davies wrote to her that 'my mind wants looking after dreadfully and I consider you responsible for it'.[42] Anna Richardson, so it would seem, offered Emily Davies something of the guidance and advice which Davies offered to her younger women friends, such as Elizabeth Garrett—but without any of the cold wind. Much of Davies's autobiographical writing takes the form of the letters she wrote to Anna Richardson. Detailed letters were sent dealing with all of Davies's feminist activities and with her social life and reading. But while Davies obviously felt great affection for Anna Richardson—as she did for Barbara Bodichon and Adelaide Manning—these relationships depended mostly on correspondence with only occasional meetings. One senses that this allowed Davies the relief of confidential communication without imposing too much in the way of emotional demands. She assured Adelaide Manning that, should she or Barbara Bodichon be ill or really need her, she, Emily Davies, would drop everything and go to them.[43] But this statement was included in a letter declining an invitation to visit Miss Manning—and thus suggests that, for everyday purposes, constant correspondence was all that Davies was prepared to offer.

Although recent feminist scholarship has concentrated on female networks and on the female friendships of feminists and other prominent women, for Davies, as for many of her contemporaries, relationships with men were just as important. Davies obviously enjoyed her female friendships, but, unlike Frances Cobbe, she

[41] Elizabeth Garrett to J. G. S. Anderson, 8 Dec. 1870, quoted in Stephen, *Emily Davies*, 124.
[42] Ibid. 54.
[43] Ibid. 308.

was disinclined to engage in public praise of such relationships or to argue that they were preferable to heterosocial contacts. Where other nineteenth-century feminists extolled the virtues of female associations and of joint female action, Davies deplored the 'tendency to increasing separation' between the sexes, seeing this as inevitably reinforcing the oppression and the inferiority of women. All such separations entailed 'drawing lines of demarcation and setting up artificial distinctions' which worked against women.

We have not yet come to it in religion, but with Ladies' Committees, Ladies' Associations, Lectures to Ladies, & the rest, one does not quite see why we should not soon have also Ladies' Churches & Chapels, in which the duties of women as such, should be specially inculcated. We have the principle already, in the double moral code, which most people believe in.[44]

What she sought instead was the possibility that men and women could become friends and colleagues, meeting as equals. Davies herself had a number of close male friends and she discussed all her feminist concerns with men. From her remaining correspondence, it is clear that she derived encouragement, sympathy, and support from men—as well as enjoying bantering arguments with them. The most important of these friends was Henry Richard Tomkinson whom she met in the early 1860s, when he was the secretary to the London Centre for Local Examinations. Tomkinson was at this time managing director of the Sun Fire Insurance Company, but he had been bursar at Marlborough and had a keen interest in education. He became involved in all Davies's projects after this, assisting and advising her in regard to the local examinations, her own election campaign for the London School Board, and all her dealings with Cambridge. He was a member of the College Committee which planned Girton and he was treasurer of the management committee until 1877. He was regarded by many as the only person who was able to make Davies change her mind about college policy and as her closest and most reliable adviser.[45]

But in regard to male friends, as to female ones, Davies preferred

---

[44] Emily Davies to H. R. Tomkinson, 6 Jan. 1869, Davies Papers, ED XVII/GC 1/7.
[45] Bradbrook, *That Infidel Place*, 65–70; Stephen, *Emily Davies*, 86–7.

to keep a certain distance. Her most recent biographer has suggested that Tomkinson, having for some years visited Davies and
her mother on a frequent and intimate basis, proposed marriage
to Davies in 1875. This caused her great distress and a general
breakdown in health. But marriage was not something Davies was
prepared to contemplate and she refused. Although there is no
direct evidence to support this theory, it does help to explain the
severe breakdown Davies suffered in that year—and the fact that
after it, Tomkinson ceased to be a member of either her social
circle or of any of her committees.[46]

Davies had other close male friends in addition to Tomkinson—
indeed each of her specific campaigns seems to have involved some
fairly constant communication and correspondence with men to
whom she explained her views and with whom she discussed the
overall situation. The campaign to have London University open
its examinations to women involved a correspondence with R. H.
Hutton.[47] The Royal Commission on Endowed Schools brought a
lengthy correspondence with its secretary, Henry John Roby.
These correspondences make entertaining reading. Davies wrote
amusing and ironical letters which were received with pleasure and
returned in kind. These friendships involved an acceptance of
difference and an exchange of opposing views. Thus Hutton made
it clear that he was opposed to women having the same education
as men, while accepting the need for proper examinations in girls'
schools. Davies regarded the offer of special examinations as a
serpent, in place of the requested fish, but felt no inclination to
cease writing to him because of it.[48] They debated the question
whether or not Davies and her committee really knew what the
average girl sought in the way of examination—with Hutton
assuming that he and the London University Senate knew far more
about this matter than Davies and her 'enlightened ladies'.[49]

Davies's correspondence with Hutton emphasizes one aspect of
her personality which is too often ignored. Her letters to him, like

[46] Bennett, *Emily Davies*, 189–93.
[47] Richard Holt Hutton (1826–97), theologian, journalist, and man of letters,
editor of the *Spectator* for many years.
[48] For their correspondence, See Davies, 'Family Chronicle', fos. 460–75.
[49] R. H. Hutton to Emily Davies, 4 June 1866, Davies, 'Family Chronicle', fo.
462.

many of her letters to other friends, both male and female, are witty, sharp, and very amusing. It is not surprising that, in the course of their correspondence, Hutton commented that he often regretted 'not meeting you now as I used often to do' in the days when he lectured at Bedford College while Davies was a Lady Visitor chaperoning the students.[50] Contact with her, like his correspondence, would presumably have added a pleasant piquancy to his daily life. Davies's sharpness of tongue and her splendid sense of humour enabled her to deal with the timidity and the criticisms which came to her daily as she attempted to expand the educational world of middle-class girls. She commented herself on her own amusement at many of the letters she received, especially those from the mistresses of girls' schools who did not want their pupils subjected to external examinations.

Some of the schoolmistresses' letters are almost illegible and very funny. One is afraid the Examinations will foster the spirit of confidence and independence which is too common amongst girls of the present day. I fancy girls must be excessively insubordinate by nature, or they never would have a grain of spirit left, after going thro' school training.[51]

Davies's irony and her sense of humour were appreciated by both her male and female friends. In thanking Davies for sending her a copy of *The Higher Education of Women*, Frances Cobbe commented that it was a '*capital* book. I have not read anything which delighted me so much this many a day—the sense, and the fun! Your quick bits of sarcasm are impayable [sic]. I think you cannot fail to do good for you have met the enemy at every point.'[52]

Davies's relative lack of involvement in personal relationships gave her all the more time to devote to the women's movement. For all that her interest was directed towards ultimate goals rather than towards individual or personal fulfilment, she had an almost unequalled dedication to her own notion of the emancipation of women. She was one of the very few full-time participants in the movement, dedicating herself to it entirely from the early 1860s until the end of the nineteenth century. The amount of labour involved in all this was quite extraordinary. Without either sec-

[50] Davies, 'Family Chronicle', fo. 463.
[51] Emily Davies to Henry Richard Tomkinson, 10 Nov. 1863, Davies, 'Family Chronicle, fo. 323.
[52] Frances Cobbe to Emily Davies, n.d., Davies, 'Family Chronicle', fo. 419.

retarial help or any mechanical means of producing or duplicating letters, Davies kept up all the necessary minute-taking and correspondence of nearly a dozen organizations. Not only did this involve constant correspondence with her own committee members and with all those individuals on the various university governing bodies whom she sought to influence, but it also meant correspondence with a vast number of local committees who were engaged in finding girls to enter university examinations or in fund-raising.

Davies was extremely efficient and methodical, keeping copies of all her own letters and copying out many of the letters she received either into her 'Family Chronicle' or into other sets of notes. Several hours in each day must have gone in writing letters or notes for her various committees and then many others were added by her own very frequent correspondence with the various friends whom she kept abreast of all the developments in her work and in her life. She undertook many different activities to advance the cause of women both in education and in public life generally. Thus, despite her relative lack of interest in primary education, she was a successful candidate for the London School Board in 1870—although the pressure of her other activities meant that she was less active once elected than she might have been.[53]

In 1869 Hitchin House, the forerunner to Girton, opened with five students. From then until 1904, the college occupied the bulk of Emily Davies's time and attention. In the beginning she selected students and decided on the curriculum as well as overseeing all aspects of college finance and administration. She was the secretary of the College Committee and even did a stint as Mistress in the early 1870s, resigning in 1875 because she felt too worn out to continue.[54] For a couple of years after this, she did go into semi-retirement as recurrent ill health confined her to home and sometimes even to bed. By the late 1870s she had resurfaced, however, continuing to be a powerful figure at Girton through her secretaryship of the College Committee and organizing two attempts to persuade the Senate of Cambridge University to admit women to degrees.

[53] See Patricia Hollis, *Ladies Elect*, 71–90 for a fascinating account of Davies and Elizabeth Garrett as candidates for and members of the Board.
[54] Stephen, *Emily Davies*, 295.

For all her dedication to Girton, Davies was a very poor college administrator. The students resented her detachment on the one hand, and her rigidity as regards the curriculum on the other. Even Barbara Bodichon agreed with their views. 'I think we all felt the lack of genial wisdom in Miss Davies,' she wrote once to her friend Sarah Marks, in response to a complaint about Davies's lack of interest in or sympathy with Girton students. 'She who has an immense love of justice for women would die to give young women what she never had herself in early life, ah, die to get it for them though she might hate every individual.'[55] Bodichon's rather strong words were echoed by many of the students who felt bitterly Davies's lack of involvement with or even concern about their lives. Her emphasis on examinations and her lack of interest in the question of tuition brought complaints from students and caused her to lose the services of first-rate scholars and teachers such as J. R. Seeley.

Reading Davies's correspondence concerning Girton, one has the sense that running the college was uncongenial to her in many ways—and that she expected from the students the same kind of self-sacrifice she made herself. What mattered was not so much the education of a few women as the establishment of the principle of university education for women and of a large and reputable college to provide it. Hence Davies was constantly concerned to enlarge the college buildings, using any new funds for this purpose and refusing even to contemplate alternative uses such as the establishment of scholarships or improvements to the library. Her interest was not so much with the internal affairs of the college as with its expansion and development and its relationship with the University and Davies made several major—but unsuccessful—attempts to persuade the University to admit women to degrees.[56]

When she resigned as College Mistress in 1875, Davies moved back to London where she lived for the rest of her life. Once the College was opened, she felt able to resume suffrage activity. She joined the London National Society for Women's Suffrage in 1886, becoming a member of its General Committee three years later. Davies's age and renown ensured that she would immediately assume a prominent place in the suffrage movement. She was an

---

[55] Quoted in Bradbrook, *That Infidel Place*, 31.
[56] See ibid. 58–72; McWilliams-Tullberg, *Women at Cambridge, passim*.

ideal person to lead suffrage deputations to Members of Parliament—and of course this kind of campaigning was the sort of
which she most approved. Davies led several such deputations
through the late 1890s and the early years of the twentieth century.
In addition, she addressed public and private meetings, wrote
constant letters to newspapers, and published brief articles explaining to Girton students why they should become involved in the
suffrage struggle. Their education, in Davies's view, made them
precisely the people who should speak and write on behalf of the
movement.[57]

Davies's involvement in the suffrage movement was no more
free of conflict in these later years than it had been in the 1860s.
She feared the advent of a large-scale campaign and, as one would
expect, was extremely hostile to the militants. Although sympathetic to the problems of working women, she was no more
prepared to accommodate an alliance between suffragists and the
Labour Party in the early twentieth century than she had been to
accept the participation of radicals in the 1860s. As we shall see,
when the National Union of Suffrage Societies finally agreed to
assist Labour candidates in elections, Davies felt that the time had
come for her to resign from the suffrage movement.

By this time, Davies was already 70 and ready to move away
from a public life and back to her family. She moved to Hampstead,
where she lived with her brother Llewellyn and her niece Margaret.
Although Davies now withdrew from active involvement, her role
in the women's movement was not forgotten. Just as her retirement
from the Girton College Committee was followed by a series of
letters and testimonials from Girton students, present and past,
and from many others who had been involved in the education
campaign, so when women's suffrage was finally granted, her role
in the fight was acknowledged. On 19 June 1917, she received a
letter, conveying the following Resolution passed by the London
Society for Women's Suffrage.

That the Organisation Committee of the London Society for Women's
Suffrage, meeting as they believe on the eve of the passing through the
House of Commons Committee of the Clause in the Reform Bill which

---

[57] Emily Davies, 'The Women's Suffrage Movement', Central Society for
Women's Suffrage, 1906. Reprinted from the *Girton Review*, 1905.

ensures the Enfranchisement of Women, sends its affectionate greeting and congratulations to Miss Emily Davies, to whose zealous and able leadership the advance of women in different fields owes so much.[58]

Davies was one of the very few pioneer members of the women's movement who lived to cast a vote—walking to the polls in 1919 to register her support—presumably for the local Conservative candidate.[59] She died two years later in July 1921.

II

How then does one establish the nature of Emily Davies's feminism? It is somewhat ironic that so little has been written about Davies's own writing because it is she who best exemplifies the long-held image of Victorian feminism as being concerned primarily with questions of the equality between men and women and not with the separate needs of women. And it is unquestionably the case that the central core of Davies's feminism lay in her belief that it was the common humanity which women shared with men that should be at the base of the social order and that this should underlie any reforms in the legal and social position of women.

Davies's insistence on the similarities between men and women ensured that one of her major targets was prevailing Victorian views on sexual difference. She addressed this question in her first published writings in 1860, in her *Thoughts on Higher Education* and in much of her correspondence about women's education in general and Girton College in particular. Davies was at one with most other feminists in stressing the ignorance and prejudice and irrationality that went into many accepted beliefs about the intellectual differences between the sexes. But she stood almost alone in her refusal to enter into any kind of adulation of conventional notions of femininity or of motherhood, and in her attempt to bypass or to play down the whole question of the ways in which women differed from men. Accurate knowledge on these questions was unavailable, in her view, and until such time as it was available, the matter should be allowed to rest.

To demonstrate how little ideas about the true nature of womanhood depended on accurate knowledge, Davies contrasted the many different ideals of feminine nature and behaviour to be found in contemporary literature.

One authority, delightfully contented with things as they are, assures us that 'humanly speaking, the best sort of British young lady is all that a woman can be expected to be—civil, intelligent, enthusiastic, decorous, and, as a rule, prettier than in any other country'.... Another, less happily constituted, asserts that 'all good judges and good teachers lament the present system of girls' education.... After all is over, girls know very little and care about less.' ... Another view is, that a woman should be 'a gentle tyrant, capricious indeed, yet generous and kind-hearted withal'...[60]

Extending beyond, to the world of literature, we have contrasts between Patmore's 'Angel in the House' who rejoices 'in her husband's ill-temper, as affording her an opportunity of dispelling it by soothing arts', but who contrasts strongly with Tennyson's Isabel, a 'stately flower of female fortitude'.

Davies began her book *The Higher Education of Women* with this discussion of feminine 'Ideals'. It enabled her to show that no one could devise an education for women based on these contradictory ideas of what they were or what they should be. But the arrogance of men in assuming that all women should be what they themselves desired did not escape her notice. In her opposition to the conventional beliefs of her society, Davies turned frequently to her religious beliefs and to the teachings and practices of the Church of England. In contrast to the views of popular writers, she argued, 'the theory of education of our English Church recognizes no distinction of sex'. In baptism, in confirmation, in the catechism the same duties are laid down for men and women. This principle is evident in the Scotish Church as well. 'The Shorter Catechism teaches that "God created man, male and female, after His own image in knowledge, righteousness, and holiness, with dominion over the creatures".'[61] Of course the Bible and the practices of the Church supplied the kind of established authority which would appeal to Davies on strategic grounds. But at the same time, it is important to recognize the importance of her religious beliefs and of the harmony between them and her feminist views.

[60] Davies, *Higher Education*, 21–6.
[61] Ibid. 16–17.

Of course Davies was not alone in addressing these questions about the differences and similarities between men and women. Everyone who attempted to expand the world of women in the nineteenth century had necessarily to attack prevailing ideas about male and female spheres. Nor was she alone in her use of humour. Like Frances Cobbe and Millicent Fawcett, she used ridicule and irony in her battles against her opponents rather than displaying anything akin to anger. Where Davies differed from other Victorian feminists was in her lack of sympathy with prevailing Victorian feminine ideals on the one hand, and in her recognition of the psychological and aesthetic appeal offered by them on the other. In her view, there were two possible human ideals. One, which was 'extensively prevalent, and probably influencing many persons who have never stated it definitely to themselves', centred on the notion that,

the human ideal is composed of two elements, the male and the female, each requiring the other as its complement; and the realization of this ideal is to be found in no single being, man or woman, but in the union of individuals by marriage, or by some sort of vague marriage of the whole race.[62]

Once this view was adopted, the alternative ideal which 'rests on the broad basis of humanity falls into the background, and there is substituted for it a dual theory, with distinctly different forms of male and female excellence'.

In Davies's view, the general acceptance of this theory of the differences between and the complementarity of the sexes was not surprising.

It gratifies the logical instinct; and many persons, hastily taking for granted that it is the only conception of the relations between men and women which recognizes real distinctions, assume it to be the only one which satisfies the craving of the aesthetic sense for harmony and fitness.

Unfortunately, this ideal did not reflect reality and hence it was not workable.

We make the world even more puzzling than it is by nature, when we shut our eyes to the facts of daily life; and we know, as a fact ... that men are by no means ciphers in the home circle—we know that a man who should

[62] Davies, *Higher Education*, 10–11.

be all head would be as monstrous an anomaly as a woman all heart—that men require the protection of law, and women are not so uniformly prosperous as to be independent of comfort and consolation—men have no monopoly of working, nor women of weeping. The sort of distinction it is attempted to establish, though not without an element of truth when rightly understood, is for the most part artificial, plausible in appearance, but breaking down under the test of experience. When overstrained and made the foundation of a divided moral code, it is misleading in proportion to its attractiveness.[63]

It was Davies's insistence on the common humanity of men and women which determined the specific demands she made and the kinds of changes she wanted for women. In the absence of any clear evidence that women had a different kind of mind from men, she sought an education for women which was identical to that given to men. In the same way, she believed that women needed a freer life generally, with access to a wide range of work, with entry to the professions and with the possibility of full participation in public activity. These demands, she hastened to assure her readers, did not emanate from any desire to interfere with or to deny distinctions of sex. That there were such distinctions, she was perfectly willing to accept. What she questioned, and what she saw all the others fighting for the emancipation of women as questioning was 'the degree in which certain qualities, commonly regarded as respectively masculine and feminine characteristics, are such intrinsically, or only conventionally.... it is not against the recognition of real distinctions, but against arbitrary judgements, not based upon reason, that the protest is based.'[64]

Davies's approach to the situation of women can be labelled in many different ways. One could obviously see her as primarily an 'equality' rather than a 'difference' or 'cultural' feminist although, as we shall see, she placed great store on feminine decorum and was never able entirely to relinquish the ideas about women's social and moral duties with which she grew up. Alternatively, one can, as some recent historians of education have done, label her views 'radical' because of her refusal to accept a special education for girls. But none of these terms really helps one to come to terms with the complex nature of Davies's feminism, as it developed

[63] Ibid. 13–14.
[64] Ibid. 159.

through the course of many struggles. Moreover none of them offer any approach to the central questions which Davies poses: namely, the relationship between feminist theory and feminist strategy in the nineteenth century and the relationship between feminist ideas and national political beliefs and attitudes. Although those who use the term 'radical' about Davies see it as a term of praise, as one who loathed radical women, she would have shuddered at the thought that anyone could apply it to her. And indeed, within the whole framework of the nineteenth-century women's movement, it is not possible to do so. While some of Davies's educational ideas might appear radical, her approach to the question of how the women's movement should proceed was definitely not, and one needs to put both these aspects of her work together in order to understand the complex whole that made up her feminism.

The freedom from conventional beliefs or values which is so marked when one reads Davies's published work is certainly not evident when one looks at her approach to feminist campaigns. Almost from the start, Davies's insistence on caution and decorum created problems within the suffrage and educational campaigns. She supported the goal of women's suffrage and was very excited about the enthusiasm for it expressed at the Kensington Discussion Society in 1865. But when that discussion led to the question of a full-scale campaign, she feared that this was premature and that the wrong kind of discussion or publicity would ultimately harm both the chances of women's gaining the suffrage and the education campaigns. If such an agitation were to go ahead, it was important in her view to ensure that the right people were involved. Only 'safe' people should be included in any committee established to campaign on the matter: 'if wild people got upon it, who would insist on jumping like kangaroos, (the simile is not flattering) they would do harm.'[65]

Davies's concern was not only a strategic one. It extended also to the whole theoretical question of what a suffrage campaign was. She did not, she explained to Henry Tomkinson, believe that 'rights ought to be seized by force'.

Take the case of Slavery. It would surely be better that the right of

---

[65] Emily Davies to H. R. Tomkinson, 14 Nov. 1865, Davies, 'Family Chronicle', fo. 441.

freedom should be restored by the people who stole it, than that it should be extracted by an insurrection of the slaves. As to the suffrage, my view is that, the object of representation being, not to confer privileges but to get the best possible government, women should be politely invited to contribute their share of intelligence in the selection of the legislative body. As to their 'asserting their rights successfully and irresistibly', the idea is, if I may say so, rather revolting to my mind.[66]

Unlike earlier Conservative feminists, such as Mary Astell, Davies accepted that there was a parallel between the situation of slaves and that of women and hence that there was a similar parallel between the campaign for the abolition of slavery and that for the emancipation of women.[67] But her Conservatism is evident in the very way in which she drew this parallel, in her ideas both about how these campaigns should be waged and about the end being sought. She was not looking for any large-scale transformation of society, but rather for slow and moderate change of very particular situations and institutions. Hence she had no sympathy for the idea of enfranchising all women. Even when Davies returned to the suffrage campaign in the 1880s, she was only prepared to campaign for the enfranchisement of single women of means.[68]

Unlike the later suffragettes, Davies did not believe that women's suffrage would bring a drastic alteration to their position in society.

Though I do not expect that any great effect of the women's vote would at once be seen in the shape of extensive legislative reform, I do expect that, gradually, laws which are unjust to women ... would disappear, and that women would gain a hearing on questions in regard to which the conditions of their lives may give them special knowledge and insight. . . . I desire the removal of the disability which in my opinion is unjustly and unwisely inflicted upon women, because I believe that indirectly, it would have a deep and far-reaching effect; that by raising the status of all women, as such, it would tend gradually to remove hindrances to their well-being,

---

[66] Ibid.

[67] In 1862, she wrote to Barbara Bodichon welcoming the idea of an anti-slavery article for the *English Woman's Journal*. 'If we exist for anything, surely it is to fight slavery, of negro as well as of women.' Emily Davies to Barbara Bodichon, 3 Dec. 1862, Bodichon Papers, B. 302.

[68] Emily Davies, 'The Women's Suffrage Movement', 3–4.

to increase their self-respect and their sense of responsibility, and to favour their development on natural lines.[69]

Davies was well aware that her position was a difficult one. When the question of an organized suffrage campaign was seriously raised for the first time, she wrote to her friend and adviser, Henry Tomkinson, to ask what he thought of the matter. Frankly admitting that while others were enthusiastic about beginning some form of suffrage agitation, she had

rather tried to stifle it.... I don't see much use in talking about the Franchise till first principles have made more way. The scoffers don't see how much is involved in improved education, but they are wide awake about the Franchise. You see I lean to compromise, tho' I would also like to keep clear of hypocrisy, and the line between the two is rather faint.[70]

Davies was not alone amongst Victorian Conservatives in being interested in reform campaigns. Moreover she followed the pre-dominant Conservative approach to questions of strategy. For her, as for Frances Cobbe, the appropriate way to begin campaigning for any measure was not to call a public meeting, but to organize a committee composed predominantly of respectable and well-known individuals. It was not popular support that she sought, but rather the quiet support of prominent people.[71] When she was campaigning for access for girls to university examinations, for example, Davies arranged for letters and petitions to be sent to the governing bodies of the universities by ladies who were teachers or who had experience of girls' education. Here, as in regard to the establishment of Girton, she always sought clergymen and titled women for her committees. This approach contrasts very strongly with that of Josephine Butler, who constantly sought the support and energy of ordinary people strongly committed to the cause. Davies could never have accepted this. She felt personally far more at home dealing with committees made up of prominent and well-born individuals whose social position gave them authority—and who knew how to behave–and she believed that such people alone could bring pressure to bear in the appropriate way.

[69] Davies, 'The Women's Suffrage Movement', 5.

[70] Emily Davies to H. R. Tomkinson, 10 Nov. 1865, Davies, 'Family Chronicle', fo. 439.

[71] See Frances Power Cobbe, *The Life of Frances Power Cobbe*, London, 1894, ii. 262.

Davies's approach did not make her own campaigns any easier. While she could combine her conservative views regarding national politics and the general state of society with an outspoken criticism of the situation of women, there were not many others also able to do so. Many of those whose names she wished to connect with her own projects were entirely opposed to her desire to transform the situation of women. When she was setting up the committee to organize Girton, for example, she was very keen to have Charlotte Yonge as a member of it. Yonge typified all that was most desirable for Davies. 'Her name is so well-known, and so well-liked by vast numbers of young ladies, and her own claims to solid culture so real.'[72] But Yonge refused to have anything to do with establishing a college for women. 'I have decided objections to bringing large masses of girls together,' she wrote, in reply to Davies's request, 'and think that home education under the inspection or encouragement of sensible fathers, or voluntarily continued by the girls themselves is far more valuable both intellectually and morally than any external education. . . . Superior women will teach themselves, and inferior women will never learn more than enough for home life.'[73]

It was not only in regard to the suffrage question that Davies's attitudes and ideas came into conflict with those of other feminists. They did so throughout the educational struggle as well. The question at the bottom of this battle involved the kind of education which women should receive in college. Davies insisted that Girton students sit for the whole range of university examinations, including the Previous which required some knowledge of Greek, and that they kept to the same schedule as male students. This approach was criticized both by the students and their teachers. The criticism was spearheaded by a group of young dons, centring on Henry Sidgwick, who were seeking to reform the syllabus and the examination system at Cambridge.

Davies's position was an extremely hard-line one and, as many people have pointed out, it testified to her lack of sympathy for learning as an end in itself. Thus she took very little interest in the

[72] Emily Davies to Anna Richardson, Dec. 1867, Davies, 'Family Chronicle', fo. 564.
[73] Charlotte Yonge to Emily Davies, 22 July 1868, Davies, 'Family Chronicle', fo. 622.

question of tuition. Indeed, she regarded tuition as something which was significant only in so far as it prepared the girls for their examinations. She was unsympathetic to the requests students made to have more lessons or to the desire of those who taught her students to extend and move beyond the basic syllabus. Ironically, most of the men who offered lessons to Girton students were, like J. R. Seeley, themselves engaged in the process of devising new ways of teaching, which they saw as being far more beneficial to the students than was the routinized learning of a narrow syllabus. Hence they necessarily came into conflict with Davies. Seeley himself withdrew from teaching Girton students at the end of 1870 because he was not prepared to give his time to the college while it continued 'the old and to me obsolete routine'. He saw Davies's approach as a narrowly conservative one and argued that it would cause her to alienate her possible supporters.

You must depend mainly, in your college, upon Liberal support. Conservatives will have nothing to say to you as it is. If then it turns out that the Education you offer is of a very narrow type, and everything but Classics and Mathematics dies out ... because ... we let examinations decide the thing for us, there will be no reason, that I can see, why the Liberals should differ from the Conservatives about you. I am quite sure that numbers of people ... will in that case decide against you.[74]

Seeley's comments echo the widely-held view that Davies's conservatism threatened her own project. But his assumption that liberal political views automatically entailed significant reform in women's education is very much open to question. In her struggle to have women admitted to Cambridge, Davies faced opposition on two fronts. On one side, there were those who disliked any form of tertiary education for women—a group rightly seen by Seeley as predominantly conservative. But on the other side were those who, while supporting the tertiary education of women in general terms, favoured an alternative scheme to Davies's and one which offered women an education which was different in its content and its requirements from that available to men. The irony in the whole situation is that it was liberals who were arguing for a special education for women, one which would not have prepared them for degrees—and one which had as one of its aims a perpetuation

[74] J. R. Seeley to Emily Davies, 18 Dec. 1869, Davies Papers, ED XVII/CC 3/13.

of that very separation between men and women to which Davies was so hostile.

Davies had no wish to be caught up in the general question of university reform which was so contentious an issue in the 1860s and 1870s. She had little interest in the question—and no sympathy for the reformers. As she made clear on a number of occasions, she had no special attachment to the existing examination system. 'We are not fighting for the existing Little-Go any more than for one part or another of the Tripos Examinations. What we are fighting for is the common standard for women and men without in the least committing ourselves to the opinion that the ultimate best has as yet been reached in any examination.'[75]

Davies's battle against those who suggested an alternative education for women at Cambridge is fully documented and discussed elsewhere and does not need to be retold here. But it is important to stress the extent to which this battle involved all the issues of her own feminist beliefs and to understand why she felt so strongly about it. As we have seen, she was not an educational reformer in any general way nor was she sympathetic to the ideas, the approach, or the youth of the group of young men surrounding Henry Sidgwick. Indeed she often wished for 'a few more old ladies like Lady Stanley of Alderley ... to counterbalance the levity of young Cambridge'.[76] Sidgwick's claim, that the standard of education at Cambridge was so poor as to make it unsuitable for anyone—and hence that instead of following in this path, women should pioneer a new and better education—left her quite unmoved. And it is quite easy to see why this should be so.

Davies could not take seriously the idea that women should pioneer the new model university education. The suggestion that they do so could, she conceded, be seriously meant by some university men. 'But this idea is so new and so bewildering to the outside world that it is simply incomprehensible. The statement of it is regarded as irony.'[77] Davies herself regarded it in this light— and indeed it was a rather cruel irony that this very university education of which she had been deprived, and which had marked the differences between her brothers and herself, should be deemed

---

[75] Quoted in McWilliams-Tullberg, *Women at Cambridge*, 77.
[76] Ibid. 42.
[77] Ibid. 128–9.

worthless by the men who had benefited from it at the very moment
when she was seeking to make it available to other women! What
struck her most forcibly was not the question of the relative merits
between proposed new schemes and existing old ones, but rather
that the new schemes then being suggested should involve giving
women a separate and different kind of education. She had long
had to contend with the idea of separate education and separate
examinations, and in all cases she insisted that those who supported
special or separate examinations or educational schemes for women
were in some way assuming that there were significant intellectual
differences between the sexes and that these were known. Through
this very process of different educations, they were perpetuating
the conventional differences while getting no closer to an understanding of what, if any, innate differences between the sexes really
existed.

It is understandable, although perhaps a little unfair, that Sidgwick's interest in educational reform and his efforts on behalf
of women at Cambridge should have received so sympathetic a
treatment from historians, while Davies is usually shown as the
intransigent, destructive, and abrasive one. But the question which,
at least by implication, she asked has only recently been posed by
others. This is the question as to why he and his supporters should
have been so timid about trying to force through their desired
changes in the ordinary Cambridge curriculum for men, choosing
instead to try to get the women students to bring these about.[78]
Apparently Sidgwick's hostility to having women sit for the Little-
Go or for the Pass examination, and his feelings about the deeply
entrenched conservatism of Cambridge itself, were so great as to
make him actively oppose the admission of women to university
degrees. Indeed, much of his behaviour in regard to the whole
question of the status of women at Cambridge and the kind of
education they should receive is hard to understand and a close
scrutiny of it makes it very easy to understand why Davies so
disliked and distrusted him, seeing him, as she said, as the viper
gnawing away at her vitals.

Davies's abrasiveness and her outspoken hostility to Sidgwick
and to the others who were involved in the establishment of special
lectures and examinations for women at Cambridge and in the

[78] McWilliams-Tullberg, *Women at Cambridge*, 86–96.

founding of Newnham is well known. But this hostility can be better understood if one recognizes that the battle at Cambridge was for Davies only one episode in a lifelong struggle against the limitations and confinement of women to what men deemed to be the appropriate education to fit them for their proper place. Prior to the battle at Cambridge, Davies had already fought to have the Oxford and Cambridge local examinations and the London University examinations made available to women. At every point, she had to contend with the suggestion that women be provided with some kind of education and examinations, but that they be different in character from those available to men. The first time this happened was in relation to London University, which agreed to provide a special examination for women in 1868. Davies explained her objections to it to R. H. Hutton. 'I don't think we object so much as you suppose', she wrote on one occasion, 'to being called "different". What we cannot help doubting is the competence of the London University to decide what the differences are, & to frame a curriculum for them.'[79] Later, she conceded that neither her committee nor London University knew what the intellectual differences between men and women were. But for that very reason, the

existing exams, having already a recognised standing, had better be thrown open without reservation & let us see what comes of it. The moment you begin to offer special things, you claim to know what the special aptitudes are. The London exams do not strike me as eminently suitable either for men or women, but if girls like to go in for them, why should they be stopped?[80]

Davies and her committee did ultimately accept the London University proposal and she was pleased to see the similarities between the programme of examinations for women and the Matriculation examination for men. 'The differences are that Greek is not compulsory, and women are to have only the *First* instead of the *First Four* books of Euclid.'[81] She could not refrain, subsequently, from expressing her lack of understanding as to why one book of Euclid was deemed sufficient for women while men

[79] Emily Davies to R. H. Hutton, n.d., Davies, 'Family Chronicle', fos. 466–7.
[80] Ibid. 472–3.
[81] Emily Davies to Anna Richardson, 27 Mar. 1868, Stephen, *Emily Davies*, 192.

studied four,[82] but she accepted the examination with good grace.

But it is scarcely surprising that Davies was less affable or accommodating when the very same question of a special and different education for women was raised at Cambridge a few years later. She disliked what she saw as an increasing emphasis on separation and division between men and women in every aspect of society. In her view,

in all departments of study boys and girls, men and women, should walk together in the same paths. Why should they be separated? . . . the whole specializing system has a tendency, so far as its influence goes, to separate—to divide where union is most to be desired. The easy way in which it is taken for granted that, as a matter of course, men care for men and women for women—that a certain *esprit de corps* is natural, if not positively commendable—must surely arise from a most inhuman way of looking at things. Conceive a family in which the brothers and sisters form rival *corps* headed by the father and mother respectively! If on the small scale the spectacle is revolting, surely it ought to be no less so in the great human family.[83]

Davies did not accept that a separate scheme of education for women should ever be accepted, even as a short-term expedient. But she came increasingly to feel that the scheme for special university lectures for women, supported by Josephine Butler and Anne Clough and backed by James Stuart and Henry Sidgwick, was not, as at first appeared, merely a stopgap measure. Rather it was the beginning of a completely separate scheme of college education, and one which made it harder for her and her supporters to argue that women needed the same education as men. In her view, a special scheme which applied a lower standard to women could only be deleterious. She rested much of her case on ideas she shared with Matthew Arnold. Davies knew Arnold and had solicited an article from him for the *Victoria Magazine* even before she corresponded with him over the Schools Commission. Arnold's approach to culture was one she clearly endorsed, and it strengthened her own sense of the importance of Greek and Latin for girls. She referred to Arnold in explaining her opposition to the courses of lectures for women supported by Sidgwick and Clough.

[82] Emily Davies, 'Special Systems of Education for Women', in her *Questions Relating to Women*, 135.

[83] Ibid. 133.

We have not found hitherto that the Lectures are paving the way for the Cambridge College, but the contrary. You see, one must take into account that when you give the choice of a difficult best, or the easy second best, the latter is most likely to be taken. It is what Mat. Arnold might call an appeal to our relaxed self, and such appeals are very likely to be successful.[84]

In a similar way, Davies repeatedly argued that women set lower examination standards than those of men would simply learn to perform to that standard rather than to set their sights any higher.

Davies's insistence that women be given the same education as men derived ultimately from her belief in the intellectual similarities of the sexes. As a woman who knew herself to lack nurturing qualities either towards individuals or to society at large, Davies questioned the whole Victorian definition of femininity with its assumption that women were naturally home-makers and carers. Her central demand was that the separation of one sex from the other be ended and their mutual and common interests and needs be emphasized.

Davies's rejection of the idea that women were innately suited for their social and domestic role went along with a very definite sense that most women were miserable within the domestic sphere. She spoke from bitter experience when she argued that, especially for the single middle-class women who were her chief concern, home and domestic duties offered no real scope. Daughters were rarely needed in any extended capacity for domestic work as most of it was done by servants. At the same time, the current age was one in which 'idleness is accounted disgraceful'.[85] Thus daughters lacked either activity or any social validation for themselves. As we have seen, home, in Davies's view, was not transformed for women on marriage. It remained a place of confinement and misery, of loneliness and isolation, lacking either purposeful activity or close and congenial companionship.

The answer to the problem of home lay for Davies in outside activity. Girls needed education and training in childhood and youth, followed by occupations and employment. Long before the establishment of Girton, Davies insisted on the need for education and occupations for women, insisting 'that the women who have

---

[84] Emily Davies to Anna Richardson, 30 Dec. 1867, Stephen, *Emily Davies*, 189.
[85] Davies, *Higher Education*, 44.

professions, or something equivalent, are happier than those who have not'.[86] In response to those who feared that, once given an education, women would all rush into masculine occupations, Davies argued that competition would solve the problem: women would not flock into areas which were not suited to them as they would be outclassed by men. But Davies felt that many existing occupations were suitable to women. Although she did not like it herself, she accepted that many women would and should engage in voluntary philanthropic and sanitary work, insisting only that the women who undertook this should be trained in the proper ways to approach social questions rather than simply responding to their own 'gushing benevolence'.[87] Moving on from this, Davies turned to the question of professions and paid occupations. Medicine headed the list here. Other more novel suggestions followed: that women could become chaplains to workhouses; that they could also engage in farming, in manufacturing, and in all forms of business. In Davies's view, middle-class girls should be treated as their brothers were, being taken into the family business rather than left at home to do nothing.

Davies's views on occupations for girls and single women were similar to those of her contemporaries, if rather more expansive in range. When it came to marriage, she was far more unusual. Where other Victorian feminists, including John Stuart Mill as well as Cobbe, Fawcett, and Butler, believed that women would and should give up any other occupation on marriage, Davies stood alongside Elizabeth Garrett in her insistence that marriage and a career were not necessarily incompatible for women.[88] Formerly, Davies argued, women did not give up their economic activity on marriage as they undertook much of the work of family and household businesses. In the present day, many literary women were married, as were many schoolmistresses, while the wives of certain men, such as clergymen, undertook a great deal of work outside the home. All in all, Davies inclined to the view that educated and trained professional women would have the requisite skills to manage a household with a minimum of effort and would

---

[86] Emily Davies to R. H. Hutton, n.d., Davies, 'Family Chronicle', fo. 477.
[87] Davies, *Higher Education*, 72.
[88] Jo Manton, *Elizabeth Garrett Anderson*, London, 1965, 213.

have plenty of time to carry on with their outside work.[89] Far from reducing the level of intimacy between husband and wife, shared interests and knowledge would be likely to increase the active sympathy a woman could give her husband—just as it would increase the range of things they could talk about.[90] Similarly, of course, a household in which both parents were educated to a similar extent would provide a much better basis for children than one where the interests and the outlook of the husband were quite different from those of the wife.

Davies's rejection of existing Victorian ideals of womanhood served both to differentiate and to alienate her from many other Victorian feminists. While the demand for equality in certain areas of political, economic, and social life was common to all feminists, many of Davies's contemporaries sought rather to buttress and expand the domestic, moral, and social sphere generally designated as women's than to eschew this sphere and demand complete equality of access to the male public world. As many historians of feminism have shown, the idea of women's nurturing capacities, their compassion, and their moral superiority to men was a central theme of much nineteenth-century feminist thought and rhetoric. It was central to the feminism of Josephine Butler, for example, and it caused her to reject utterly the ideas and the approach of Emily Davies. In Butler's view, Davies was one of the 'masculine aiming women' who sought to obliterate sexual differences and hence were bound to fail in their quest. 'I dread their failure,' she explained to her friend Albert Rutson in the midst of the educational battle, 'because it clogs the wheels and blocks up the path of us who are driving towards a different and a higher goal. I pray for Miss Davies constantly, and for all like her, that a wise heart may be granted them in time, and that God may gently turn them back from error.'[91]

Butler's description of Davies as 'masculine aiming' has a certain degree of truth. For Davies differed from Butler, as indeed she differed from Frances Cobbe, not only in her lack of sympathy with any form of idealization of femininity, but also in her lack of interest in or sympathy with women's groups and women's

[89] Davies, *Higher Education*, 102–4.
[90] Ibid. 112–13.
[91] Josephine Butler to Albert Rutson, 23 May 1868, Butler Papers.

networks. Where Cobbe extolled the virtues of female friendship
and an exclusively female domestic world and Butler stressed the
importance of female solidarity in the Contagious Diseases
agitation, Davies rejected the view that women should organize or
campaign separately from men. Davies did not eschew all female
groups: she was after all the secretary and the mainstay both of the
Kensington Discussion Society and of the London Association of
Schoolmistresses. But both of these groups met quite specific needs
and when the need was no longer present, she had neither regrets
nor any sense that women's groups were a necessary or beneficial
thing in themselves.

This aspect of Davies's outlook is made evident in all her campaigns, in her rejection of unsuitable women, and in the pleasure
she took in working with sympathetic or challenging men. There
is clearly an element of personal preference here and it follows
quite closely from Davies's lack of really close or intimate women
friends. But there was more to it than that, as is made clear in her
many discussions of the need for women and men to learn to work
together. Davies articulated these ideas most clearly in the early
1860s, when she was editor of the *English Woman's Journal*. Davies
had grave doubts about the merits or even the utility of the journal.
Its small circulation made her feel that it was entirely ineffective
as it was preaching only to the converted. She had no sympathy at
all for the view, expounded by Bessie Raynor Parkes, that the
journal had to exist as a means of communication between women
and as an indication of what women could do, working by themselves. In Davies's view, this was absurd. Had Parkes

been brought up among either Church people or orthodox Dissenters,
who between them, constitute the great mass of English society, she would
know that there is nothing at all new in women's working together. All
over the country, there are Ladies' Associations, Ladies' Committees,
schools managed by ladies, Magazines conducted by ladies &c. &c., which
get on well enough. The new and difficult thing is for men and women to
work together on equal terms.[92]

Ultimately the journal folded and Davies felt no regret, seeing
it as much more important to have the arguments for the eman-

---

[92] Emily Davies to Barbara Bodichon, 17 Jan. 1863, Bodichon Papers, B. 309.

cipation of women included in general periodicals which were widely read.

Davies's lack of interest in women's relationships and women's groups was matched by her disinclination to engage in any issue which pertained specifically and exclusively to women and which did not allow for a demand that women be given the same freedoms or resources as men. Thus while campaigning for women's access to education, to the medical profession, and to the suffrage, she refused ever to address any issue involving the sexual oppression or exploitation of women. She had no sympathy for the Contagious Diseases agitation nor did she ever discuss the question of domestic violence. Although she had a detailed knowledge of the ideas about women held by medical men and clerics, she never followed Frances Cobbe in exploring the ways in which doctors and priests extended the subordination of women. Where Millicent Fawcett and Josephine Butler saw the sexual oppression and exploitation of women as the major underlying issue which needed to be addressed, Davies focused her attention on the confinement of women to a prescribed sphere which made no allowance for their personality and which denied their full humanity. In her view, the sexual double standard in itself was simply an extension of the idea that men and women should live separately, behave differently, and be regulated by different standards.[93]

The question of how one approaches or labels Davies's feminism remains a very vexed one. In some ways, one could argue that her insistence that the education of women be identical with that of men, and her rejection of certain aspects of Victorian domestic ideology have a radical tinge. Certainly one would be hard pressed to label them 'conservative'. But Davies's apparently radical analysis was accompanied by an extreme dislike of anything to do with political or social radicalism. She wanted her committees always to be composed of members of the Establishment—and preferably of those with known Conservative sympathies. It was her dislike of being associated with the radical wing of the Liberal Party which made her resign from the suffrage movement in 1867. 'The more I see of them [Radicals] the worse they appear,' she wrote to Anna Richardson, adding rather ambiguously, 'No doubt some of them

---

[93] Davies, *Higher Education*, 14.

have the domestic virtues.'[94] For all this, Davies's own campaigning could be hard-nosed and ferocious: there was nothing hesitant or compromising in her attacks on Henry Sidgwick or on the scheme for special lectures for women—and, although Davies refused to let anyone prominent in the suffrage movement be associated with the committee to establish Girton College, it was clear throughout her dealings with Cambridge that she had a particular feminist vision for women's education and that she was going to fight to carry it out.

A certain tension between Davies's analysis of the situation of women and her demands for change on the one hand, and her approach to the actual behaviour of women on the other, is evident throughout her life. Nowhere is it more clearly illustrated than in relation to the students at Girton. Davies's insistence that Girton students undertake the same education as was available to men at Cambridge was not accompanied by the belief that they should share in the daily life or be accorded the freedom that their brothers enjoyed. Indeed, Davies—like Anne Clough at Newnham—demanded standards of propriety and decorum which were much narrower and more rigid than those of the homes from which the students were drawn.[95] She commented on the fact that college women were of an age when they might well have been married and running homes, but she never contemplated offering them the authority or the responsibility which would have devolved on them had they in fact been married and running homes of their own. Indeed, in her college management, one sees all the small inconsistencies and the insistence on minute gradations between the acceptable and the unacceptable which is evident in all those discussions of women to which Davies objected so strongly. Thus climbing on the large lawn roller and being pulled along was an acceptable outdoor sport—Emily Davies even joined the students the first time they did it, but playing football on their own lawn was not.[96] Shakespeare readings were acceptable—but having girls take male parts and dress in male attire was definitely not. Women were to be intellectually and politically equal to men, but they were not in any way to forsake their socially prescribed roles. Thus her

[94] Stephen, *Emily Davies*, 118–19.
[95] Vicinus, *Independent Women*, 134.
[96] Stephen, *Emily Davies*, 224–5.

students were faced simultaneously with the demands that they follow absolutely the curriculum and the time-scale deemed appropriate for male students—while at the same time they were required to behave at all times and in all ways as young ladies. Davies wanted a 'fair field with no favour', in all matters pertaining to education and to work. But this demand was not accompanied by any fundamental re-examination of the female role in society which they were expected to fulfil.

As we have seen, Davies had strong views about the misery these roles entailed on women and rejected the notion that they suited some intrinsic female nature, seeing them simply as the result of social convention. But she sought to assist certain women to avoid them rather than subjecting them to any overall analysis. It is moreover clear that, for all her rejection of conventional ideas of femininity, Davies was bound in the same ways as her contemporaries to certain aspects of these ideas. She could deny that all women were nurturant, but not that they all exercised a beneficial moral influence. Indeed, some of her demands for an extension of the range of employments open to women depend greatly on this quality. Thus, for example, Davies argued that factory work was suitable even for middle-class women and that such women would raise the moral level of factory life. Women of the factory owners' class could well, in her view, be employed to supervise other women workers. 'Such an example, such an ideal, brought within the immediate and daily contemplation of women and girls of the labouring class, would be more effectual in rectifying their standard of morals and refinement than any philanthropic agency.'[97] The womanly qualities of women were, in Davies's view, demanded by convention rather than being innate. But for all that, she regarded some of them as unavoidable and on the whole desirable.

Davies's sense of the importance of female decorum was evident in her own behaviour. When she wrote a paper for the National Association for the Promotion of Social Science on 'Medicine as a Profession for Women' in 1867, it was delivered for her by Russell Gurney. Yet in that very year, several other women whom Davies knew—including Bessie Raynor Parkes, Emily Faithfull and

---

[97] Davies, *Higher Education*, 89.

Frances Cobbe—all delivered their own papers.[98] Indeed women had been delivering papers since the National Association for the Promotion of Social Science began: Mary Carpenter addressed its first annual conference and was probably its most regular contributor. Hence Davies was not required to break new ground, but only to do what other advanced women had already made acceptable in certain situations.

It is hard to avoid the conclusion that her caution was exacerbated and extended by her work in the women's movement. Because of her role as secretary of the various committees campaigning for the admission of women to university examinations and for Girton College, she came constantly into contact with the opponents of the movement. Like Millicent Fawcett, Davies was probably only able to bear this because of her sense of humour. But it would have been surprising if it did not take its toll. It is probable that the efforts of out-and-out opponents had little impact. The clergymen and doctors on the London University Senate, from whom Davies anticipated hostility, would, one hopes, have simply supplied amusement. The Rev. E. R. Condon, for example, feared that admitting women to university degrees would result in situations in which the weary surgeon coming home for dinner would find his wife dissecting dead bodies (presumably on the dining-room table). His fear that educating women would 'make the next generation of women a large-brained, cold-hearted, hard-working, mathematical Greek and Latin race of Logicians, but unmotherly and untender'—although shared by the majority of the Senate was something that Davies had already anticipated.[99] What was probably more difficult to deal with was the qualms of those whom she wanted as supporters. Thus, for example, when she approached the Dean of Canterbury, Dr Alford, seeking his support and participation on the committee she was forming to press for the admission of girls to the Cambridge Local Examinations, she received the following reply.

The only hesitation which remained after your last kind letter was owing to something I saw in your circular or letter about aiming at obtaining *degrees* for ladies. Much as I should wish to deepen the foundation of

---

[98] *Transactions of the NAPSS*, London, 1867, *passim*.
[99] Davies papers, Box II, 3/21, Admission of Ladies to University Examinations. Report of the Meeting of Convocation at Burlington House, 12 May 1863, fo. 96.

female education and furnish ladies with the elements of sound knowledge,
I should deprecate introducing anything like *competition* or personal public
designation into the characteristic of female society in England—believing
that any personal eminence would be dearly bought at the sacrifice of that
unobtrusiveness, which is at the same time the *charm* and the *strength*, of
our English women.[100]

The need to deal with both men and women with views like
Dean Alford was, at least to some extent, something which Davies
imposed on herself. Her rejection of anyone whose views even
smacked of being radical or unconventional meant that she was
always working with people whose social views were more conservative than her own and who constantly reinforced her sense of
the dangers of confronting existing standards of female behaviour.
At the same time, reading her correspondence and her reports of
debates on the education question, one begins to see why she was
so insistent that women students and members of the women's
movement generally should refrain from doing anything which
would give rise to the suspicion that they were becoming unwom-
anly or indecorous.

But Davies's emphasis on decorum and on women's staying
within the bounds of propriety at all times had positive as well
as negative consequences. Her conservatism in matters of social
conduct is often seen as something which contrasts, and even
conflicts, with her feminism—as she attempted at one and the same
time to change the world for women, and to keep its fundamental
outlines as they were. There is undoubtedly some truth in this
argument. But one could equally well argue that it was only because
of her conservative social and political framework that Davies was
able to be as radical as she was on the education question. Her
insistence that there be complete equality in the education of men
and women involved jettisoning all assumptions about the gendered basis of innate mental and emotional attributes. She rejected
entirely the Victorian ideal of nurturant womanhood and in so
doing subverted the existing framework for family life and for
social order. It was only possible for Davies to take these positions
if she saw these issues as relatively discrete, as matters which could
be dealt with in themselves without requiring a radical reordering

---

[100] Dr Alford to Emily Davies, 22 July 1864, 'Family Chronicle', fo. 367.

of society. Her Conservative political beliefs allowed her to treat these questions as isolated ones, which could be discussed and dealt with without raising any broader questions about the nature of society. She did not propose to alter the constitution of society— only that of the position of women. Hence, far from Davies's feminism being limited by her conservatism, one could well argue that the very condition of her radical ideas about women was her adherence to the status quo in other respects.

4

Frances Power Cobbe

WHILE Emily Davies's ideas have been almost totally neglected, those of Frances Power Cobbe have been greeted with considerable enthusiasm in recent years.[1] And, indeed, it is precisely because of the differences between Davies and Cobbe that this has been so. Where Davies's feminism stressed equality Cobbe's centres on sexual difference. Where Davies directed her attention largely to the public sphere and to gaining reforms in institutions, Cobbe paid a great deal of attention to private and domestic life. Thus while Cobbe shared Davies's interest in women's education and in the suffrage question, it is not her ideas on these questions which have attracted notice,[2] but rather her discussions of marital violence and of women's domestic subordination on the one hand, and her defence of celibacy and of female domestic companionship on the other. These interests, like her concern about women's health and about the role of doctors in perpetuating their subordination, speak directly to twentieth-century feminist concerns and have thus been taken up by twentieth-century writers.[3]

---

[1] Frances Power Cobbe, 1822–1904. There is as yet no biography of Cobbe. The most complete details of her life are to be found in Frances Power Cobbe, *The Life of Frances Power Cobbe*, 2 vols., London, 1894. See also *The Dictionary of National Biography*; Olive Banks, *Biographical Dictionary of British Feminists*, Brighton, 1985, 53–4; and Helen Caskie, 'Frances Power Cobbe: Victorian Feminist', 1981, unpublished typescript available at Fawcett Library.

[2] But see Jane Lewis, ed., *Before the Vote was Won: Arguments For and Against Women's Suffrage*, London, 1987, which includes two of Cobbe's suffrage speeches: 'Our policy: an address to women concerning the suffrage' and her 'Speech at the women's suffrage meeting, St George's Hall, 13 May 1876'.

[3] See e.g. Carol Bauer and Lawrence Ritt, ' "A Husband is a Beating Animal"—

That Cobbe's writings have been widely reread is no more than their due. She was unquestionably the ablest and most prolific writer amongst the mid-Victorian feminists and her very distinctive wit and style continue to make her articles fascinating. Cobbe contributed to almost every aspect of the nineteenth-century debate about the situation, the nature, and the rights of women. Not only did she discuss marital violence and the merits of celibacy for women, but she dealt also with the whole range of legal, social, economic, and medical problems which women faced. She took a particular interest in exposing the treatment women suffered at the hands of doctors, clerics, philosophers, and social theorists. Indeed, in her recognition of the connection between the many different forms of female oppression evident within the family, the Church, and the intellectual and professional worlds, Cobbe came closer to propounding a theory of patriarchy than did any other Victorian feminist. At the same time, and unlike Emily Davies, she accepted many of the prevailing beliefs about the differences between men and women and about the sexual roles which followed from these differences.[4]

Despite the interest in Cobbe's ideas that is now evident, she still awaits a biographer. One unusual feature of Cobbe, which helps to explain why no biography has been written, is the fact that she was not a great feminist activist. She inaugurated the public debate about university education for women, she was a member of the Married Women's Property Committee, she campaigned for women's suffrage, and she played an important part in bringing about the 1884 Matrimonial Causes Act, but she did not lead any of these campaigns, nor was she closely associated with their day-to-day affairs. To date it has mostly been the leaders of these campaigns who have found biographers. Within the nineteenth century Cobbe's ideas were probably better known than those of

Frances Power Cobbe Confronts the Wife-Abuse Problem in Victorian England', *International Journal of Women's Studies*, 6 (1983), 99–118; Nina Auerbach, *Woman and the Demon: The Life of Victorian Myth*, Cambridge, Mass. and London, 1982, 122–5, 144–7; Dale Spender, *Women of Ideas and What Men Have Done to Them: From Aphra Behn to Adrienne Rich*, London, 1982, 310–17; B. Caine, 'Feminism, Suffrage and the Nineteenth-century English Women's Movement', *Women's Studies International Forum*, 5 (1982), 537–50.

⁴ See e.g. the discussion of Cobbe in Martha Vicinus, *Independent Women: Work and Community for Single Women, 1850–1920*, London and Chicago, 1985, 15–18.

almost any other feminist. She was a very well-known journalist,
publishing articles in a very wide range of Victorian periodicals in
addition to her regular 'leader' in a popular daily paper, the *Echo*.[5]
Hence she carried the ideas of the movement to the world at large.
Ironically, the very fact that Cobbe was a professional journalist,
and needed to be paid at market rates, meant that none of the
struggling journals set up by the women's movement could afford
to pay for her services.[6]

Cobbe's interest in philosophical and religious questions, and
her quite substantial reputation in these fields, made her see herself
as the philosopher of the women's movement and as one particularly well qualified to write in very general terms about the
nature of women and about their social role and responsibilities.[7]
This view was accepted by some of her contemporaries who argued
that, 'excepting John Stuart Mill, she has done more than anyone
else to give the dignity of principle to the women's movement'.[8]

Although obviously dedicated to the women's cause, this was
not the only movement in which Cobbe was interested. She had
been an active philanthropist since her girlhood and continued
her philanthropic activities in adult life, becoming particularly
involved in the Workhouse Visiting Society and in the Societies
for Friendless Girls, which attempted to keep a benevolent and
controlling eye on workhouse girls who went into domestic service.[9]
In the 1870s she became very closely involved with the antivivisection campaign. Indeed, a recent history of this movement
claims that 'in the public mind', Cobbe was 'the personification of
anti-vivisectionism'.[10] She established and ran the Victoria Street
Society, the most important organization in the campaign, and

---

[5] A number of these leaders were republished in Frances Power Cobbe, *Re-
echoes*, London, 1876.

[6] Emily Davies regretted that she could not afford to pay Cobbe to contribute to
the *English Women's Journal*, Emily Davies to Barbara Bodichon, 2 Jan. 1863,
Bodichon Papers, B. 302.

[7] See esp. Frances Power Cobbe, *The Duties of Women*, London, 1881. This was
a series of lectures first delivered in London in 1880 and subsequently published
many times in both England and the United States.

[8] Walter Lewin, 'Life of Frances Power Cobbe', *Academy*, 46 (1894), 321.

[9] See Frances Power Cobbe, 'Friendless Girls and How to Help Them: being an
Account of the Preventive Mission at Bristol', From a paper read at the NAPSS
Congress in 1861, London, 1862.

[10] Richard D. French, *Antivivisection and Medical Science in Victorian Society*,
Princeton, NJ, 1975, 62.

edited its newspaper, the *Zooopholist*. For her, as for a number of
other Victorian feminists, there was a close connection between the
antivivisection and the feminist movements. Not only were both
fighting to protect defenceless creatures from the limitless powers
of men—but there was a strong sense of identification amongst
women with the animals who were subject to the vivisector's knife.
Indeed the suggestion was often made that those very men who
participated and even delighted in experimentation which involved
the torture of animals were more than likely to engage in the sexual
exploitation and the cruel treatment of women.[11]

Cobbe always emphasized the close connection between her
feminist concerns and her involvement in these other philanthropic
and reform movements. Stressing this connection enabled her to
insist that her concern about women was a philanthropic one,
directed towards her unfortunate suffering sisters, and having
nothing to do with herself.

It was not till I was actively engaged in the work of Mary Carpenter at
Bristol, and had begun to desire earnestly various changes of law relating
to young criminals and paupers that I became an advocate of 'Women's
Rights'. It was good old Rev. Samuel J. May, of Syracuse, New York,
who, when paying us a visit, pressed on my attention the question *'Why
should you not have a vote?* Why should not women be enabled to influence
the making of laws in which they have as great an interest as men?'[12]

Cobbe's insistence on the philanthropic impetus behind her
concern with women's rights cannot be denied. Philanthropy was
one of her passionate and life-long interests. At the same time in
emphasizing that it was philanthropic impulses that turned her
attention to the sufferings of unfortunate women, Cobbe was participating in an agreed strategy within the women's movement.
Lydia Becker spelled out this strategy quite unequivocally in a
letter explaining to a colleague how necessary it was for the women's
movement to recruit women whose 'own domestic bliss is perfect'.

However miserable a woman may be, if she makes that the ground of
agitation for an amelioration of the condition of her sex—though she is
undoubtedly right in doing so, yet it may be said that self-seeking is at

---

[11] See Coral Lansbury, 'Gynaecology, Pornography and the Antivivisection
Movement', *Victorian Studies*, 28 (1985), 413–38.
[12] Cobbe, *Life*, ii. 209. Emphasis in the original.

the bottom of her efforts. But when women who have nothing to ask for, so far as they personally are concerned, exert themselves in the cause of their suffering sisters, the voice of reproach is silenced.[13]

In seeking to gain support for the women's movement by insisting that it was essentially a philanthropic one, Becker was attempting to build on the Victorian adulation of female self-sacrifice rather than making any attempt to challenge it. As we have seen, this approach was rejected by Emily Davies, but it was heartily endorsed by Cobbe and by Josephine Butler, both of whom felt a genuine call to engage in philanthropy and found that their philanthropic interests did expand their concern about the situation of women. In what seems almost like an echo of Becker, Cobbe argued that 'Happily circumstanced women', like herself, would

have been very poor creatures had we not felt bitterly those [wrongs] of our less fortunate sisters, the robbed and trampled wives, the mothers whose children were torn from them at the bidding of a dead or living father, the daughters kept in poverty and ignorance while their brothers were educated in costly schools and fitted for honourable professions.[14]

Cobbe's insistence that it was philanthropy which made her aware of the plight of women deserves serious attention. For her, as for Josephine Butler, philanthropic activities did indeed provide an insight into the lives and sufferings of poor women which was available in no other way. At the same time, it is not possible to accept Cobbe's attempt to explain her feminism simply through her philanthropic impulses. Philanthropy may well have provided the pathway for many nineteenth-century women to break out from the domestic into the public sphere.[15] But of the thousands of women who engaged in philanthropy, only a handful became actively involved in the women's movement. Several of those whom Cobbe knew or with whose work she became involved, including Mary Carpenter and Louisa Twining, did not take up the question

---

[13] Cited in Helen Blackburn, *Women's Suffrage*, London, 1902 (repr. New York, 1971), 41.

[14] Cobbe, *Life*, ii. 210.

[15] For discussion of this, see Jessica Gerard, 'Lady Bountiful: Women of the Landed Class and Rural Philanthropy', *Victorian Studies*, 30 (1987), 183–211; F. K. Prochaska, *Women and Philanthropy in Nineteenth Century England*, Oxford, 1980; Anne Summers, 'A Home from Home—Women's Philanthropic Work in the Nineteenth Century', in *Fit Work for Women*, ed. Sandra Burman, London and Canberra, 1979.

of women's rights—despite Cobbe's attempts to convert them to
her viewpoint. Thus while accepting the importance for Cobbe's
own feminism of her philanthropic interests and activity, one still
needs to ask how the two came to be connected.

A close look at Cobbe's ideas about the role of women in philanthropy reveals the fact that they contained a particular feminist
edge. She insisted that women decide for themselves what kind
of philanthropic activities they undertake and that they follow their
own inclinations and wishes. She disliked both monastic charity
and the attempt to organize the work of women into large-scale
societies. Cobbe disapproved strongly of all forms of asceticism, so
monastic life was something which she was quite unable to accept.
She insisted that it was wrong in itself and destructive, involving
not only self-mortification for the individual, but also a denial of
common life and ordinary relations.[16]

Monastic life shared with large charitable societies one thing
which Cobbe particularly disliked: both involved women in
obeying a set of regulations and requirements which were set
by others and thus denied them the autonomy which Cobbe saw
as essential. Hence for her, 'the healthiest and best form of all
female philanthropy is the care which the wife and daughters of a
squire or mill-owner take of the workers and tenants with whom
they are naturally connected.'[17] Both her social origins and her
social attitudes are of course clearly evident in this statement, but
they are combined with a strong sense that philanthropy is engaging
and interesting for women only in so far as it allows them the
exercise of their own initiative. She was particularly hostile to
the ways in which both monasteries and large scale charitable
organizations involved the subordination of women to male
superiors.[18]

Although Cobbe offers no direct answer to the question of how
and why she combined philanthropy with feminism, a careful
reading of her autobiography suggests an answer. It is one which
requires a rather different interpretation of her life from the one

[16] Frances Power Cobbe, 'Female Charity—Lay and Monastic', *Fraser's Magazine*, 66 (1862), 774–88.
[17] Frances Power Cobbe, 'Woman's Work in the Church', *Theological Review*, 2
(1865), 516.
[18] Ibid. 516–17.

which she so carefully presents. Indeed, contrary to her insistence on the absolute independence of her feminist commitment and her own life, one might well argue that, more than any other Victorian feminist, Cobbe's feminist ideas derive from and reflect her personal experience. Her philanthropy merged with her feminism because by the time she began working with Mary Carpenter, she had already begun not only to struggle against the constraints which she faced as a woman, but to theorize and generalize her own struggles. Her philanthropic work served to show her a range of problems and constraints which were not part of her own experience, but which other women faced. But Cobbe's feminism had begun while she lived in her family home and it was articulated in the fight for religious autonomy, which she waged against her autocratic father. In the course of this battle, Cobbe established her own sense of the limits of obedience which daughters owed parents and of the need for women to learn how to combine familial duty with intellectual and moral independence.

Cobbe's father died while she was in her thirties, leaving her free at a time when she was still young enough to travel and explore the world for herself. In the course of her travels, she met many new people, especially women, and experienced a wide range of different social and personal situations. It was these, alongside her earlier closeness to her mother, which gave Cobbe her insight into the richness of female life and the possibilities open to single women. Thus when indignation at the social, legal, and political wrongs of women began to be voiced, Cobbe was quite ready to join in. What she added as her distinctive contribution was precisely the views she had come to through her own experiences: on the one hand, the need to accept the unavoidable constraints of womanhood, and on the other, a sense of the pleasures which were to be found in female companionship and in a female sphere which rejected either the intrusion of or the need to serve men. Indeed Cobbe's own life offered her the basis for the celebration of womanhood which is the most distinctive feature of her feminism.

I

Although Cobbe was a very welcome participant in the campaigns to reform the property laws, concerning married women, and to gain women's suffrage, she was in background and outlook very different from most of her colleagues. In a movement largely recruited from the professional middle class, Cobbe was one of the few who came from the gentry. Born in 1822, Frances was the only daughter of Charles Cobbe and Frances Conway of Newbridge, County Dublin. She came from a wealthy and distinguished Anglo-Irish family and never lost her pride in her family or her sense of their affluence—especially in her later years when this contrasted strongly with her own more straitened circumstances.

Although she came from a much wealthier family than did Emily Davies, this discrepancy was little evident when the two women met as adults. Cobbe grew up on a large estate, but when she left her paternal home, she did so with an annual allowance which permitted her to live only in the most modest way. The contrast between her straitened independent life and her wealthy youth was something of which she was very conscious. Sometimes when she visited her brother, 'it comes over me there in the stately old rooms and beautiful gardens that I was born a gentlewoman and have rather made a downfall in becoming a hack, scribbling for a half-penny newspaper. But the scribbler is happier than the idle lady was (if indeed I was ever idle) and my regrets always end in a laugh.'[19] For many years Cobbe supplemented her income by writing. In her final years, however, she commented ruefully on the fact that the £5,000 she had earned by a lifetime's journalism was less than her oldest brother received annually from the family estate.[20]

Apart from two years at boarding school and one year with a brother in Donegal, Cobbe spent her first thirty-six years living in the family home. Her life there was often solitary as her three brothers were very much older than her and the family had few close neighbours. Her childhood was happy despite this, or so she

[19] Frances Cobbe to Mary Somerville, 6 Sept., no year given, but the letter was attached to a newspaper cutting dated 1871, Somerville Papers, MSFP, II.
[20] Cobbe, *Life*, ii. 76.

later wrote, because of her very close relationship with her mother
and because of the pleasures she derived from her comfortable
home and the freedom she was given to roam the surrounding
countryside.

For the details of Cobbe's life, one is dependent on the autobiography which she wrote a decade before she died. This is a most
readable and entertaining work, quoted often, especially by those
interested in the education of girls in the nineteenth century. But
like most autobiographies, it contains a carefully shaped and edited
'life' and it needs to be treated with care by historians. Cobbe is
consistently vague and even incorrect about details and she selected
very carefully from her past incidents to be told and others to be
omitted.

From the very beginning her book is cast in the 'epic and heroic
mould' regarded by Nina Auerbach as one of the significant features
of the autobiographies of Victorian spinsters.[21] Cobbe glories in
her single state, insisting that hers was absolutely a 'Life Worth
Living' and making quite clear her intention to depict her own life
as an illustration of how rewarding the life of a single woman could
be. 'Perhaps if this book be found to have value it will partly consist
in the evidence it may afford of how pleasant and interesting . . . a
life is open to a woman, though no man has ever desired to share
it, nor has she seen the man she would have wished to ask her to
do so.'[22] One consequence of this emphasis is that Cobbe boasts
constantly not only about her own achievements, but also about
the notable people she has known. Her acquaintance amongst men
and women of letters, as indeed amongst famous people in all walks
of life constitutes the substance of at least three chapters.

It is perfectly clear that the autobiography was written with
particular political ends in mind. Shortly before she began writing
it in the early 1890s, Cobbe wrote to tell her old friend Lydia
Becker that she was 'planning to write, for a last book a sketch of
my life in which I shall make a point of showing how I came to be
concerned with Women's Rights and why I support them'.[23] By
this time, she had retired from active involvement in the movement.

---

[21] Auerbach, *Woman and the Demon*, 122.

[22] Cobbe, *Life*, i. 5.

[23] Frances Cobbe to Lydia Becker, 12 June, no year, Manchester Public Library,
NUWSS Collection, M50/1. 2/49.

Nearing 80 and in poor health, Cobbe had moved from London to North Wales. This book was her last contribution to the Cause. It also offered an opportunity for explanation and justification after Cobbe had retired battered and exhausted from the antivivisection battles of the 1870s and 1880s.

In some cases, the tensions between the propagandist functions of the book and Cobbe's actual feelings are suggested by curious formulations which raise the very questions they were ostensibly intended to answer or to prevent. In the chapter on 'Childhood', for example, Cobbe offers the first of many disavowals that she had any personal experience of the grievances suffered by so many women—albeit in a way which undermines the statement at the very moment that it is made. 'If I have become in mature years a "Woman's Rights Woman" it is not because in my own person I have been made to feel a woman's wrongs. On the contrary my brothers' kindness and tenderness to me have been unfailing from my infancy.'[24] But what, we feel compelled to ask, of her father, to say nothing of the legal and social institutions which ensured that it was always the brothers who were in a position to be kind and charitable to Cobbe not least because, as she makes quite plain in the text, they inherited so much more of their father's property than she did?

Similar questions are raised by her discussion of the women's movement. The chapter dealing with this subject is called 'The Claims of Women', and it is strategically placed so that it comes immediately before the chapter dealing with the antivivisection campaign and called 'The Claims of Brutes'. Cobbe's discussion of the women's movement constantly emphasizes her concern with 'our less fortunate sisters, the robbed and trampled wives, the mothers whose children were torn from them at the bidding of a dead or living father, the daughters kept in ignorance and poverty while their brothers were educated at costly schools and fitted for honourable professions'.[25] In keeping with this emphasis, her discussion of her own involvement in the women's movement stresses her concern with the suffrage campaign, her part in the campaigns to reform the laws pertaining to the property of married women and her campaign to have 'aggravated assaults' made

[24] Cobbe, *Life*, i. 31.
[25] Ibid. 210.

sufficient grounds for a woman to obtain a legal separation from her husband.

Even a cursory reading of Cobbe's account of her introduction to and subsequent involvement in the women's movement shows it as inaccurate and misleading. This is made immediately evident both by the incorrect sequence of her own activities and by her disregard of others involved in similar campaigns. Thus, for example, Cobbe writes as if she were the only member of the women's movement to take up the question of marital violence, totally ignoring the many articles and speeches by Lydia Becker, J. S. Mill, and others on the subject—and ignoring equally the sustained publicity given by the *Women's Suffrage Journal* to this problem.[26] Cobbe insists, moreover, that it was the issue of women's suffrage which first brought the whole question of women's rights to her attention when she was working with Mary Carpenter in 1859.

In fact the suffrage question did not really surface in England until the mid-1860s and although she supported it, Cobbe was so hesitant about the wisdom of any large-scale campaign at that time that she resigned from the first Executive Committee of the London National Society for Women's Suffrage within weeks of its being formed. Like Emily Davies, she found 'the different ideas of Radicals and Conservatives as to what is advisable ... more various than I had imagined' and felt unable to accept either the radical viewpoint or the thought of being associated with particular women whom she disliked. The suggestion of an amalgamation between the London Society and its Manchester counterpart also horrified her as she feared being associated with any statement or action 'whose good taste might be questionable'. She explained her position to Helen Taylor: 'this woman question is precisely the one on which it is hardest and also most imperative to preserve the strictest dignity and on which I could trust only those I knew most

[26] For Cobbe's account of her work, see ibid. 218–25; see also John Stuart Mill's speech in 'Speeches of Mr Jacob Bright, M.P., Mr Robert Lowe, M.P., Mr J. S. Mill, M.P., and Mr Shaw Lefevre, M.P., in the Debate on the Second Reading of the Bill to Amend the Law with Respect to the Property of Married Women', Manchester, 1868, 18–20. The *Women's Suffrage Journal* carried articles about marital violence and regularly published notices about particular cases of violence to wives and about the penalties imposed on husbands. After 1884, it also noted the many cases in which women who were subject to aggravated assaults were not in fact granted a separation.

thoroughly to take any steps of importance.'[27] Like Davies, she was vehemently opposed to any large-scale organization or any vocal campaigning for the suffrage at this time and did her best to dissuade others from undertaking it.

The record of Cobbe's publications serves further to question her account of the early years of her involvement in the women's movement. For it was not women's suffrage that she wrote about during the early 1860s, but rather the question of celibacy versus marriage. In these years, Cobbe entered spiritedly into the debate about redundant women which was sparked off by W. R. Greg's suggestion that those women who were not married should be shipped to the colonies to find men to serve.[28] Cobbe offered powerful and cogent arguments in favour of women remaining single, insisting that such women be able to lead full and satisfying lives. The defence of single women, like the advocacy of a greater and more independent role for women in philanthropy, were matters of immediate personal relevance for Cobbe and she showed none of the hesitancy here which characterized her early attitude to women's suffrage.

As we have seen, Cobbe's autobiography was written in 1896, a long time after the crucial years 1859-60, during which she first became involved in the women's movement. It is both possible and probable that she had forgotten some of the details of how things were in her earlier years. Women's suffrage had become the central issue in the women's movement by the mid-1890s, and it is this which explains the prominence which Cobbe gave it in her book. At the same time, her philanthropic activities serve, as she wished them to do, to legitimize the demand.

Having rejected one of Cobbe's versions of the connection between her philanthropy and her feminism, one is tempted to look further into her personal and family life to see if one cannot, despite her disclaimers, find other sources for her later feminist views. And indeed there is in the autobiography itself much that suggests it

[27] Frances Cobbe to Helen Taylor, 4 Dec. 1867, Mill–Taylor Collection, vol. xii, fos. 339–41, British Library of Political and Economic Sciences.

[28] Frances Power Cobbe, 'Celibacy v. Marriage', *Fraser's Magazine*, 65 (1862), 228-35, and 'What Shall We Do with our Old Maids?', *Fraser's Magazine*, 65 (1862), 594–606. For a discussion of this debate, see J. A. Hammerton, *Emigrant Gentlewomen: Genteel Poverty and Female Emigration, 1830–1919*, London, 1978, and Vicinus, *Independent Women*, 10–45.

was in her family home, and through the rebellion she staged against her father's attempt to dictate her religious beliefs and observances, that Cobbe established the basis for her feminist beliefs. The careful statements she made about the kindness of her brothers also gains an added meaning when contrasted with the father, who is conspicuously omitted.

Frances Cobbe had, or so she tells us, a happy and indulged childhood, surrounded by maternal and fraternal affection and knowing no want. In her early teens she left home to spend two years at an exclusive girls' boarding school in Brighton. Those years, though intellectually profitless and barren of enjoyment, were expensive and had been intended by her parents to give her the best education available. Cobbe's well-known description of them serves as a set piece for anyone wishing to comment on the appalling state of girls' schooling in the first half of the nineteenth century. She returned home with great relief, free now to continue her education unhampered by the noise, the frivolity, and the senseless routine of school. Her return also enabled her to resume her very close relationship with her mother, who was by that time a bed-ridden invalid.

On her return, Cobbe took over most of the responsibilities for running the house. This was for her a period of great enjoyment. Her time of trial came some years later when her mother died, leaving her in her early twenties as housekeeper and sole companion to her father. Cobbe's father plays little part in her recollections of childhood. He had apparently little interest in his only daughter, confining his attention to his wife and his sons. By the time she was an adult, Frances Cobbe was very well aware of the complete lack of interest or affection which existed between her and her father. To be his companion was an onerous task and she did not attempt to bring to it the care and concern she had shown for her mother. Indeed she engaged almost immediately in a deliberate confrontation with her father which increased the distance between them, but gave her a small area of autonomy.

During the last years of her mother's life, Frances Cobbe had experienced the loss of her religious faith. This had been a long-drawn-out process, beginning when she found herself doubting the veracity of accounts of Christ's miracles—at the age of 11. Little by little, she rejected the morality of the Old Testament, and then turned her attention to the New. Like so many other Victorian intellectuals, it was the 'scheme of the Atonement' which she found particularly unacceptable.[29] By her early twenties, Cobbe had rejected all the basic tenets of Christianity. She spent some time as an agnostic, although this position was one which brought her little peace of mind. Finally, with the help of her own reflections and of much theological reading, she established a new set of beliefs based on the idea of a just and rational God whose moral law was evident to everyone through their own intuition.

Cobbe's particular form of Theism was directly related to her own experience. Her mother had died while she was still in her agnostic phase and Cobbe found the idea that this death sundered her permanently and immutably from the person she loved most intolerable. Hence, as she was herself well aware, she began seeking a religious position which would contain the idea of immortality but did not return her to the fold of Christianity. She found help in her quest through reading the American Transcendentalists. Theodore Parker's *Discourse of Religion* was 'the epoch-making book' for her. Cobbe insisted that she had already come to most of Parker's conclusions before she read his work, but that it none the less 'threw a flood of light on my difficult way'.

It was, in the first place, infinitely satisfying to find ideas which I had hammered out painfully and often imperfectly, at last welded together, set forth in lucid order, supported by apparently adequate erudition and heart-warmed by fervent piety.... in the second place, the Discourse helped me most importantly by teaching me to regard Divine Inspiration no longer as a miraculous and therefore incredible thing; but as normal and in accordance with the natural relations of the infinite and finite spirit.[30]

Although Cobbe did not refer to this in her Autobiography, her later comments on Parker suggest that other aspects of his thought met deeply-felt needs of which she was becoming increasingly aware. Cobbe had grown up in a home dominated by an imperious and arrogant man who expected—and received—unquestioning obedience to all his commands. He had never shown either interest in or affection for her—indeed, it is not clear that he expressed

---

[29] Cobbe, *Life*, i. 89.
[30] Ibid. 97–8.

or showed genuine warmth to anyone. Her carefully measured summing up of her father after his death leaves one in little doubt as to how she felt about him.

His mistakes and errors, such as they were, arose solely from a fiery temper and a despotic will, nourished rather than checked by his ideas concerning the rights of parents, husbands, masters, and employers; and from his narrow religious creed. Such as he was, everyone honoured, some feared, and many loved him.[31]

By contrast, Cobbe adored her mother, a woman who was gentle, affectionate, refined, and compassionate. She typified for Cobbe the highest form of femininity.

At the very moment when Cobbe was wrestling with her different feelings about her parents, she found something very similar to her own feelings translated by Parker on to a theological plane. For Parker's *Discourse on Religion* contained a powerful critique of the masculine brutality evident in the Christian God. This God was both King and Judge, but he showed in the exercise of his absolute power cruelty, jealousy, selfishness, vindictiveness, and a complete lack of tenderness or compassion. In contrast to this, Parker put forward his own notion of a God who was, 'not a king but a Father and Mother, infinite in power, wisdom and love'.[32] Parker's God combined both masculine and feminine qualities and thus incorporated reverence for women as well as for men.

Cobbe referred explicitly to this idea in the Preface to the *Collected Works of Theodore Parker*, which she wrote in the early 1860s. Here she singled out Parker's idea of God as including both parents as one of his most significant contributions to religious thought.

All the power and care and forethought and inexorable loving severity which we attribute to the Fatherly character is fulfilled in Him. And all the inexhaustible forgiving love and tenderness which a mother's heart reveals is His also.... Too long has the Catholic Church separated off the Mother side of Deity into another object of worship; and more fatal still, has been the error of the reformed Churches who in rejecting the Madonna, have rejected all that she imaged forth of the Divine mansuetude

---

[31] Cobbe, *Life*, i. 206–7.
[32] Theodore Parker, 'Discourse on Religion', in *The Collected Works of Theodore Parker*, ed. Frances Power Cobbe, London, 1863, i. 306.

and tenderness. God is Himself and alone (as Parker often rightly addressed Him in his Prayers) 'The Father and Mother of the World'.[33]

For Cobbe herself, these ideas and Parker's authority laid the basis on which she declared her independence from her own father. Although her religious doubts had caused her great anguish during the entire time she nursed her mother, she had forborne to tell her mother this, not wanting to grieve a woman already burdened by ill health—and certainly not wanting to create a barrier between herself and her cherished parent. By contrast, Cobbe wasted no time in telling her father of her position, waiting only a short time after her mother's death before apprising him of her religious doubts. Having told him that she had ceased to accept the tenets of Christianity, she refused either to attend church or to participate in family prayers. Thus in the very statement of her position Cobbe indicated to her father that she would no longer obey his directions in regard to her religious observances. While her father presided over his assembled sons and servants, Frances roamed the garden alone, engaging in her own religious observances: the reciting of a series of prayers which she had written for and read to her mother.

Cobbe was severely punished for her apostasy by being sent away from home for several months, left uncertain all the while as to whether or not she was going to be disinherited. Finally she was recalled and reinstated as housekeeper although she refused to make any concessions. The arrangement, while it met the basic needs of both herself and her father, was never comfortable. She was 'all the time in a sort of moral Coventry, under a vague atmosphere of disapprobation wherein all I said was listened to cautiously as likely to conceal some poisonous heresy'.[34] She outraged her father even more a couple of years later by writing a book.

The Theory of Intuitive Morals, Cobbe's first book, was intended to expound her religious and philosophical beliefs. Cobbe's stated aim in writing this book was a desire to establish a basis for morality which was independent of Christian revelation. She wanted to insist that there is a moral law which is evident to everyone through intuition. But her ideas on the nature of morality served also to justify the area of independence she demanded from her family.

---

[33] *The Collected Works of Theodore Parker*, 14 vols., London, 1866, vol. i, p. xviii.
[34] Cobbe, *Life*, i. 105.

Cobbe's belief in a rational and righteous God led her to argue that the true end of human life was not happiness, but the 'perfecting of human souls'.[35] Hence the duty an individual owed to God took precedence over any other duties to family or friends, important though these might be.[36] For Cobbe, as earlier for Mary Wollstonecraft, a personal belief in a rational God provided the basis on which women could claim intellectual and spiritual equality with men while not rejecting their familial or domestic duties.

Like most other Victorian women writers, Cobbe had to do her own work in secret at night, after her domestic duties were fulfilled. She hid all trace of manuscript or proof and, when her father found out about the book, promised to publish it anonymously to avoid any public embarrassment he might suffer. As this shows, while rejecting her father's religious authority, Cobbe never questioned the duty she owed as a daughter. Once widowed, her father was quite entitled to demand that she become his housekeeper and his companion. She did what was required, but did not see that she had to love him or to abnegate her own beliefs or moral values.

In 1857, after some years of illness, Charles Cobbe died. Frances Cobbe, now in her mid-thirties, was finally free of familial duties. Her freedom, however, took the form of dispossession as the house which she had overseen for so many years now passed to her eldest brother and his wife assumed the role of housekeeper. Not only was she effectively turned out of the home she loved, but she found herself in very straitened circumstances. Either to punish her for heresy, or as a sign of his views about the place and entitlements of women, her father left her only £200 per annum. This was a lot of money by some standards, but it was less than the pin money which Cobbe had received while running her father's home.[37] It certainly was not enough to allow her an independent life similar in comfort to that she had known at Newbridge House. Cobbe rejected absolutely the idea of becoming a resident maiden aunt dependent on her brother's family. A few weeks after her father's death, she embarked on a long trip to Europe and the East, visiting Egypt, Lebanon, Palestine, and Syria as well as Italy and Greece.[38]

---

[35] Frances Power Cobbe, *Theory of Intuitive Morals*, London, 1885, p. vi.
[36] Ibid. 4.
[37] Cobbe, *Life*, i. 214.
[38] Ibid. i. 220–71.

Although she took a certain pride in her intrepidity as a traveller, relishing the fact that she had gone to Egypt long before Cook's Tours made it a regular stop for English tourists, Cobbe did not directly connect the experiences of this year or the following ones to the development of her feminist ideas. Yet it would seem to me that they are crucial for it was at this time that Cobbe began to experience the full range of pleasures which were available in the later nineteenth century to single women of means.

In the course of her first trip, particularly during the months she spent in Italy, Cobbe came into contact with a group of women whose lives were quite unlike what her own had been and who combined close friendships with the pursuit of intellectual, artistic, and philanthropic interests. The central figures in this circle were the American actress Charlotte Cushman and the sculptors Harriet Hosmer and Emma Stebbins. Isa Blagdon, the close friend of the Brownings, was another pivotal figure in this group.[39] Hosmer and Stebbins were in Rome largely in order to work with John Gibson. While in Rome, Cobbe met several other women connected with this circle: those who were particularly significant were Mary Somerville, who became her very close friend, and Mary Lloyd, another sculptor, who later became Cobbe's domestic companion.

Some of these women, such as Blagdon, had independent—albeit limited—means. Others, such as Cushman and Hosmer, earned considerable amounts through their work. All were unmarried and living lives which were regarded by many of their compatriots as excessively independent. Elizabeth Barrett Browning accepted that Hosmer lived in a 'house of emancipated women' but argued that her behaviour and her charm removed anything that might have been objectionable from the notion of emancipation.[40] But others, like the painter William Storey, felt that Hosmer was 'very willful and too independent by half'. He objected to the freedom with which she roamed the streets and rode alone on horseback and altogether disliked her companions.[41] Within the larger group of

[39] For details of this group, see *Harriet Hosmer: Letters and Memories*, ed. Cornelia Carr, London, 1913; *Charlotte Cushman: Her Letters and Memories of Her Life*, ed. Emma Stebbins, Boston, 1879; and *Dearest Isa: Robert Browning's Letters to Isabella Blagdon*, Austin, Texas, 1951.

[40] This phrase was used by Elizabeth Barrett Browning; Maisie Ward, *Robert Browning and His World: The Private Face (1812–1861)*, London, 1968, 221.

[41] William Wetmore Story to James Russell Lowell, 11 Feb. 1853, in *Browning*

women, there were several pairs living in intimate relationships. In the early 1850s, Cushman had lived with Matilda Hayes.[42] When the Brownings met them in 1852, Elizabeth Barrett Browning described them to her sister.

Oh—there is a house of what I call emancipated women—a young sculptress—American—Miss Hosmer, a pupil of Gibson's, very clever and very strange—and Miss Hayes, the translator of George Sand, who 'dresses like a man down to the waist' (so the accusation runs). Certainly there's the waistcoat which I like—and the collar, neckcloth, and jacket made with a sort of wag-tail behind which I don't like.[43]

After her relationship with Hayes came to an end, Cushman established a similarly close relationship with Emma Stebbins. At the time Cobbe met them, their household included Harriet Hosmer as well. Blagdon and Hosmer, while having very close friendships with women, do not seem to have set up permanent relationships similar to that of Cushman and Stebbins. But Cobbe certainly met other women who had done so. One of these was Rosa Bonheur who also visited the Italian colony. Her rejection of men as lovers or husbands was made quite explicit. Questioned once about the propriety of riding with a male friend unchaperoned, Bonheur replied, 'the fact is, in the way of the male, I like only the bulls I paint.' Her emotions were fully engaged by her friend and companion Natalie Mica.[44]

These close female friendships were not the first that Cobbe had encountered. Her one-time neighbour and close friend, Harriet St Leger, lived for many years with a female companion, Dorothy Wilson, in an intimate and affectionate relationship.[45] Cobbe was openly envious of these relationships and sought a close friendship with another woman for herself. Her first attempt in this direction

to His American Friends: Letters between the Brownings, the Storys and James Russell Lowell, ed. G. R. Hudson, London, 1965, 262–72.

[42] For a discussion of this relationship, see Lillian Faderman, *Surpassing Love of Men*, London, 1980, 223–4. Hayes subsequently went to London and worked with Bessie Rayner Parkes on the *English Woman's Journal*. See Rendall, *Equal or Different: Women's Politics 1800–1914*, Oxford, 1987, 114–16.

[43] Elizabeth Barrett Browning to Henriette Barrett, 30 Dec. 1853 in *Elizabeth Barrett Browning: Letters to her Sisters, 1846–59*, ed. Leonard Huxley, London, 1932, 196.

[44] See *Reminiscences of Rosa Bonheur*, ed. Theodore Stanton, New York, 1910, 366.

[45] Cobbe, *Life*, i. 214.

ended in disaster. On her return to England in 1858, Cobbe was seeking both an occupation and a place to live. Friends assisted and arranged for her to go to Bristol to work and live with Mary Carpenter. Cobbe's brief and amusing account of her attempts to accommodate herself to the Spartan regime which sufficed for Carpenter makes it clear that this arrangement did not last. She was unable either to become really interested in the street children to whom Carpenter was devoted or to cope with the diet of bread and salt beef which met Carpenter's minimal needs. But she also sought far more from this relationship than Carpenter was able or willing to give. Carpenter was prepared to have someone live in her house to assist her but, as Jo Manton has shown, she 'was looking for a competent subordinate not for a woman friend, still less a lesbian lover'.[46] Cobbe, by contrast, was looking for an emotional base and she did her best to make Carpenter provide one. After a few months, she could not bear the strain and she left Bristol several times during 1859 in an effort to restore her health and her equanimity.

During these absences, she wrote frequently to Carpenter and although her letters have not survived, a number of Carpenter's replies have.[47] These make it clear that she constantly demanded affection and commitment of a kind which Carpenter was only able to give to her cause. Again and again, Carpenter's letters explain her own position. She was grateful for Cobbe's love, but quite unable to return it:

My work and my cause require and must have the devotion of all my heart and soul and strength. I have not nearly enough to do what I wish; I could do nothing without the revelations which the Father has given me throughout. I am very glad you are enjoying yourself in Florence. I thank you much for your love, and know that you think much better of me than I deserve.[48]

Finally, towards the end of 1859, it was agreed that Cobbe would leave Red Lodge. She could no longer bear to be in a situation where her feelings were not responded to, and she resented Carpenter's devotion to Rosanna, the little girl she had adopted. Throughout

[46] There is an interesting discussion of their relationship in Jo Manton, *Mary Carpenter and the Children of the Streets*, London, 1976, 148–51.

[47] These letters are part of the Cobbe Papers at the Huntington Library.

[48] Mary Carpenter to Frances Cobbe, 28 Nov. 1859, Cobbe Papers, CB 70–89.

December, Carpenter wrote almost daily, assuring Cobbe that she was welcome to remain with her for as long as she chose, regretting that her way of life was injurious to Cobbe's health—but insisting that since this was the case it did provide a 'definite reason why you should feel it necessary to remove from my house', categorically denying that she would seek another companion to replace Cobbe and thanking her again for her love.[49] One cannot but feel that Carpenter breathed a sigh of relief when Cobbe finally moved into lodgings of her own, allowing Red Lodge to go back to its accustomed regime.

Cobbe did not have to wait very long after this to find a companion. She had met Mary Lloyd some time in 1858 or 1859 and a very short while after that, in 1860 or 1861, she and Lloyd began living together. In her autobiography Cobbe mentions Lloyd, but refuses to discuss her or their relationship. 'Of a friendship like this, which has been to my later life as my mother's affection was to my youth, I shall not be expected to say more.'[50] But there is, of course, much more to be said. The tenor of their friendship was known and discussed in their circle. Cobbe's letters to close friends, such as Mary Somerville, have a proprietorial tone in regard to Mary Lloyd which underlines the extent to which this was a 'female marriage'. Thus, for example, she refers to Lloyd as her 'better half'. In the early 1860s she complained—playfully—about Lloyd's absence and her independence:

Whenever I grumbled and groaned at Mary's desertion I was always silenced by hearing that she was going to you—and now the little villain has got into Rome and indulges its fascinations and goodness knows when she will go further. I hope you and Martha will be very stern and peremptory by and by, especially if you hear of a recommencing of Roman fever and make her go to Naples at once. Poor old darling. I am comforted by knowing she is happy and enjoying her little fling. Her life can never have too much of that to make up for the past—but I am very lonely without her.[51]

Cobbe had been unable to go to Italy with Mary Lloyd. She had, by this time, become a regular Leader writer for the *Echo*, and a

[49] Mary Carpenter to Frances Cobbe, 6 Dec. 1859, Cobbe Papers.
[50] Cobbe, *Life*, ii. 31.
[51] Frances Cobbe to Mary Somerville, 27 Dec., no year, Somerville Papers, MSFP II.

lengthy trip to Europe would have meant giving up this job—and the £300 per annum which it earned her.[52]

Other separations were forced on the two women by family commitments. Each of them visited family in the summer, which meant that Cobbe returned to Ireland, while Lloyd went to North Wales. Mary Lloyd had a brother who was a chronic invalid and for several years during the 1860s she spent time nursing him. For part of this period, he lived in London so that she continued to live with Cobbe and to return to their home each evening. Finally he moved to Wales, however, and she spent time with him there. Lloyd inherited property in Wales, and this, too, required her attention. In the early 1860s, Cobbe wrote to Mary Somerville about having paid

Mary a visit in her cottage which she had taken for 14 years and where she means to spend her summers near her own estate which always seems to want looking after. It is a charming cottage on a sort of terrace over a lovely brook ... and she has made it as usual at once comfortable and artistic. I am happy to think my dear pet is in so delicious a spot—since I cannot have her with me.[53]

Although doubts were later expressed by some members of the women's suffrage movement about the influence Lloyd had over Cobbe, it seems clear that it was Cobbe's interests and activities which decided how they lived. She continued to engage in all the activities she had taken up since leaving Bristol: she wrote articles for innumerable periodicals, worked in the women's movement, followed her many philanthropic interests, and became a leading figure in the antivivisection campaign.

Lloyd, by contrast, does not seem to have engaged in any independent activities. Although she was originally in Rome in order to work at sculpture with John Gibson, she seems to have done no work after she returned to London with Cobbe. She remained very friendly with Gibson and with Harriet Hosmer. Indeed she and Hosmer were with Gibson when he died. But her own working days were over. A curious sidelight on her relationship with Cobbe is thrown by her letters to Gibson, the only part of her cor-

[52] Frances Cobbe to Mary Somerville, 27 Dec., no year, Somerville Papers, MSFP II.

[53] Frances Cobbe to Mary Somerville, 6 Sept., no year, Somerville Papers, MSFP II.

respondence which seems to have survived.[54] In these, while she
comments on her life in London and talks about her brother and
his illness, no mention is made of Cobbe, with whom Lloyd was
living at the time. Gibson knew Cobbe and others amongst his
correspondents, such as Hosmer, wrote to him about visits she
made to their home. But Lloyd's letters indicate a very strong
devotion to Gibson and give one the sense that she chose to preserve
this link with her past as one part of her life which she would not
surrender to Cobbe.

Mary Lloyd lived with Frances Cobbe in London from the
early 1860s until the mid-1880s. In the course of that time Cobbe
participated in many activities of the women's movement. She was
a member of the Kensington Discussion Society to which she
contributed papers. She was also a member of the Married
Women's Property Committee and, for a short time, a member
of the Executive Committee of the London National Society for
Woman's Suffrage.

The growing diversity of the women's movement in the early
1860s is demonstrated by Frances Cobbe and her activities. Unlike
Davies, Cobbe did not become known to the Langham Place Circle
through meeting members of it, but rather through her writing.
After she had made her spirited intervention in the debate about
'superfluous' women, extolling celibacy as an option for women
delivered her paper entitled 'The Education of Women and how
it would be affected by University Examinations' at the National
Association for the Promotion of Social Science Conference in
London in 1862,[55] she was sought out by women such as Barbara
Bodichon and Lydia Becker. Informal female networks make it
likely that Cobbe was already known about at this time. Her trips
to Rome in the late 1850s brought her into contact with circles
which overlapped with the Langham Place group and her friendships with Fanny Kemble, Mary Carpenter, and Louisa Twining
would have given her an introduction to many women active in all
areas of public life.

Unlike Davies, Cobbe was not careful or methodical in the

---

[54] The letters from Mary Lloyd to John Gibson are part of the Gibson Papers,
G1/1/221–226, at the Royal Academy.

[55] This article was subsequently published in Frances Power Cobbe, *Essays on
the Pursuits of Women*, London, 1863.

keeping of notes. Although there is a collection of the letters she received from some of her correspondents, few of her own letters remain. And the autobiography which might serve in lieu is, as we have seen, extremely inaccurate and vague as to the actual details of her life and activity. Davies's letters, however, make it quite clear that Cobbe was an accepted member of the feminist network and a valued friend of Davies herself by 1863. In her letters to Barbara Bodichon throughout the 1860s, Davies referred frequently to Cobbe: to the state of her health, to her writing, to the home she set up with Mary Lloyd, to her ideas on religious questions. Thus Davies offers a much more complete picture of Cobbe's life in regard to the women's movement in the 1860s than Cobbe herself ever provided. Unfortunately Davies's comments ceased during the 1870s when her friendship with Cobbe seems to have come to a bitter end.

Despite her enthusiasm and her many talents, it is clear that Cobbe was a somewhat difficult colleague within the women's movement. Not only did she demand support for her anti-vivisection campaign from feminist colleagues, but she also attempted to get the formally non-party National Union to follow her in supporting the Conservative Party.

Although Cobbe rejected her father's religious beliefs—and his views about women—she retained the general social and political views of her childhood. Thus she had a strong sense of the importance of social hierarchy and she was almost automatically a Tory. On the whole, Cobbe took less of an interest in national politics than did the other feminists in this study. She once commented that all her definite politics centred on the question of the woman's franchise, and this would seem to have been the case. Although she recorded her social life and her philanthropic and feminist activities in her autobiography, she says little about national politics except for the question of Irish Home Rule which, as one would expect from the daughter of an Anglo-Irish landowner, she strongly opposed.[56] Even before the Home Rule crisis of the 1880s, however, she had felt an intense dislike and distrust of Gladstone. Where Butler sympathized with his constant agonizing, Cobbe was disgusted by it. She complained to Mary Somerville of his general demeanour: 'He goes about holding his head in both hands and

[56] Cobbe, *Life*, ii. 212.

crying that he is distracted!! That is a nice picture of the Prime Minister of England.'[57] She also felt that Gladstone's opposition to the emancipation of women had had a disastrous impact on the suffrage question.

Cobbe's general political views only became problematical for the women's suffrage movement when, in the mid-1880s, she joined the organization designed to increase the following of the Conservative Party at a constituency level, the Primrose League.[58] Not content simply to join it herself, she attempted to persuade other women to follow suit. Some of her reasons for doing so were explained to Lydia Becker. 'I have very little hope left to live to see our suffrage carried. Gladstone has been our ruin and I wish all the women of England would join the Primrose League to keep him and his party out of office for ever. Sir C. Dilke will be no help to us.'[59] It is not clear, either from this letter or from anything else Cobbe wrote, what exactly she thought the Primrose League would do to help in the gaining of women's suffrage. Although some Tory leaders supported women's suffrage, the party as a whole certainly did not—but presumably keeping Gladstone out of office was enough. Indeed, apart from this, and her sense of the importance of social hierarchy, it is very hard to see how she could ever have associated herself with it. Cobbe was an outspoken critic of established religion and believed that the 'divine right' of husbands and fathers should follow the divine right of kings—out of the realm of current beliefs. Thus she was at odds even with the very broad beliefs which underlay the League.[60] But neither this nor her inability to persuade the League to support women's suffrage disturbed her. On the contrary she followed up her letter to Becker with a broad appeal to other suffrage supporters to turn their backs on the Liberal Party and to support the Tories. That she did this using the letterhead of the National Union of Women's

[57] Frances Cobbe to Mary Somerville, Fri 25, no other date given, Somerville Papers, MSFP II.
[58] For a discussion of the Primrose League, see Martin Pugh, *The Tories and the People, 1880–1935*, Oxford, 1985, 43–69. For Cobbe's membership, see Cobbe, *Life*, ii. 230.
[59] Frances Power Cobbe to Lydia Becker, 5 Aug., no year given, but the letter came from Hengwrt, Dolgelly, N. Wales where Cobbe moved in 1884. NUWSS Collection, M50/1, 2/54, Manchester Public Library.
[60] See Pugh, *The Tories and the People*, 70.

Suffrage Societies created a furore which it required all Fawcett's
firmness and tact to quell.[61]

Fortunately for Cobbe, the altercations that were evident in some
of her public activities seem not to have entered into her home life.
She found with Mary Lloyd a domestic harmony which lasted for
decades. Cobbe was unquestionably the dominant partner and it
was her needs which dictated where and how they lived. It was
for her that they remained in London. Her journalistic output
depended on her being in the capital and, as Fanny Kemble noted,
she liked 'its perpetual interest and movement'.[62] Mary Lloyd, by
contrast, hated London and yearned constantly for her native
Wales. Cobbe was aware of Lloyd's inclinations and of the sacrifice
which she made. In a letter to Mary Somerville, she noted that
'Mary Lloyd is going to Wales for the autumn. She is very well
and enjoying her scenery and her mountains poor darling. I am
greatly inclined to think we ought to go and live in the country.'[63]
But of course they did no such thing, at least not until the late
1880s when Cobbe was ailing and exhausted after the fierce antivivisection battles of that decade. At this point they retired to
Lloyd's property in Wales.

Cobbe's retirement did not mean that she ceased to take an
interest in the antivivisection movement or to work for it: by 1892
she found that she had written 320 books, pamphlets, and leaflets
for this cause![64] Nor did she end her active support of the women's
movement, writing pamphlets and essays, attending and addressing
suffrage meetings and meetings of the national Vigilance Association. It was while she was in retirement that she also wrote her
autobiography.

Cobbe's final years were ones of material comfort. She had given
up her most lucrative journalism in order to devote herself to the
antivivisection movement in the 1870s and had consequently been
forced to rely on her very small paternal legacy. Immediately

---

[61] See Frances Power Cobbe to Millicent Garrett Fawcett, 24 July 1886, Fawcett
Library Autograph Collection, vol. i; and Millicent Garrett Fawcett, copy of letter
'to all London Con [sic] papers and the Times', 10 Nov. 1885, NUWSS Papers,
M50/2, 1/63, Manchester Public Library.

[62] Frances Anne Kemble, Further Records, 1848–1883, London, 1890, ii. 41.

[63] Frances Cobbe to Mary Somerville, only dated 'Aug', Somerville Papers,
MSFP II.

[64] Cobbe, Life, ii. 309.

after her retirement, however, her colleagues in the Victoria Street Society collected £1,000 with which they purchased an annuity of £100 for her. Shortly after this, she inherited a quite considerable sum of money from a devoted antivivisection supporter, sufficient to enable her to pay for the upkeep of Mary Lloyd's large house, Hengwrt, which had been leased out for some years as neither Lloyd nor Cobbe could afford its upkeep. The two women lived together at Hengwrt until Mary Lloyd's death in 1896.

Lloyd's death was a devastating blow, as Cobbe indicated in her reply to a condolence letter from Millicent Garrett Fawcett.

The end of such a friendship—thirty four years of mutual affection—is of course almost a mortal blow, and I have yet to learn how I am to live without the one who has shared all my thoughts and feelings so long. But I am very thankful that the pain and loneliness is mine—not hers as it would have been had I gone first and she been left alone. She died calmly and bravely resting on my arm and telling me we should not long be separated.[65]

It is a trifle ironic that Cobbe, who had prevented Mary Lloyd from living in Wales, should have spent the last ten years of her own life there without Mary Lloyd.

These final years were in many ways very bitter. Cobbe broke from some of her earlier feminist colleagues over their differing ideas on vivisection—and, to her regret, was unable to recommend that her niece attend Girton because of what she saw as its support for vivisection. But Cobbe's uncompromising approach, and her refusal to countenance any form of animal experimentation led not only to breaks with the women's movement but even to a complete breach with her own Victoria Street Society. Cobbe had always demanded the total prohibition of vivisection and sought parliamentary legislation along these lines. In the face of constant failure to have this measure made law, the Victoria Street Society decided in the 1890s to accept lesser measures which, they hoped, would outlaw cruel and painful experiments while allowing those conducted under anaesthetics to continue. Cobbe regarded such a position as a betrayal of the most fundamental principles of the movement and when it was adopted in 1898, resigned from the

---

[65] Frances Cobbe to Millicent Fawcett, 11 Nov. 1896, Autograph Collection, vol. 8, part 6, Fawcett Library.

Victoria Street Society altogether.[66] Thus her last years were spent
without either her lifelong companion—or the cause to which she
had devoted so much of her energy and her time.

II

The task of assessing Cobbe's feminism is complicated by the
immense range of her writing and by the fact that most of it took
the form of separate journal articles, many of which have not been
collected. It is important, however, to see Cobbe's work in its
entirety for unless one does so, it is possible to picture her as a
radical separatist, arguing for a total rejection of the demands of
men, and the setting up an independent female community.[67] That
this picture is not one that she would have recognized is made
abundantly clear in *The Duties of Women*, in her insistence that
women retain all their old virtues when given new rights.

If women were to become less *dutiful* by being enfranchised,—less conscientious, less unselfish, less temperate, less chaste,—then I should say:
'For heaven's sake, let us stay where we are! *Nothing* we can ever gain
would be worth such a loss'. But I have yet to learn that freedom, which
is the spring of all the nobler virtues in man, will be less the ground of
loftier and purer virtues in women.[68]

In her espousal of these values, Cobbe's writing offers a curious
paradox. For while she was obviously strongly committed to the
emancipation of women, some of her ideas resemble closely those of
the best-known exponents of women's domestic role. But although
Cobbe accepted many of the tenets of Victorian domestic ideology,
the framework for her ideas differed greatly from that of writers
such as Sarah Ellis. Where Ellis wrote of women entirely in terms
of their various roles as daughters, mothers, or wives, Cobbe wrote
of women as individuals, with a range of duties to themselves and

[66] The circular issued by the society and containing the resolution of the change
in policy as well as Cobbe's letter of resignation and a rejoinder to her from the
Hon. Stephen Coleridge, who had replaced her as honorary secretary, was printed
in the *Woman's Signal*, 17 Feb. 1898. For a description of her last years, see the
Introduction by Blanche Atkinson to Frances Power Cobbe, *The Life of Frances
Power Cobbe*, posthumous edn., London, 1904.

[67] See e.g. Spender, *Women of Ideas*, 310–17.

[68] Cobbe, *The Duties of Women*, 11–12. Emphasis in the original.

to others. She began with their personal duties and then went on to explore their social duties: those which derived from their familial relationships with parents and siblings, those which were the result of contracts, such as marriage, and those which came to them as citizens.

Hence where most of Ellis's work was devoted to expounding the view that women were 'relative creatures', defined only in terms of their relationship to men, Cobbe rejected absolutely the idea that women existed to serve or meet the needs of others. She had no time for any of the various theories of 'woman as Adjective', propounding instead the theory of 'woman as Noun', for whom the first end of being was one proper to herself.[69] But by the very fact of delineating women's lives in terms of their roles, Cobbe suggested a similarity between her ideas and those of writers such as Ellis. Moreover while insisting on the primacy of women's moral autonomy, she did little to question conventional ideas about their familial and social duties. By centring on the maternal nature of all women, Cobbe established her view of the basic differences between the sexes. All women were potentially mothers, whether or not they had children, and thus they were all nurturant, compassionate, and moral—possessing the qualities which mothers needed. These qualities would tend to direct their choices, either into the domestic life of wife and mother, or into the public one of philanthropist. Cobbe was well aware that not all single women chose philanthropy as an occupation or a career. But she thought that even those women who did not and who chose art or literature instead showed in their work womanly and compassionate qualities.[70] She rejoiced that it was no longer the case that 'the Church of Rome monopolizes the truth, that on a woman who has no husband, parent, or child, every sick and suffering man, every aged childless woman, every desolate orphan, has a claim. She has not fewer duties than other women, only more diffused ones.'[71]

The core of Cobbe's feminism, then, lay in her belief in the moral autonomy of women on the one hand, and in her strong sense of sexual difference on the other. She insisted that women

[69] Frances Power Cobbe, 'The Final Cause of Woman', in *Woman's Work and Woman's Culture*, ed. Josephine Butler, London, 1869, 21.

[70] Cobbe, *The Duties of Women*, 5.

[71] Cobbe, 'Celibacy v. Marriage', 233.

were rational beings with responsibility for their own conscience and with a primary duty to themselves and to their God and it was this point that serves to distinguish her from the proponents of domestic ideology. At the same time, Cobbe had no doubt about the extent or the importance of the innate mental and moral differences between the sexes.

The issue which had allowed her to rebel against paternal despotism while still remaining a dutiful daughter became the central point in her general theoretical discussion of the nature and the problems of women. It is scarcely surprising that the clearest formulation of her ideas on the relationship between the moral autonomy of women on the one hand, and their social and familial duty on the other, are to be found in her general discussions of daughters.

In 1865 Cobbe offered a long discussion paper to the Kensington Discussion Society on the subject, 'The Limits of Obedience of Daughters'.[72] In this she explored all the various questions which had been significant for herself and she laid down the general line of argument which she kept to throughout her life. In the first place, Cobbe stressed the obligation daughters were under to care for and tend parents and the primacy of this relationship over all others. In her view, the needs of a spouse or of friends took second place to parents who, as a result of the care they had bestowed, were entitled to 'primary benevolence' from their children. This entitlement meant that parents could impose on children many demands, including in general terms the sacrifice of the child's wishes, should such a sacrifice be genuinely needed in order for the parent's needs to be met. There was no question that, should a parent want domestic companionship or care from a daughter, the daughter must provide it.

The daughter had no right to demand an autonomous life, should her parents need her services or her presence. But this did not mean that the daughter had to relinquish everything for her parents or that she should offer absolute and unquestioning obedience. The daughter herself, in Cobbe's view, had a moral responsibility to ensure that the parent's demands were reasonable and just, and

---

[72] Emily Davies copied out Cobbe's paper carefully by hand. See Frances Power Cobbe, 'The Limits of Obedience of Daughters', Kensington Discussion Society, 1863, Emily Davies Papers, ED IX/KEN5.

that they were in fact conducive to the parent's well-being. The daughter had no obligation to obey demands which did not comply with these guidelines. Parents had no right to direct the course of action of grown-up daughters in matters which pertained directly to the daughter's well-being. They had no right, for example, to demand that a child renounce a career, enter into an engagement, or refrain from reading a particular book merely as a matter of arbitrary will. If a child is convinced that this course of action is not necessary to ensure the well-being of the parent, he or she is 'always free (and may be morally bound) to resist such a demand and to act to the best of his or her judgement independently thereof'.[73] What is perhaps most interesting about Cobbe's discussion is that while her central concern was with daughters, she believed that in many instances the situation of daughters was, or should be, the same as that of sons.

Cobbe followed her discussion on daughters with an article on 'Self-Development and Self-Abnegation'.[74] In this she addressed the problem of parental selfishness and female self-abnegation. Attacking the idea that female self-abnegation was a morally good or beneficial thing, she argued that the parental selfishness which prevented daughters from developing their own intellects and interests was morally wrong and reprehensible. A parent was entitled to require that a child see to the parent's needs and comfort, but not to deprive the child of moral or intellectual liberty—indeed, once a child was grown up, Cobbe argued that the parent had no right to command a daughter, any more than a son, in regard to their own affairs.[75]

These arguments and ideas, which were taken up again in Cobbe's widely read lectures on *The Duties of Women*, point to the continuity in her ideas. They also illustrate the centrality of the position of daughters in her analysis of the situation of women. Of all the various roles and relationships of women, that of daughter comes closest to being universal. In the nineteenth century, as Cobbe knew only too well, the fact of being a daughter determined how a woman could live and what she could do. This was so in an

---

[73] Ibid.
[74] Frances Power Cobbe, 'Self-Development and Self-Abnegation', in her *Studies New and Old of Ethical and Social Subjects*, London, 1865, 65–85.
[75] Ibid. 74.

immediate and practical sense in her own life. While her parents needed her, she remained in their home. When they were dead, she was free to travel, to establish an independent life, to enter into a whole new domestic relationship. Had her father survived for longer than he did, these possibilities would not have existed for her. Thus it was only when daughters were released from parental ties that they could enter into any other relationship or form of life.

It is important to note that Cobbe did not regard the restrictions which women faced through their daughterhood as either unjust or as changeable. She would have regarded it as morally inexcusable for a daughter to leave ailing parents in order to establish an independent life, even had she had the means to do so. What she offered instead was a moral scheme which allowed daughters to insist on and to retain their moral autonomy at the very time that they were devoting themselves entirely to the care of their parents. Thus her analysis of the position of daughters offers a kind of limiting case: it establishes the minimum level of self-determination which women should have—and, in the process, points to ways in which even daughters with uncongenial parents can render their situation tolerable.

Cobbe's sense of the absolute nature of a daughter's duty to parents is a central defining feature of her feminism. For the role of daughter, unlike any other female role, is both universal and inescapable. Cobbe's insistence on the primacy of this role shows very clearly her own sense of the differences between the familial and social roles and responsibilities of men and women and of the limited possibilities for change. She attacked the 'claustration' of women, protested against their exclusion from education, physical activities, interesting occupations and social and political responsibility.[76] She was an uncompromising critic of the ways in which most middle- and upper-class families distributed their wealth amongst their children, providing everything needful to educate and set up their sons, while leaving their daughters relatively impecunious and without the skills to support themselves. But it never occurred to her to suggest that sons have exactly the same duty to care for parents as do daughters.

While Cobbe acknowledged and accepted many aspects of pre-

[76] Cobbe, *The Duties of Women*, 8.

vailing Victorian beliefs about the duties of daughters, she rejected radically those pertaining to wives. It was not only the actual situation and sufferings of married women that Cobbe attacked, but the entire legal and moral framework of marriage itself. The moral autonomy of women was the central issue here as both the marriage ceremony and the legal situation of married women denied this autonomy. In Cobbe's view, the vow of obedience required of a bride was 'irreconcilable with the fundamental basis of morality'.[77] An adult's conscience and moral responsibility could not be handed to another person. Cobbe argued that if marriage necessarily involved total obedience even when it came to matters of conscience, then she would hold it unlawful for any woman to marry. For Cobbe, as for Mill, the existing framework of marriage was not only wrong in itself, but encouraged the development of further wrongs. It had a deleterious moral effect on both men and women, encouraging selfishness, despotism, and even violence in men while it made women passive, dependent, and devious.[78]

Integral to Cobbe's view of marriage was the problem of domestic violence. The fact that women lacked legal and political rights and that they were regarded not only as inferior and subordinate to their husbands, but as the property of those husbands, led directly, in her view, to many forms of ill-treatment of women. Although she only began to campaign on this question of domestic violence in the late 1870s, Cobbe had long shared the concern felt by Lydia Becker and many other feminists on this question.[79] Her earliest articles dealing with the question of celibacy and marriage, published in the early 1860s, already contain references to domestic violence. In these Cobbe pointed to the fact that this problem was not confined to the working class: even cosseted wealthy women— supposedly married to gentlemen—'might be called on to endure from their husbands the violence and cruelty we are accustomed to picture exercised only in the lowest lanes and courts of our cities'.[80] But Cobbe's sense of the extent and the severity of this

---

[77] Ibid. 107.

[78] Ibid. 109.

[79] The *Women's Suffrage Journal*, ed. Becker, made a regular practice of reporting cases of marital violence—with comments on the leniency of the sentences usually given to the violent husband. See, e.g. 'Lancashire Husbands', *Women's Suffrage Journal*, 2 Oct. 1871, 107.

[80] Cobbe, 'Celibacy v. Marriage', 234.

problem became more and more pronounced in later years.

'Wife Torture in England' is understandably one of Cobbe's best-known articles. Written when she was in the midst of the antivivisection campaign, it contains the fullest expression of her sense of the ultimate victimization of women. The problem, as Cobbe points out, is one not confined to the private realm of the home: individual acts of cruel behaviour were condoned and even encouraged by the widespread acceptance of domestic violence in society and in English culture generally. The popularity of Punch and Judy shows, as of *The Taming of the Shrew* were of a piece with the fact that any mention of wife-beating tends 'to conduce rather than otherwise to the hilarity of a dinner party'.[81] It was this general framework which allowed the further development of the aggravated or brutal assaults with which Cobbe was particularly concerned. She noted that some 1,500 of these cases in which women were not only beaten, but also kicked, burnt, blinded, and maimed came to the attention of the courts each year, and estimated that this made up about one-third of the total number of cases.[82]

On the basis of court records, Cobbe designated certain areas as the 'kicking districts'. These were usually ones with high population density, overcrowded housing, and uncertain wages. She saw this behaviour as being closely linked to such living conditions and to drunkenness—especially that caused by adulterated drinks which 'literally sting the wretched drinkers into cruelty'.[83] She saw the behaviour itself, and more especially the tolerance of it by successive governments as being a direct result of women's lack of political rights. But she sought, as a remedy, the reform of the Matrimonial Causes Act so that such violence was accepted as grounds for granting to women a separation. Cobbe was one of the few people who, after taking up this question, rejected as a solution the flogging of the male perpetrators of such violence. The existence of such punishments would act as an additional disincentive to the women concerned to give testimony against their husbands. What they needed was to be released from the power of these men.[84]

[81] Frances Power Cobbe, 'Wife Torture in England', *Contemporary Review*, 32 (1878), 57.

[82] Ibid. 72.

[83] Ibid. 65.

[84] Ibid. 82.

Cobbe usually paid lip-service to the notion that 'for the mass of mankind, marriage is the right condition, the happiest, and the most conducive to virtue'.[85] But she immediately undermined this proposition by pointing not only to the unhappiness evident in many specific marriages, but to the ways in which all women suffered as a result of the structure of marriage. She made the point most clearly in regard to questions of health, pointing to the well-known ill health of married women, but suggesting that this was partly caused by the fact that all their time and energy was devoted to the care of others, while no one paid any attention to their needs. She wrote at length about the problem of domestic disharmony, seeing women as more likely than men to suffer from an unhappy marriage because of their lack of outside interests and activities. 'Bad husband headache' was one of the many ailments to which such women were liable. Domestic disharmony was, in her view, not only a result of personal incompatibility between particular husbands and wives, but also consequent upon the nature of male demands and expectations of female service in the home. Any home, particularly one with a fussy male head, had a holiday atmosphere when the paterfamilias was away for a few days, leaving all the women of the household to relax together.[86]

All of Cobbe's discussions of marriage gain added point from being contrasted with the celibate lives possible for women of independent means. Unmarried women, in her view, lost few of the pleasures of their married sisters. Their homes could be as comfortable as those of their married sisters, as 'a woman makes her home for herself, and surrounds herself with the atmosphere of taste and the little details of housewifely comforts'.[87] All women, in her view 'inherited the blessed power of a woman to make true and tender friendships, such as not one man's heart in a hundred can even imagine'.[88] This capacity meant that unmarried women need neither be lonely nor emotionally deprived. She could share her life and her home with a companion who shared her interests, who understood her nature, who offered her affection and support—and who gave her what a woman could otherwise never

---

[85] Cobbe, 'What Shall We Do with our Old Maids?', 595.
[86] Frances Power Cobbe, 'Tarry-at-home Husbands', in *Re-Echoes*, London, 1876, 273–8.
[87] Cobbe, 'Celibacy v. Marriage', 233.
[88] Ibid.

have: the inestimable comfort which came from having a wife![89]

What is clear from all of this is that, while Cobbe accepted much of what is generally termed Victorian domestic ideology, she rejected the notion that women were designed to serve men. Hence for her, women's domestic role became the basis for female community and solidarity. Men were obstacles and hindrances to the establishment of a comfortable home—not the central focus of that home.

Cobbe's powerful article, 'Wife Torture', was written at the height of her involvement in the antivivisection campaign. She, like many other Victorian feminists, saw this campaign as closely allied to the movement for women's emancipation. Women, like animals, were subject to the power and the callousness of doctors and scientists and to the brutality of many men. Conversely, the maternal and nurturing qualities of women would cause them to be repelled by vivisection. And Cobbe did find her antivivisection work supported by many of those with whom she campaigned on behalf of women.[90] Others, such as Josephine Butler, did not join in her campaign, but shared her general outrage at the practice.[91] Unfortunately for Cobbe, however, not all of those active in the women's movement shared her total antipathy to any form of animal experimentation—and her ties with some of her friends and indeed with the whole education campaign were severed as a result of this.

Cobbe had been the first woman to speak publicly about the benefits women would gain from university examinations and she had been an early supporter of Emily Davies. But her friendship with Davies and her support of Girton College ended in the late 1870s in the course of a controversy over vivisection and animal experiments at Girton.

In line with her general insistence that Girton students follow the normal Cambridge curriculum, Davies and the rest of the Girton Committee agreed that those students preparing for Physiology in the Natural Sciences Tripos should attend lectures and see the lectures illustrated through experiment at the university

[89] Frances Power Cobbe, 'The Little Health of Ladies', *Contemporary Review*, 31 (1878), 289.

[90] French, *Antivivisection and Medical Science*, 239–50.

[91] Josephine E. Butler, *An Auto-biographical Memoir*, ed. George and Lucy Johnson, Bristol, 1909, 261.

Laboratory. In a memo written to set out and to defend the Girton position, Emily Davies insisted that 'No vivisection whatever is practised at the College'. The students attend lectures and, for the more advanced part of the course, see certain demonstrations. 'Some of these are performed by a mechanical apparatus, some are preparations seen under a microscope, some are performed on dead animals, and some—a very small proportion—on living animals rendered insensible by anaesthetics.'[92] For Davies, for Barbara Bodichon, and the others on the College Committee, the fact that anaesthetics were used and that the experiments were carried out only by licensed members of the university staff made it acceptable for Girton students to attend and to see them.[93]

Cobbe could not accept this view of the matter at all. Fearful of the damage which Girton would suffer if Cobbe publicly attacked it for supporting vivisection, Barbara Bodichon sent Adelaide Manning, a friend both of hers and of Emily Davies, to see and talk to Cobbe. Miss Manning made little headway. Cobbe, she wrote, regarded the existence of these experiments 'as the worst crime possible', and felt that their existence 'makes for a degree of breach with her friends'.[94] Cobbe refrained from expressing her outrage in public at this time, but the question did not die.

A new agitation occurred in 1891 when the question arose again in regard to Somerville College at Oxford. Cobbe again broached the question of vivisection at Cambridge, but this time, she accepted Millicent Fawcett's assurance that no vivisection was done by the girls themselves.[95] At Oxford this appeared not to be the case and Cobbe protested publicly about the involvement of women in this activity.[96]

Although Cobbe could not carry the whole women's movement with her on the antivivisection question, her own writings about women in the late 1870s and 1880s bear the clear imprint of her concerns with 'the claims of brutes'. When she was writing her

[92] Emily Davies, Memorandum, Girton College Cambridge, 30 Apr. 1887. Bodichon Papers, B. 438.
[93] See Note from Sedley Taylor to Barbara Bodichon, n.d., Bodichon Papers, B. 441 *a* and *b*; Mary A. Ewart to Barbara Bodichon, 8 Apr., Bodichon Papers, B. 440.
[94] Adelaide Manning to Barbara Bodichon, 10 Apr. and 23 Apr., Bodichon Papers, B. 444–5.
[95] See letters from Frances Power Cobbe to Millicent Garrett Fawcett, 16 Jan. 1891 and 16 Mar. 1891, Fawcett Library, Autograph Collection, Part IV.B.
[96] French, *Antivivisection and Medical Science*, 276.

article, 'Wife Torture', Fanny Kemble noted that Cobbe had turned away from other animals to write about the torture men inflicted on 'those dumb animals, their wives'.[97] And it is very evident that in the years of this campaign, the aspects of the woman question which Cobbe wrote about did change. Her earlier focus on the merits of celibacy and the avenues open to single women gave way to a more intense concern with their physical health and well-being. She moved from discussing the problems women faced as a result of the ways in which their needs were neglected or ignored to looking at the infliction on them of cruel and barbarous forms of treatment both in the home and in the medical arena. Cobbe also expressed great concern about the effects on men of their conduct in regard to women and to animals. She saw as one of the causes of brutality to wives the existence of a 'little recognized passion, which rude men and savages share with many animals, and which ... consists in anger and is cruelly excited by the signs of pain'.[98] This passion, which she termed 'heteropathy', was one she saw as dying out slowly as civilization advanced. At the same time, she believed that those doctors and scientists involved in vivisection were not only unmoved by the pain and suffering they inflicted, but that they were brutalized by the very acts in which they were engaged—and in many cases, that they began to find excitement and even pleasure in their pursuit. Husbands who engaged in brutality to their wives deprived themselves and their sons of any possible moral influence which their wives might have. In a similar way, doctors and scientists, by engaging in vivisection, destroyed their own humanity and the humanity of all those with whom they came into contact.

The parallel between the sufferings of women and those of animals becomes even more pronounced in Cobbe's other writings, in which she turned her attention to the ways in which women suffered at the hands of doctors who were, of course, her target in the antivivisection campaign. The extent to which the health and happiness of women lay in the hands of the medical profession was something about which Cobbe had long been concerned. She believed her mother had lived as an invalid for many years as the result of medical incompetence and that she herself had been

[97] Frances Anne Kemble, *Further Records*, ii. 80.
[98] Cobbe, 'Wife Torture', 65–6.

incapacitated and almost crippled as a result of the incorrect treatment of a bad sprain. But as on the question of domestic violence, she did not engage in any broad discussion of the question until the late 1870s and early 1880s. When she did, all her sense of the arrogance and the cruelty of the medical and scientific profession which had developed in the antivivisection campaign was clearly evident. Throughout her discussion of doctors, there is a constant reference to the question of medical experimentation and to the ways in which the needs of the patient are sacrificed to the doctor's desire to acquire either knowledge or manipulative skills.[99]

Cobbe's attack on the medical profession, like so much of her other writing, shifts back and forth between values and ideas which have no place in current thinking, but which she shared with many of her own contemporaries, and arguments which could take their place, unaltered, in mid-twentieth-century feminist writing. Like Josephine Butler, Cobbe was very aware of and very concerned about the growing power of the medical profession in all areas of life. The Medical Council and the medical press provided an increasingly arrogant public voice. But even on the level of daily life, 'as medical officers in parishes and unions, factory and prison surgeons, public vaccinators, medical officers of health, inspectors of nuisances, and very commonly as coroners, the doctors are daily assuming authority which, at first, perhaps, legitimate and beneficial, has a prevailing tendency to become meddling and despotic.'[100] But one reason for Cobbe's fear of this process was the agnosticism of many medical men. Like Butler, and like many other Victorians, Cobbe did not believe that any form of morality was possible unless it was based on some kind of religious faith. Thus for her, 'few prospects are more profoundly alarming than the advance to ubiquitous influence of an order of men who, as a rule, reject and despise those ultimate faiths of the human heart in God and Duty and immortality, which ennoble and purify mortal life as no physiological science can ennoble, and no physical "sanitation" purify.'[101]

There are interesting similarities and contrasts between Cobbe's

---

[99] Frances Power Cobbe, 'The Medical Profession and its Morality', *Modern Review*, 2 (1881), 296–326.

[100] Ibid. 297.

[101] Ibid. 308.

ideas on the medical profession and those of Josephine Butler. Both saw women as the main victims of the medical profession and as providing the basis for the assertion of their power. But there are significant differences between the way they focus and articulate this shared belief. Cobbe included their role in originating and supporting the Contagious Diseases Acts in her list of ways in which doctors exerted power over women and made them suffer.[102] But she did not ever engage in detailed discussion of this question. She wrote at much greater length of the trials which all working class women underwent at the hands of the callous and uncaring medical men they confronted in public hospitals.[103] But she was most concerned about the way in which doctors treated women of her own class—making them into a sex of patients who required constant attention and thereby subsidized for ever the very men who prevented them from enjoying or taking control of their own lives.

The prevailing medical views about women, which saw them as constantly liable to ill health, and defined female functioning as pathological, filled Cobbe with fury.[104] She was quite unable to accept that the rational deity in whom she believed could have 'designed a whole sex of Patients—that the normal condition of the female of the human species should be to have legs which walk not, and brains which can only work on pain of disturbing the rest of the ill-adjusted mechanism—this is to me simply incredible'.[105] She noted, with some sarcasm, that the women deemed to be victims of female valetudinarianism 'are precisely the human beings who, of our whole mortal race seem naturally most exempt from physical want or danger and ought to have enjoyed immunity from disease or pain of any kind'. They have never been in want, nor suffered exposure to hardship or toil.[106] They were all able to pay the physicians who attended them handsomely. She wondered whether women would receive quite as much medical attention if England adopted the old Chinese custom whereby patients paid doctors a salary so long as they were in health and ceased to pay when they were ill![107]

---

[102] Frances Power Cobbe, 'The Medical Profession and its Morality', 321–2.
[103] Ibid. 311.
[104] For a selection of these views, see *Women from Birth to Death: The Female Life Cycle in Britain 1830–1914*, ed. Pat Jalland and John Hooper, Brighton, 1986.
[105] Cobbe, 'The Little Health of Ladies', 278.
[106] Ibid. 278–9.   [107] Ibid. 294.

In Cobbe's view, the way that doctors treated women as patients was closely tied up with their fight to exclude women from the profession. Like many other feminists, she commented on how much happier women would be if they were able to be treated by doctors of their own sex. She noted the connection between the campaign for the entry of women to the medical profession and the widespread medical concern about the effects on women of excessive study. When it became clear that women might enter the market as competitors,

the doctors grew earnest and made a grand discovery—namely, that mental labour is peculiarly injurious to the weaker sex—much worse, it would appear, for the feeble constitution, than any amount of ball-going and dissipation; and that, in short, a term at Girton was worse than five London seasons. Women would perish, and the human race cease to multiply, if female intellects ascended from gossip to Greek![108]

Much of Cobbe's attack on the Victorian medical profession, so far as women were concerned, is supported by recent historians who have investigated this field.[109] But it also contains some elements which serve to underline her general social and political ideas. Thus one of the points to which she devotes considerable attention in her general discussion of the morality of the medical profession is the social origin of doctors. In England, she noted, unlike the situation in much of Europe, medical men were not generally recruited from the higher ranks. 'As a rule, it appears that the majority of British doctors are either the sons of men of the secondary professional classes or of tradesmen, and in some cases ... of professional artisans.' Medicine is 'a parvenu profession, with the merits and defects of the class'. Chief amongst the defects is the tendency to hang together and to make common cause against outsiders—in a way similar to that of trade unions. Doctors were of a lower social origin even than lawyers—and hence less to be trusted.[110] It is somewhat ironic that Butler saw doctors as coming from a quite different social class. To her they were

---

[108] Ibid. 322–3.

[109] See e.g. Lorna Duffin, 'The Conspicuous Consumptive: Woman as Invalid', in Delamont and Duffin, eds., *The Nineteenth Century Woman*, London, 1978, 26–57.

[110] Cobbe, 'The Medical Profession and its Morality', 300.

aristocrats and came from the class which she saw as being most likely to exploit women sexually.[111]

Cobbe's sense of social superiority to the doctors whom she castigated was very important. It has a curious, even quaint touch to it. But at the same time, it was the only basis Cobbe had which allowed her to address doctors from the superior position she needed, if she was to dismiss their grandiose claims and their pretensions to infallibility. It was only her sense of social superiority which gave Cobbe a speaking position from which to attack the medical profession. Without this, she could merely have voiced her fears—as Butler did—in letters to friends. But with it, she was able to make public statements of an apparently impersonal kind. Class was the only basis women like Cobbe had for asserting their superiority over particular groups of men whose own claim to authority was based on knowledge and professions from which women were excluded. Emily Davies refrained from replying to the medical attacks made on higher education for women, much though they angered her, because she knew that all she had at her disposal was her own beliefs. Her strategy was to have Elizabeth Garrett Anderson reply, thus inserting into the debate a contrary medical opinion. Cobbe, by contrast, entered the debate herself, making use of her experiences and the knowledge she gained from the antivivisection campaign, but framing all of this with the assumption of an authority gained through her privileged social position.

As we have seen, Cobbe never lost her sense of herself as a member of the landed gentry. It remained an integral part of her identity throughout her life and she appealed to it constantly. Whereas Josephine Butler looked for support amongst working-class men, Cobbe sided with Emily Davies in believing that, if one wanted to get anything done, it was necessary to be supported by prominent, and preferably by titled, people. She stated her opinion most clearly in regard to the antivivisection campaign. At the very start of that campaign, Cobbe was invited to attend a meeting of the vivisection subcommittee of the RSPCA. She had hoped that this body would take up the question publicly and in Parliament. Her first glance around the table, however, demonstrated that this was not so.

[111] See Josephine Butler to Mr Edmundson, 28 Mar. 1872, Butler Papers.

On entering the room my spirits sank, for I saw around the table a number of worthy gentlemen, mostly elderly, but not one of the more distinguished members of the committee or (I think) a single Peer or Member of Parliament. In short, they were not the men to take a lead in such a movement and make a bold stand against the claims of science.[112]

Once she took over the leadership of the antivivisection movement, she did her best to ensure that peers and Members of Parliament were always prominent.

This sense of the need to work largely, if not exclusively, with titled and wealthy people who were widely known and highly regarded within society served also to illustrate Cobbe's Conservatism. Like Emily Davies, she inherited a set of Conservative political beliefs and ideas in childhood and, despite the changes in her religious views, retained them throughout her life. As we have seen, she became a Dame of the Primrose League and did her best to persuade others to follow suit. For all this, it is clear that for Cobbe, as for Davies and indeed for a large number of other Victorian Tories, Conservative political views were as much a matter of sentiment, of preferred companions, of belief in a particular style and way of doing things as they were a set of political principles. Indeed, Cobbe rejected even the most basic Conservative beliefs, rejecting entirely the Tory adherence to the Anglican Church or their belief in the sanctity of the patriarchal family. In regard to the women's movement, Cobbe preferred a discreet method of campaigning for the suffrage and avoided public contact with radical individuals or causes. Her philanthropic commitments were also very important here, providing a useful framework for discussing the situation and problems of women without overtly connecting her demands with the broader question of natural rights or with the debates about universal franchise.

At the same time, Cobbe does serve further to show the limited utility of labels derived from national or party politics in describing or analysing Victorian feminism. One could call her beliefs about the nature and duties of women conservative. But what does one do then with her critique of marriage and of the role of science and of medicine in exacerbating women's oppression? These issues were not part of the framework for national politics and hence

[112] Cobbe, *Life*, ii. 557–8.

terms such as 'liberal' or 'conservative' are very problematical in relation to them. Seeking to place Cobbe on a conservative/liberal axis seems ultimately much less rewarding than examining the range of interests which fed into her feminism or the complexity of the feminist ideas she propounded.

Taken in their entirety, Cobbe's views offer interesting insights into the connection between feminist ideas and the broader intellectual and social context in which they developed and into the importance for feminism not so much of a coherent political theory as of a distinctive female perspective. For Cobbe was very closely integrated into the mid-Victorian context, accepting many common Victorian ideas about the nature of womanhood and about the appropriate sphere and roles for women. She differed from her non-feminist or anti-feminist contemporaries in her absolute rejection of the idea that women were 'relative beings' whose purpose in life was to serve men. For her, women had the same moral worth as men and were independent moral beings. Hence while accepting the idea of separate spheres, she also saw men, both individually and collectively, as oppressing women.

In dealing with Cobbe, one is continually forced to recognize the vast differences which underlie the apparent similarities between Victorian feminist approaches and our own. Cobbe shows this contrast with particular force because of her recognition of the institutional basis of women's oppression as it operates through marriage and family life, through religious organizations, and through scientific, medical and sociological knowledge. But despite this, Cobbe's endorsement of so much of the framework of Victorian domestic ideology combined with her religious beliefs to prevent her from articulating fully a modern theory of patriarchy. As we have seen, for all her criticism of excessive paternal power, Cobbe accepted absolutely the idea that daughters should sacrifice themselves for their parents, although she set limits on the extent of this sacrifice. The result, however, was that Cobbe refrained from arguing directly that it was the family as an institution which oppressed women. In a similar way, while showing clearly how the medical and scientific professions oppressed women, Cobbe saw the cause of their behaviour as residing in their atheism and materialism. She saw this as the reason why they were able to ignore suffering both in women and in animals—hence while recognizing

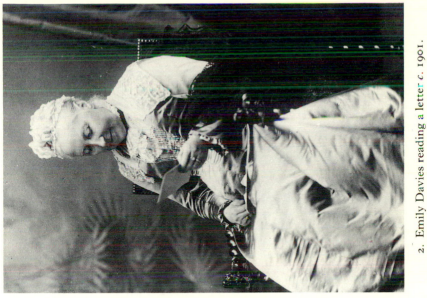

2. Emily Davies reading a letter *c.* 1901.

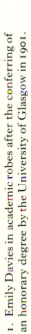

1. Emily Davies in academic robes after the conferring of an honorary degree by the University of Glasgow in 1901.

3. Newbridge House, Co. Dublin. The home of the Cobbe family.

4. Charles Cobbe, 1857.

6. George Butler, *c.* 1880.

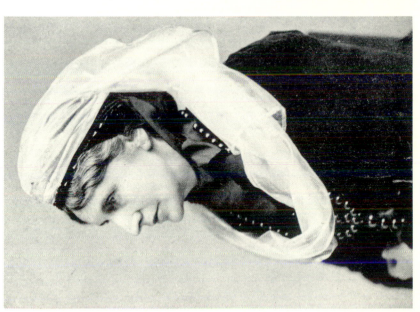

5. Josephine Butler, *c.* 1891.

7. Frances Power Cobbe, 1894.

8. Josephine Butler, 1903.

10. Henry Fawcett, 1867.

9. Millicent Garrett Fawcett in 1867, the year of her marriage.

12. Millicent Garrett Fawcett, c. 1909.

11. Philippa Fawcett, c. 1880.

13. Mrs Fawcett leading the procession to the Albert Hall, 1908.

14. Millicent Fawcett and Agnes Garrett leading a procession to lay flowers on the statue of J. S. Mill in May 1927.

the power they exercised over women, she saw the only possible solution as a moral and religious reform for individual men.

Cobbe's strong sense of the institutional basis of male power did not make her hostile to all men as individuals. As we have seen, she was greatly indebted to Theodore Parker, and throughout her life there were a number of men like John Stuart Mill or James Martineau whom she regarded as teachers, colleagues, or friends. But all of these men had played a part in her intellectual development and in her fight for her own autonomy and all were concerned about and offered ways of supporting the battle for the rights of other women. Hence their stature in her eyes was a direct consequence of her sense of them as friendly to the women's cause. Indeed, after Mill's death, Cobbe wrote to her close friend Martha Somerville that this event was 'a terrible loss to all women—and personally a grief to me. He was one of the two or three men in the world whom I ever felt one could love and honour as if they were good women.'[113] Cobbe's all-embracing interest in women and the woman's perspective which she applied to her analysis and evaluation of men provides the final part of her feminist programme. For her men were distinctly and essentially 'other' and their autonomous lives and activities were of relatively little interest. In much of her writing, they are shown primarily as intruders and invaders of women's sphere, demanding attention and satisfaction, denying women's needs or interests. Cobbe's ideal domestic life was one from which men were absent, temporarily if not altogether.

Cobbe's critical attitude towards men and her rejection of the idea that they embody the highest human values is augmented by her frequent references to actual women who embodied her ideal of active, energetic womanhood. Where Mary Wollstonecraft inveighed angrily against female frivolity, weakness, and lack of moral fortitude, Cobbe often presented images or examples of female strength, dignity, courage, and intellectual acumen. This is not to say that she was never critical of women: indeed female incapacity and lack of practical as well as managerial skill was a frequent target of her wrath. Like several other mid-nineteenth century feminists, she argued that those men who opposed

[113] Frances Power Cobbe to Martha Somerville, New Park Villas, 1873. Somerville Papers, MSFP vol. 18.

improvements in female education should be condemned to spend their lives with women who were the product of the appalling education deemed adequate for girls in private schools. But her alternative was always posed in terms of women who showed the benefits of knowledge, intelligence, and experience.

Here, as elsewhere, Cobbe's own experience was crucial as she could refer to her close friends, Mary Somerville, Mary Carpenter, Louisa Twining, or Harriet Hosmer whenever the occasion demanded. All of these women were exceptional, but through their very existence they demonstrated the potential women had for artistic, intellectual, and socially useful lives. That all but one were single simply added emphasis to the arguments Cobbe put forward about the connection between celibacy and a satisfying life. At the same time, their work and their manifold talents enabled her to put forward an ideal of female excellence which served both to question any notion of masculine superiority and to exhort women to greater efforts.[114]

Cobbe's positive view of womanhood, her admiration for many individual women and her enjoyment of the kind of life which women could share with each other combine to give her feminism an energy and an enthusiasm which is the necessary counterpoint to her dark vision of the sufferings women often experience at the hands of men.

Cobbe's feminism involved placing considerable emphasis on the differences between men and women and on establishing what would now be called a 'woman-centred' view of the world. But for all this, she did not eschew the battle for women's legal and political rights. Her ultimate goal was not simply a society in which men and women would be equal, but one in which women could develop their specific capacities to the full, unhampered by legal, social, and economic restrictions and supported in their efforts by other women who were able to share their enthusiasms and ideals. It was an ideal based on the notion of women's moral autonomy and on the ways in which this autonomy could be asserted in every situation which women faced. But of course this very autonomy was impossible if women were subject to legal or political disabilities which limited their freedom or their capacity for independent

---

[114] Cobbe, *The Duties of Women*, 147–8, see also the Dedication in Frances Power Cobbe, *Essays on the Pursuits of Women*, London, 1863, p. iii and pp. 81–9.

action. Both equality and difference were thus integral not only to her feminist strategy but to her overall feminist vision. Without equality, women would continue to be unable to develop to the full their potential—or their differences from men.

5

Josephine Butler

THE place of Josephine Butler within the history of nineteenth-century English feminism has long been the subject of disagreement.[1] Butler has always had a heroic status amongst Victorian reformers. Her beauty, eloquence, and enormous charm, the physical and moral courage evident in her capacity to face hostility, ostracism, and threats of real physical and sexual violence, combined with her frail health, her very feminine demeanour, and her spiritual radiance to make her a quite compelling figure. One of her colleagues in the Ladies' National Association for the Repeal of the Contagious Diseases Acts recalled that the first time she heard Butler speak she felt that here was 'a Woman Christ [sent] to save us from our despair'. Another commented that Butler's hold over the members of the Ladies' National Association was such that 'the mere thought of her being ill paralyses some of our workers, who almost exist by her inspiration'.[2]

But while no one would deny that Butler was an extraordinary woman with great powers of persuasion and of leadership, this does not in itself make her a feminist. Indeed, in the twentieth century, although several of those who have written about her seem to share something of the admiration for her evident amongst her followers,

---

[1] Josephine Elizabeth Butler, 1828–1906. There is no recent biography of Butler. The fullest accounts of her life are still to be found in Josephine E. Butler, *An Autobiographical Memoir*, ed. George and Lucy Johnson, Bristol, 1909; and A. S. G. Butler, *Portrait of Josephine Butler*, London, 1954.

[2] Cited in Judith Walkowitz, *Prostitution and Victorian Society: Women, Class and the State*, Cambridge, 1980, 114.

a number do not regard her as a feminist at all. The first of the
recent studies of the Contagious Diseases agitation queries whether
this term can be applied to Butler—'except in the broadest sense'—
because of her lack of interest in either the suffrage movement or
the question of the legal rights of married women.[3] Butler's deep
religious feeling and her insistence that she was called by God to
help and protect fallen women has contributed to the placing of
her alongside the other great Victorian 'social reformers motivated
by religious insight' such as Octavia Hill, Mary Carpenter, and
Florence Nightingale rather than alongside the pioneer feminists:
Emily Davies or Millicent Garrett Fawcett.[4]

There is, however, a contrasting view of Butler in which she is
seen as the most complete and in some ways the most advanced
Victorian feminist. Millicent Fawcett was one of the first to argue
both that Butler was 'the most distinguished English woman of the
nineteenth century' and that her ideas and principles had particular
relevance for twentieth-century women.[5] Recently several historians have pointed to the extent of Butler's feminist concern,
insisting on the need to see the connection between her involvement
in the Contagious Diseases agitation and her broader analysis of
the oppression of women.[6] Some would go further, arguing that it
was Butler who shifted both the analysis and the strategic approach
of Victorian feminism in ways which anticipated the developments
of its mid-twentieth-century counterpart.[7]

Few would now seriously question the intensity of Butler's feminist commitment, but the precise nature of her feminism and her
place in the nineteenth-century women's movement continue to be
problematical. Many of those active within that movement did not

---

[3] Glen Petrie, *A Singular Iniquity: The Campaigns of Josephine Butler*, London,
1971, 63. Petrie claims that Butler had 'absolutely no interest whatever in the
question of female suffrage'. This is simply not the case: from the early 1870s
onwards both Butler's published works and her correspondence refer frequently to
her recognition of the importance of women's suffrage.

[4] Deborah M. Valenze, *Prophetic Sons and Daughters: Female Preaching and
Popular Religion in Industrial England*, Princeton, NJ, 1985, 50.

[5] Millicent Garrett Fawcett and E. M. Turner, *Josephine Butler: Her Work and
Principles, and their Meaning for the Twentieth Century*, London, 1927, 1.

[6] See e.g. Walkowitz, *Prostitution in Victorian Society*, 116–17.

[7] Jenni Uglow, 'Josephine Butler: From Sympathy to Theory', in Dale Spender,
ed., *Feminist Theorists: Three Centuries of Women's Intellectual Traditions*, London,
1983, 147; and Dale Spender, *Women of Ideas and What Men Have Done to Them*,
London, 1983, 346.

see Butler as part of the central core of feminist agitation and felt
that her ideas and objectives differed from their own. As we have
seen, Emily Davies regarded Butler's insistence on special education for women as directly destructive of her own attempts to
establish equal and identical tertiary education for men and women.
In a similar way, Mill and others who supported his belief in the
primacy of the suffrage movement saw Butler's leadership of the
Contagious Diseases agitation as fragmenting the whole women's
movement and as impeding the broader movement for the emancipation of women.[8]

Butler made no attempt to integrate herself into all the campaigns
of the women's movement, showing little inclination to follow or
to accept the leadership of any other women. Where Millicent
Fawcett saw the women's movement as a multi-faceted one with a
variety of different leaders,[9] Butler really only believed in her own
leadership. Thus she constantly bemoaned the fact that the suffrage
movement was led by Lydia Becker, a plain woman who 'has not
the gift of winning'[10] or decried Fawcett's lack of warmth and
charismatic appeal.[11] Fawcett and Becker may have acknowledged
Butler's powers and her leadership of the moral crusade, but she
certainly did not regard them as her leaders in the suffrage question.

In part this is a reflection of Butler's whole approach to political
agitation. The campaigns she undertook were in her view not
simply political campaigns, but great reform campaigns with moral
and religious overtones. They were intended to bring about not
only changes in laws, but moral and social transformations. Butler's
own contribution was that of providing spiritual leadership and
inspiration. Her addresses to the Ladies' National Association in
form and in imagery bear a closer resemblance to a great sermon
than they do to a campaign speech. Her words were cherished by
her followers and were circulated both by her and by them. Her
own ideal of leadership hence centred on the quality of inspiration
rather than organization. Thus while accepting Fawcett as competent, she always regarded her as somewhat cold and lacking in
the absolute faith which was for Butler the prerequisite for a leader.

[8] B. Caine, 'John Stuart Mill and the English Women's Movement', *Historical Studies* (1978), 61–3.
[9] Millicent Garrett Fawcett, *What I Remember*, London, 1925, 117.
[10] Josephine Butler to Miss Priestman, 18 Nov. 1873, Butler Papers.
[11] Josephine Butler to the Misses Priestman, 4 Nov. 1896, ibid.

Unlike either Becker or Davies, Butler had no interest in organizing committees or in doing the detailed daily work that went into the mounting of a campaign. This was done either by paid agents or, in a voluntary capacity, by other women. Butler often let these people know her views, assuming that they would be acted upon, but she did not enter into the detailed daily work herself.

Butler's lack of method or careful application is as evident in her approach to feminism as it is in her running of her campaigns. Although she had many insights into the nature of women's oppression, and expressed many of them in moving and eloquent ways, Butler did not ever integrate these insights into a coherent feminist theory.[12] And for all the novelty of some of her views, they were combined with adherence to many conventional views about women. Despite her cogent arguments about the need for female solidarity and for specifically female methods of campaigning, her ideas about women embody perhaps more of Victorian domestic ideology than is evident in any other Victorian feminist—including the notion that service to others was an integral part of women's nature. Finally while Butler was very eloquent about the need for all women to unite in order to fight their oppression, she was equally eloquent in disavowing her belief or participation in anything that could be called a sex war, and in insisting that her battles all fitted within a liberal reforming tradition which was concerned about individual rights, regardless of sex.

It is the relationship of Butler's liberalism to her feminism which is of most interest here. For within Victorian feminism, it was Butler and her campaigns which most dramatically illustrated both the connections and the conflict between these two ideologies. When one is looking at Emily Davies and Frances Cobbe, the question about the relationship between national politics and feminist politics is a relatively minor one. They illustrate the connection between party affiliation and ideas of strategy on the one hand, and the complete disjunction between such party affiliation and ideas about the nature of women on the other. Like most other mid-Victorian conservatives, Davies and Cobbe shared the basic tenets of economic and political liberalism, combining them easily enough with their critiques of the domestic and legal oppression of women. The caution and the sense of decorum which prevented

---

[12] See Uglow, 'From Sympathy to Theory', 149–51.

either Davies or Cobbe from addressing questions pertaining to prostitution or the sexual control of women enabled both of them to avoid the one issue in which liberal beliefs and feminist beliefs really came into conflict: the question of sexual hierarchy and of the sexual control of women by men. It is Butler who faced and who elucidated this conflict most clearly.

It is ironic that Millicent Fawcett is usually represented as the leading nineteenth-century liberal feminist since Josephine Butler was in fact a much more ardent liberal and felt much more at home within the Liberal Party than Fawcett ever did. The daughter of a prominent Liberal who was active both in the battle for the 1832 Reform Act and in the movement for the abolition of slavery, she was herself part of a large group of provincial radical Liberals, many of whom shared both her views on economic and social questions and her feminism. While Fawcett severed her connection with the Liberal Party when it committed itself to Home Rule in 1886, Butler supported this position.[13] She was a member of the Women's Liberal Association throughout the 1880s and 1890s.[14]

Butler's support for the Liberal Party even extended to an enthusiasm for Gladstone, despite his constant opposition to all of the aims of the women's movement.[15] Where Cobbe despised and Fawcett always disliked and distrusted Gladstone, Butler was both fascinated by and sympathetic to him. He typified her ideal of the conscientious political leader, concerned with great moral and religious questions. There is more than a hint of identification in her description of his 'great solitary heart, fighting for truth, and leaning on God and hated with a deadly hatred by many, misunderstood by so many more, and so calm and so generous in the midst of abuse'.[16] She even managed to forgive his intransigent opposition both to the Contagious Diseases campaign and to the whole question of the emancipation of women.[17]

[13] See Josephine E. Butler, *Our Christianity Tested by the Irish Question*, London, 1887.

[14] See e.g. Josephine E. Butler, 'Women and Politics', speech delivered at a meeting of the Portsmouth Women's Liberal Association, 11 Apr. 1888, Butler Papers.

[15] See Ann P. Robson, 'A Bird's Eye View of Gladstone', in *The Gladstonian Turn of Mind: Essays Presented to J. B. Conacher*, ed. Bruce Kinzer, Toronto, 1985, 63–96, for a discussion of feminist attitudes to Gladstone.

[16] Josephine Butler to Edith Leupold, 15 June–23 Aug. 1866, Butler Papers.

[17] For a discussion of Butler's attitude to Gladstone, see Petrie, *A Singular Iniquity*, 145–6. For her final evaluation, see Josephine Butler to Stanley Butler, Dec. 1905, Butler Papers.

Butler's liberal beliefs and her sense of the Contagious Diseases agitation as a great Liberal reform campaign allowed her to work closely with a very supportive group of provincial radical Liberals.[18] But it was not long before enormous tensions developed between her liberalism and her feminism. The state regulation of prostitution, as Butler said again and again, proceeded from the assumption that men were naturally unchaste and that women had to be sacrificed to meet male sexual needs. Thus constructions of male sexuality were a major target of the Contagious Diseases campaign. In addition, Butler's investigations of the actual operation of the various systems for regulating and controlling prostitution throughout Europe made her very aware of the co-operation of police, medical practitioners and brothel-keepers in keeping them going.

The general silence imposed on women about sexual matters and the sexual violence with which Butler and her colleagues were threatened when they campaigned against the Contagious Diseases Acts increased their sense of the ways in which men banded together, across class, religious, and normal social barriers in order to silence and control women. Moreover the tensions between men and women within the repeal movement, the tendency of men to attempt to direct the agitation, to exclude women from policy formation, and to limit their role within the Contagious Diseases agitation itself demonstrated the differences between male and female approaches to the question of prostitution.[19] Butler's discussion of these matters, isolated and partial as they are, amount in the end to a fairly extensive critique of masculinity and of the sexual basis for women's oppression.

There is then a constant tension between Butler's liberalism on the one hand, and her feminism on the other. Liberalism provided the framework for Butler's whole social and political approach. It was an integral part of her feminism. Without it she would never have been able to undertake the Contagious Diseases campaign as it alone provided her with a way to tackle prostitution as a major political question, rather than in terms of rescue work directed towards individual women. But liberalism as a theory did not

[18] Walkowitz, *Prostitution and Victorian Society*, 99–104.
[19] Ibid. 139–41.

address questions about sexuality or desire, nor could it offer a
critique of the exchange and the control of women's bodies by men.
Butler herself was unable to resolve this tension—except by resort
to religion. Her constant use of religious terminology and her belief
that some kind of religious cataclysm was imminent reflect of course
both her own personality and certain aspects of the religious culture
with which she grew up. But they also suggest that she saw no
solution to the sexual oppression of women as being possible until,
as she said, the kingdom of God was established on earth.

I

The major facts of Josephine Butler's life are fairly well known.
Born in Northumberland in 1828, she was the fourth daughter and
the seventh of the nine children of John Grey and Hannah Annett.
John Grey was a distant relative of one of the great Whig families.
Hannah Annett, by contrast, was the daughter of a French
Huguenot family, silk-weavers by trade, who had been forced to
leave France by the revocation of the Edict of Nantes. Grey had a
small estate in Northumberland, and the family lived first at Mill-
field Farm in Glendale, where Josephine was born, and then at
Dilston after 1833, when John Grey was appointed manager of the
extensive northern estates of the Greenwich Hospital in Northumberland and Cumberland. A large new house was built for
him and his family when he took up this position, and in her
childhood and youth, Josephine Butler shared with Frances Cobbe
the experience of living as the daughter of an influential and
respected figure amongst the landed gentry.

   Like most girls of her class, Josephine Grey was educated mostly
at home, by her mother and by governesses. She had as a constant
companion her beloved sister Harriet. 'We were one in heart and
soul, and one in all our pursuits,' Josephine wrote many years later.
'We walked, rode and played together. When one was scolded,
both wept; when one was praised, both were pleased.'[20] They lived
a free outdoor life, becoming excellent horsewomen and having a
fond attachment to many pets. Their mother supervised them

[20] Butler, *Memoir*, 8–9.

closely, insisting that their work be done thoroughly, that they aim at excellence, and that their reading be accompanied by thorough understanding.[21] Their education was completed by two years at a girls' school in Newcastle where Harriet's dislike of learning was readily accepted by a sympathetic mistress who discerned in her a 'spark of genius' and gathered up for preservation her discarded writing and drawings. Butler tells us nothing about what, if anything, she gained at school nor how she felt about it.

Recent work on Butler has tended to stress the fact that she 'grew up conscious of a network of supportive women'.[22] Within her own family there were three women who contributed directly to her development: her mother, whose religious influence and supervision of Josephine's education were so important; her strong-minded and intelligent aunt, Margaretta Grey, an outspoken critic of the constraints faced by women and of what she saw as the shrinking circle of women's activities; and her sister Harriet Meuricoffre, who was Josephine's closest friend in childhood and who worked with her in all campaigns to abolish the regulation of prostitution.[23] Moreover, once Butler became involved in the Contagious Diseases agitation, she became part of a large female network. The Ladies' National Association, as Judith Walkowitz has argued, 'gave political expression to a supportive female subculture in the mid-Victorian period' and the leading women in that campaign established very close relationships with each other.[24]

But while these female networks were of great importance to Butler, her speeches, pamphlets, and books emphasize the contribution of her father—and later of her husband—to her public work. Her convictions, she explained on many occasions, 'dated from her childhood, and were inherited in part from her dear father, who often gave his political lessons to his daughters with his hand resting on the family Bible'.[25] This picture of her father was greatly extended in the *Memoir of John Grey*, which Josephine

[21] Ibid. 12–13; Butler, *In Memoriam: Harriet Meuricoffre*, London, 1901, 9.

[22] Uglow, 'From Sympathy to Theory', 148; Walkowitz, *Prostitution and Victorian Society*, 115.

[23] See Butler, *Harriet Meuricoffre, passim*.

[24] Walkowitz, *Prostitution and Victorian Society*, 113.

[25] Butler, 'Women and Politics'.

Butler wrote in 1869, just after her father had died.[26] When George
Butler died in 1892, Josephine coped with her loss in a similar way
by writing her *Recollections* of him, stressing her indebtedness to
him in her work.[27] It is interesting in this context to note that
Butler refrained from writing a memoir of either her mother or her
aunt and that she made only a few comments about them. These
were certainly filled with praise and suggest she felt affection and
respect for both women, but she does not seem to have felt about
them as intensely or to have connected them as closely with her
work. Butler did write a memoir of Harriet Meuricoffre, which
suggests that Harriet belonged alongside John Grey and George
Butler as the three people who mattered most in her life. But where
the memoirs of her father and husband contain detailed statements
of her indebtedness to them and of the ways in which she gained
her sense of the public world and of political and social reform
from them, the memoir of 'Hattie' consists largely of excerpts from
Harriet's letters.[28]

Josephine Butler's account of her childhood suggests that the
Grey family was an unusually harmonious and devoted one, the
affection of her parents for each other being extended also to
all the children. In demonstrating the harmony of family life,
particularly of her parents' marriage, Butler shows their mutual
concern and protectiveness: the tender way her father nursed her
mother through a serious illness; the longing and affectionate letters
he wrote when separated for any time from his wife and children;
and the way in which his wife supported and advised him on
business and family matters. Although she says very little about
any of her siblings apart from Harriet Meuricoffre, Butler makes
it clear that they remained in constant contact throughout their
lives and that all of them remained on terms of intimacy and
affection with their parents.[29]

Religion was central to the Greys' family life. Hannah Annett was
a Moravian and had grown up in a deeply religious but essentially
ecumenical household in which members of all denominations were
welcome. John Grey had not grown up with any particularly devout

---

[26] Josephine E. Butler, *Memoir of John Grey of Dilston*, Edinburgh, 1869, 157.
[27] Josephine E. Butler, *Recollections of George Butler*, Bristol, 1892.
[28] Butler, *Harriet Meuricoffre*.
[29] Ibid., *passim*, and Butler, *John Grey*, 255–69.

religious feelings, but in the course of a serious illness when he was in his twenties, he had become deeply imbued with religious feeling and had taken to reading the Bible frequently. The Grey household was thus a religious one, but theirs was a non-sectarian religion concerned rather with states of feeling than with particular doctrine. Nowhere is the sense of family unity and affection more evident than in Butler's account of the way that family prayers and church attendance bound them all together. Far from being a duty, religious beliefs provided the basis for social action and the language in which affection was expressed in the Grey family. John Grey read the Bible every Sunday, but he managed to communicate to his children his enjoyment of its language and its epic quality. There was, moreover, much discussion of what he read so that the weekly Bible readings were a source of stimulation and pleasure for them all.[30] There is no suggestion in Butler's account of the Sabbath gloom which was so often a part of Victorian family life.

The central role of John Grey in Josephine Butler's account of her family's religious observance is significant. It establishes the general pattern for her perception of her parents: her father is always depicted as the active partner and as the really important one in her own life. Her mother, by contrast, is always in the background. Butler traced her own social origins entirely through her father. She described his family at some length, concentrating particularly on his sister Margaretta to whom both he and Josephine were very close. But nothing is said about her mother's parents or siblings, and little about her mother's personality. Mention is made of her mother's social background, but it receives no elaboration. Butler even attributes her recognition of poverty and suffering to her father and to his concern about agricultural labourers—rather than to any hardships suffered by her mother's family as migrant weavers.

As a young child, she became aware of the social problems of the 1830s and 1840s by reading with her father government 'blue books' and reports about the new Poor Law and the treatment of paupers in workhouses. In her correspondence Butler acknowledged the importance of her mother's religious views: the Moravian upbringing of Hannah Annett and the openness to all forms of Christianity which existed in her home served as a basis for

[30] Ibid. 49.

Butler's own ecumenical approach.[31] Hannah Annett's moral training and insistence on excellence amongst her children is shown as
standing all of them in good stead.[32] But these small details pale
into insignificance beside the loving and detailed portrayal of John
Grey.

Butler's *Memoir* of her father carefully establishes his social
position, his connection with all the great reform issues of the first
half of the nineteenth century, his strength, his integrity, and his
almost heroic status amongst those for whom he worked. His first
active political campaign was in support of the movement for the
abolition of slavery. He worked to gain signatures for the petition
to end the slave trade in the border country and he accompanied
Lord Brougham on his anti-slavery tour of Northumberland and
Cumberland in 1826. He campaigned for Catholic Emancipation
and for the 1832 Reform Act, using his considerable local influence
at election times. Although his direct political activity ended after
1833, he took a great interest in the repeal of the Corn Laws and
the establishment of free trade. Butler made it perfectly clear that
her father was the embodiment of Liberalism as she understood it.

God made him a Liberal; and a Liberal in the true sense he continued to
be to the end of his life. In conversation with him on any public questions,
one could not but observe how much such questions were matters of
feeling with him. I believe that his political principles and public actions
were alike the direct fruit of that which held rule within his soul,—I mean
his large benevolence, his tender compassionateness, and his respect for
the rights and liberties of individual man.[33]

Butler traced her connection with her father in very specific
terms. Her first awareness of injustice derived from his concern to
abolish first the slave trade and then the whole institution of slavery.
She constantly insisted that her father's horror at slavery and at
the particular sufferings borne by slave women affected her own
later outlook.

When my father spoke to us, his children, of the great wrong of slavery,
I have felt his powerful frame tremble and his voice would break. . . . sad
and tragical recitals came to us from first sources of the hideous wrong

[31] See letter from Josephine Butler to 'Dear Friend', Miss Priestman, 17 Jan.
1883, Butler Papers.
[32] Butler, *Harriet Meuricoffre*, 8.
[33] Butler, *John Grey*, 47.

inflicted on men and women. I say women, for I think their lot was particularly horrible, for they were almost invariably forced to minister to the worst passions of their masters, or to be persecuted and die.[34]

The parallels between her own battle against the Contagious Diseases Acts and the work of those engaged in fighting for the abolition of slavery was stressed by Butler throughout her campaign. The Contagious Diseases Acts, like any form of regulated prostitution, 'secured the enslavement of women'[35] in her view and she referred frequently to the Contagious Diseases Acts as a 'slave code'.[36]

The continuity between her father's concerns and her own is demonstrated also in Butler's discussion of John Grey's sympathy with women. He regarded the women in his own family as his intellectual and spiritual equals, supporting all moves to improve the education of women and signing the petition for reform of the laws pertaining to the property of married women. In his role as magistrate and overseer, he sympathized greatly with the plight of women who faced domestic difficulties.

I can recollect many a time seeing some poor woman weeping at his office-door or in the kitchen, waiting to tell her woes to him, and also I can recall the cheered look and light step with which such poor women often went their way after he had spoken to them. In cases of misunderstandings between husbands and wives, it was always remarked that his love of justice came out strongly, though his tenderness, perhaps, made him lean, in sympathy, a little to the woman's side.[37]

Where Beatrice Webb argued that her father's interest in the ideas of the women of his family made them all into non- or anti-feminists,[38] Josephine Butler establishes a natural progression from an egalitarian family with social commitment and a high evaluation of women to her own dedication to the women's cause. There is something ironic in Butler's description of her father's tenderness to women. So pained was he by any mention of sexual impropriety

---

[34] Butler, *Memoir*, 14.
[35] Josephine E. Butler, *Personal Reminiscences of a Great Crusade*, London, 1898, 37.
[36] See e.g. Josephine Butler, 'Letter to the Members of the Ladies National Association', Aug. 1875, 7 and 14, Butler Papers.
[37] Butler, *John Grey*, 329–30.
[38] Beatrice Webb, *My Apprenticeship*, Harmondsworth, 1971, 35.

or immorality that few spoke of such things in his presence.[39] One of the few mentions of her mother's activity, as distinct from her father's feelings about her mother, occurs here, as it was her mother who always asked the Grey daughters not to mention any local sexual scandal in their father's presence for fear of distressing him! 'Fashionable vice or villainy . . . were not even understood by him.' He thus avoided entirely the burden which his daughter's detailed knowledge of the many sexual, legal, and economic practices involved in prostitution entailed—while retaining, through this very fact, a heroic status in her eyes. At the same time, it is clear that the problems which neighbouring women experienced through sexual oppression or exploitation was something that the women in the Grey home had to deal with.

Butler's picture of her early life suggests that her family life was far more affectionate and harmonious than was that of Davies, Fawcett, or Cobbe. She thoroughly enjoyed the education she received from her mother and found her home life stimulating and enjoyable. But this harmonious picture is upset by the story of the religious crisis which she underwent in her late adolescence. She described it to friends just before her death.

It was my lot from my earliest years to be haunted by the problems which more or less present themselves to every thoughtful mind. Year after year this haunting became more tyrannous. . . . A strange intuition was given to me whereby I saw as in a vision, before I had seen any of them with my bodily eyes, some of the saddest miseries of earth, the injustices, the inequalities, the cruelties practised by man on woman. . . . For one long year of darkness the trouble of heart and brain urged me to lay all this at the door of God, whose name I had learned was love. I dreaded Him—I fled from Him—until grace was given me to arise and wrestle, as Jacob did, with the mysterious Presence who must either slay or pronounce deliverance. . . . I fought the battle alone, in deep recesses of the beautiful woods and pine forests around our home. For hours and days and weeks in these retreats I sought the answer to my soul's trouble and the solution of its dark questioning.[40]

Butler always described her religious crisis in entirely biblical terms, with little detail as to exactly when and how it happened. However vague it is, her account makes it clear that it was quite

[39] Butler, *John Grey*, 339–40.
[40] Butler, *Memoir*, 15–16.

unlike those of Frances Cobbe, or George Eliot or of so many Victorian intellectuals, whose spiritual agony centred on their inability to believe in the God of revealed religion. About this fundamental truth Butler was apparently never in doubt. Rather what bothered her was how to make sense of human injustice and how to accept that she had a particular God-given responsibility to fight it.[41] Her crisis was thus similar to those of several other notable Victorian philanthropists and reformers such as Mary Carpenter, in that it centred on how one faced the implications of having been chosen by God to dedicate one's life to His service. In her late adolescence, the precise nature of this service was unclear and this in itself added to her distress. However when she was approached to undertake the leadership of the Contagious Diseases agitation, she immediately thought that this might after all be 'the very work, the very mission, I longed for years ago and saw, coming afar off, like a bright star'.[42]

Butler's sense of her own part in a family tradition as well as her sense of isolation and separateness are both evident in her whole approach to the Contagious Diseases agitation and to her role in it. Just before taking up this cause in 1869, she wrote the *Memoir* of her father. Her presentation of him, especially her description of the ways in which her own understanding of the world derived from his, suggests the intensity of her identification with him. His activities and beliefs both legitimated and established the framework for her own. Butler thus presents herself as having inherited the mantle of her father. But this inheritance was not an easy matter. In regard to public work, as in regard to wealth, it is the son and not the daughter who inherits directly from the father. The Grey household exemplified Victorian notions of separate spheres for men and women, with John Grey leading a public life, while his wife offered him help and support and devoted her energies to the care of the children and the household.

This ideal of family life was deeply ingrained in Josephine Butler herself. Hence the taking up of a public role involved her in a series of conflicts. She had first to establish her special fitness to undertake her father's work. Like Catherine Beecher or Mary Carpenter, both of whom were devoted to powerful fathers whose religious beliefs

[41] For more discussion on this point, see Petrie, *A Singular Iniquity*, 27–30.
[42] Diary from Sept. 1869, quoted in Butler, *Memoir*, 91.

and public work they strove to extend or to complement, she had to negotiate with a masculine tradition and to establish that she had been specially chosen to undertake a public role.[43] And Josephine was so chosen through the religious crisis she experienced when she was just 17. There has been some discussion amongst Butler scholars as to why and how this religious crisis occurred: whether it was the result of the shock she sustained when she saw the body of a man who had hanged himself or whether it had some other intellectual or emotional origin. But the precise cause of it seems less important than its function in enabling her, as a woman, to follow in her father's footsteps by undertaking a public role.

Butler's veneration of her father was almost matched by that for her husband. Where her father's example provided the framework for her campaign, George Butler helped her to understand clearly the issues that were involved in it and to maintain a balanced judgement about them. The adulatory *Recollections* of her husband which she wrote shortly after his death in 1892 contain a detailed discussion of his part in her work.

My motive in writing these recollections is to tell what he was—my husband—and to show how ... he was of a character to be able from the first to soothe the spirit of the companion of his life when 'the waters had come unto her soul'.... he was even more to me in later life than a wise and noble supporter and helper in the work which may have been called more especially my own. He had a part in the creation of it, in the formation of the first impulses towards it. Had that work been purely a product of the feminine mind, of a solitary, wounded and revolted heart, it would certainly have lacked some elements essential to its becoming in any way useful or fruitful.[44]

There is more than a touch of conceit in Josephine Butler's assumption that what made George Butler most interesting to his contemporaries was his marriage to herself and there is perhaps a suggestion running through the *Recollections* that George Butler did not quite reach the position to which his abilities entitled him— and thus that his merits needed to be enumerated.

[43] For a fascinating discussion of the difficulties faced by one nineteenth-century woman seeking both a sphere of action, and paternal approval, see Kathryn Kish Sklar, *Catherine Beecher: A Study in American Domesticity*, New Haven, Conn., 1974.

[44] Butler, *George Butler*, 2–3.

George Butler was obviously a man of considerable intellect and originality, an innovative teacher, and a man of great courage. He and Josephine were apparently extremely devoted to each other, sharing many interests and able to offer each other considerable support. Indeed theirs is one of the close and companionate marriages now used to question the whole idea of a repressive and paternalistic Victorian sexual morality.[45]

George Butler was one of that large and very unusual group of Victorian men who devoted much of their time and energy to advancing the cause of women. He was active in the campaigns to improve the education of women and to extend their employment opportunities. He also gave his whole-hearted support to Josephine Butler's campaign against the Contagious Diseases Acts, disruptive as this was both to his career and to his domestic life. Josephine Butler placed particular emphasis on his help and support in her work with prostitutes: on those occasions when she brought one of them back to her home, usually in order to provide a more comfortable death than was possible in the workhouse, George Butler worked with her, showing the women concerned the respect and the care which he would accord to any lady visiting his home.

But while George Butler loved and admired his wife, he was unable to protect or to defend her against the world in which he made her live. When they first married in 1852 the Butlers lived in Oxford, where George was a university examiner. It was in these years of their marriage that Josephine Butler first experienced the problems faced by many able and intelligent women of her own class, as she was surrounded by men who regarded her thoughts and ideas with contempt and made it perfectly clear that she was a member of the inferior sex.

Although they were apparently very happy together, Oxford had what Josephine Butler later described as its 'shadow side'. She had come from 'a large family circle and from free country life to a university town—a society of celibates, with little or no leaven of family life'. There was no female companionship for her, as college fellows were not permitted to marry, and the University offered neither scope for her abilities nor recognition of her ideas. With

[45] F. B. Smith, 'Sexuality in Britain, 1800–1900: Some Suggested Revisions', in *A Widening Sphere: Changing Roles of Victorian Women*, ed. Martha Vicinus, Bloomington, Ind., 1977, 187.

something of an understatement, Butler noted that the lack of home life or of social interaction between 'the academical portion of the community and others' fostered 'a one sided-ness of judgement . . . an exaggeration of the purely masculine judgement on some topics, and a conventual mode of looking at things'. Even in her own home, she was silenced by her husband's friends. 'I sat silent, the only woman in the company, and listened, sometimes with a sore heart; for these men would speak of things which I had already revolved deeply in my own mind, things of which I was convinced, which I knew, though I had no dialectics at command with which to defend their truth.'[46] It was particularly when conversation turned to questions of sexual morality that Butler was shocked by the cynicism, the levity, and the brutality of these men who had no compassion for the women whom she saw as the victims in sexual encounters, and who endorsed the existing double standard which regarded sexual immorality as acceptable in men but utterly unacceptable in women.

George Butler's part in all this is particularly interesting. In her memoirs Josephine maintains that he helped her through this period by showing a pitying disdain for his male colleagues with their limited understanding of social and moral questions. The poor fellows, he explained, knew no better. Josephine Butler ostensibly sought to show how deep her husband's sympathy and under- standing was. His blessed common sense 'came to the rescue to restore for me the balance of a mind too heavily weighted with sad thoughts of life's perplexing problems'. But, looking back from the vantage-point of the late twentieth century, it is hard not to see his sense that his friends deserved pity as something which she would find hard to swallow. Moreover, while George Butler disagreed with his friends, especially when discussions turned to moral and sexual questions, he does not seem to have indicated this to them or to have supported his wife's position. In later years, he publicly attacked the double sexual standard and supported Josephine's approach to moral questions, but in their early years, he seems rather to have counselled her to be patient. As was so often the case with Josephine Butler, it was religion that brought her peace. After George's friends left their Oxford home, the Butlers read the Bible together, praying 'that a holy revolution might come about and the

[46] Butler, *Memoir*, 30.

Kingdom of God might be established on the earth'.

Butler's recollections of her early married life were written in order to provide the context for her 'great crusade'. Hence they stress those spiritual and moral questions which led her to it. But as a result of this, they contain a curious omission. While presenting herself as one who came from a close and affectionate family and then created another through marriage, Butler reveals nothing about the formation of this family—about the birth of her three sons or how this affected either her health or her life in Oxford. Her daughter is present, but really only through the story of her tragic death which served to propel Butler into her involvement with prostitutes. In her own terrible grief, she found the only possible solace in contact with 'other hearts which ached night and day' as hers did. Butler's other comments about this event emphasize the extent to which the loss of her daughter meant the loss of her daily companion as both her husband and sons were engaged at work and school, leaving her alone. She makes very few comments about her sons—about their upbringing, education, or relationship with their parents. She seems to have been like Fawcett in gaining the support of her children for her activities. They did not become champions of her cause, but they certainly seem to have accepted her involvement in it and to have remained close and devoted to her. In her later years, especially after the death of George Butler, she wrote to her son Stanley frequently and at extraordinary length, discussing with him every aspect of her life and thoughts. She was also very affectionate to and warmly regarded by her grandchildren, one of whom wrote a memoir of her.[47]

The death of Butler's daughter led to the family moving to Liverpool, where Butler began her work with prostitutes. This move also brought her into contact with a large group of able and energetic women dedicated to improving the situation of their sex. Several feminist campaigns were under way by the late 1860s and Josephine Butler was very soon involved in most of them. In 1867 she became the President of the North of England Council for Promoting the Higher Education of Women and a year later she wrote a pamphlet on 'The Education and Employment of Women' which looked at the plight of single women in particular and at their great need for better education and for a wider range of

[47] A. S. G. Butler was her grandson.

employment opportunities.[48] She worked with Jessie Boucheret and the Society to Promote the Employment of Women to expand the training and work opportunities for women.

In the same year, she joined Lydia Becker and Elizabeth Wolstenholme in preparing a memorial to the Council of the Social Science Association, seeking its support in pressuring Parliament to reform the laws which deprived married women of the ownership and control of their property or earnings.[49] The following year, the Married Women's Property Committee was formed with Becker as treasurer and Elizabeth Wolstenholme as secretary. Butler joined the committee and remained on it until the passage of the Married Women's Property Act in 1882 brought its dissolution.

In her own accounts of these years, Butler stresses her work amongst prostitutes. She began to frequent the various resorts of active prostitutes and the bridewells, hospitals, refuges, and penitentiaries where she found aged, ailing and infirm ones. Some who were terminally ill she took home to die and when the numbers of these sad cases threatened to overflow the space available, she opened a special 'House of Rest' for the purpose.[50]

Although Liverpool and her involvement in the women's movement brought Butler into contact with other women, it did not end her close friendships with men. In these years, although Butler became quite friendly with Elizabeth Wolstenholme, Jessie Boucheret, and Lydia Becker, her closest friends—and the ones to whom she wrote about her concerns on behalf of women—were men. Her feelings about the connection between prostitution and the lack of work for women, for example, was most clearly articulated in letters to her devoted friend, Albert Rutson. Rutson had been a university friend of George Butler's and had met Josephine when the Butlers lived in Oxford. It was to Rutson that Josephine Butler wrote to express the horror she felt at having to discuss details about her body with male doctors, and her relief at finding a woman doctor, once Elizabeth Garrett began to practise. It was

---

[48] Josephine E. Butler, *The Education and Employment of Women*, London, 1868.
[49] The other three signatories to the memorial were Jessie Boucheret, Mrs Gloyn, and Elizabeth Wolstenholme. See 'Report of the Married Women's Property Committee Presented at the Final Meeting of their Friends and Subscribers', 18 Nov. 1882, Manchester, 1882, 12. See also Philippa Levine, *Victorian Feminism, 1850–1900*, London, 1987, 128–49.
[50] Butler, *Memoir*, 61–2.

he, too, to whom she wrote concerning her ideas about the need for greater employment opportunities for women. Rutson assisted directly in her feminist activities, helping her to draw up the memorial on the situation of married women, and offering advice on the question of the industrial employment of women for her pamphlet.

At this stage, in the late 1860s, Josephine Butler showed no sign either that she felt the lack of female support or indeed that she had any sympathy with the idea of women organizing by themselves to fight their own oppression. On the contrary, she quite clearly opposed such an approach. In 1868, when she was becoming very concerned about the economic situation of women, she wrote to Albert Rutson about the need to combat prejudice and to establish what work women could do. But she took care to emphasize that she was not suggesting that women work separately from men. 'Monopolies must be avoided. Let us women at least avoid all exclusiveness and trade union spirit.'[51]

Even in her later years, Butler always emphasized the fact that her involvement in the various campaigns for women occurred at the behest of men and that it involved working alongside them. This was so even in regard to the Contagious Diseases agitation. Emily Davies gained both her introduction to the women's movement and her first knowledge that like-minded women existed through her contact with the Leigh Smith sisters, and Cobbe became involved in feminist activities while engaged in philanthropic work carried out alongside a group of able and energetic women in Bristol. Butler, by contrast, insisted that she was actually asked to undertake the leadership in the battle against the Contagious Diseases Acts by 'a group of medical men, who (all honour to them) had for some time been making strenuous efforts to prevent the introduction in our land of the principle of regulation by the State of the social evil'.[52] She omitted to note that the specific form of her leadership was suggested by women: Elizabeth Wolstenholme approached her as soon as the Ladies' National Association for the Repeal of the Contagious Diseases Acts was established in December 1869, and Butler soon emerged as its leader.[53]

---

[51] Josephine Butler to Albert Rutson, 19 June 1868, Butler Papers.
[52] Butler, *Memoir*, 89–90.
[53] See Walkowitz, *Prostitution and Victorian Society*, 93.

Although Butler only became involved in that agitation in 1869, the Contagious Diseases Acts had been first passed in 1862 and then extended in 1864. The Acts, which were ostensibly intended to improve the health of the armed services, were only in force in specified garrisons and naval ports. In accordance with them, any woman who was identified as a common prostitute by a member of the metropolitan police was required to undergo medical examination. If found to be venereally diseased, she could be detained in a hospital for up to three months. A woman could voluntarily accept the examination, but if she refused, she could be brought before a magistrate and then bound by his orders to submit. Hence the Acts established a system of supervision and surveillance of prostitutes in specified areas.

The morality, the constitutionality, even the efficacy of the Acts were a source of concern to many.[54] The Acts did not define what a common prostitute was. Prostitution was not illegal, so that no charge of breaking a law was involved when a woman was forced to appear before a magistrate. Prostitutes were thus entirely denied the legal rights and protection enjoyed by others in England. Moreover the Act applied only to women and not to male clients. Hence the campaign for repeal of the Acts was directed towards removing the restraints it imposed on prostitutes and restoring their legal rights.

Although opposition to the Acts had existed amongst medical men and amongst some national political groups from their first introduction, it was only when Butler became the leader of the Ladies' National Association that this opposition became vocal or widely known. Her connection with this body brought great changes for Butler too, disrupting her family and occupying much of her time for many years.

The Contagious Diseases campaign offered Butler not only a political framework in which to address the question of prostitution, but also a wide network of supportive men and women who shared her own political beliefs. Butler was one of a large number of radical liberals engaged in moral and political crusades at the time, and she joined forces with many others who shared her intense opposition to the expanding role of government in regard to matters which had previously been seen as private. The Ladies' National

[54] Walkowitz, *Prostitution and Victorian Society*, 69–112.

Association for the Repeal of the Contagious Diseases Acts which Butler led worked alongside the all-male National Association for the Repeal of the Contagious Diseases Acts, sharing offices and sometimes jointly paying agents. As Judith Walkowitz has shown, the leading figures in both the National Association and the Ladies' National Association were middle-class men and women drawn from the same social constituency that supported other mid-Victorian reform groups working for a variety of morally-based political and social reforms including temperance, universal education—and opposition to compulsory vaccination.[55]

The political beliefs of this group were underlined when many of them joined to establish the Vigilance Association for the Defence of Personal Rights in 1871. This organization was established to keep an eye on legislation which infringed individual liberties.[56] It was overtly feminist, and its major activities were carried out by its Committee for Amending the Law in Points wherein it is Injurious to Women.[57] It offered Butler the forum which many of the London-based feminists found in the National Association for the Promotion of Social Science, but which was closer to her own political views. She personally disliked the Social Science Association because while it 'ought to have done so much good' by enquiring into legislation, it 'has done about an equal degree of mischief, by stimulating legislation in matters which had much better not be legislated about, but ... left to the common sense of the English people'.[58] The Vigilance Association included amongst its other founder members several radical MPs: Peter Alfred Taylor, Jacob Bright, Charles McLaren, Passmore, William Shaen, all of whom supported the emancipation of women, but who were active in other campaigns as well. Butler supported them in their opposition to compulsory vaccination and in their outspoken criticism of legislation which limited the hours and attempted to control the conditions of working women.[59]

[55] For the membership and social make-up of the repeal campaign, see Walkowitz, *Prostitution and Victorian Society*, 67–148.

[56] For the aims and the formation of this association see the *Report of the Conference of the Association for the Defence of Personal Rights*, Manchester, 1871. There is a copy in the Butler Papers.

[57] Ibid.

[58] Ibid. 24.

[59] See report entitled 'The Vigilance Association' in the *Journal of the Vigilance Association for the Defence of Personal Rights*, 1, 15 Jan. 1881, 1.

It was only when the Contagious Diseases agitation began that Butler found a close female network. The leadership of the Ladies' National Association soon became a close-knit body, with a great deal of mutual loyalty and support. Butler found these women more congenial than her earlier feminist colleagues. Their intense religious faith probably played some part in this as did the way in which they exemplified what she regarded as the most desirable features of womanhood. In her *Personal Reminiscences of a Great Crusade*, Butler wrote about the women to whom she had been closest.

The sisters Priestman and Margaret Tanner, with Miss Eslin and others closely associated with them ... have been to me, personally, through this long struggle ... a kind of body guard, a *corps d'élite* on whose prompt aid, singleness of purpose, prudence and unwearying industry I could and can rely at all times.[60]

Butler wrote often to these women and was on close and affectionate terms with them, but it is clear that these were not relationships of equals. Her leadership and pre-eminence were always recognized. It is not without significance that she mentioned as particularly notable qualities in those colleagues who became her friends 'the utter absence ... of any desire for recognition, or any vestige of egotism in any form'.[61]

The existence of this network did not end her close friendship or association with men. Even within the Contagious Diseases agitation, she worked closely with men. Henry Wilson, James Stansfeld, and James Stuart were the recipients of her communications and of her ideas quite as often as were the other women in the Ladies' National Association. But, as we shall see, it was in the course of the this agitation that she came to realize very clearly that male support could be a liability as well as a help to women.

For all her friends, and for all the difficulties Butler faced in the early years of her marriage, her greatest support continued to come from her husband. His importance in her life is evident not only in the way she wrote of him, but in the fact that his death brought to an end any kind of settled life for her. George Butler's health was

[60] Butler, *Personal Reminiscences*, 104; see also Walkowitz, *Prostitution and Victorian Society*, 113–36.
[61] Butler, *Personal Reminiscences*, 105.

poor for some years from the mid-1880s onwards and Josephine Butler's anxiety about him was enormous. When he died in 1892, it was as if her roots were severed. She gave up a settled home, living instead a peripatetic life, visiting relatives in England and in Europe and living in lodgings until her own death in 1905.

The years after George's death were trying and difficult ones for Butler, publicly as well as privately, as she lived to see herself at odds with those who had long been her closest supporters—and even to see them insist that she was doing her own cause great harm. Butler continued to participate in the abolitionist movement for much of the 1890s, throwing most of her energy into the campaign to end the regulation of prostitution in India. For some of that time, she continued to be a popular, even an inspirational figure. Reporting on the International Conference of the British and Continental Federation for the Abolition of the State Regulation of Vice in July 1898, the feminist journalist Florence Fenwick Miller described Butler in terms of adulation very similar to those used by her followers in the Ladies' National Association some thirty years earlier.

Never was there such an exhibition of silent power as Mrs Butler gave. Her presence, her beautiful saintly face, her magnetic inspiring power, were felt throughout, though in consequence of her delicate health she spoke little and seldom. At first I thought it was too sad that she ... should have lived to see the subject revived. But now I see that it is most necessary that we should have still had with us those who have borne and suffered ... in order that they might call together and inspire and set in order the newer hosts on whom the brunt of battle will fall.[62]

But this veneration for Butler was soon over. By 1901 there was a revolt against her within the abolitionist movement. When her close friend Fanny Forsaith suggested republishing some of Butler's speeches and articles in the *Shield*, Henry Wilson wrote to say that it was quite impossible. He doubted if Miss Forsaith had any idea of 'the intensity of feeling amongst a great many (I should say the great bulk) of the friends and supporters of the British Committee'. The reason for this hostility lay in the fact that Butler had come out as a strong supporter of the Government over the Boer War. By contrast, most of the abolitionists were pro-Boer.

---

[62] 'The Abolitionists Federation', *Woman's Signal*, 21 July 1898, 457.

That Butler should adopt this position was indeed extraordinary. She had been at one with her provincial radical colleagues
in her support for Home Rule in Ireland and they could not
understand how she could now support what they saw as the quite
unjustified entry of Britain into a war with South Africa. As Wilson
wrote, 'many are astounded that it could be possible for Mrs Butler
to take the line she has.'[63]

Butler's response to the Boer War remains very hard to understand. She was severely critical of British conduct in South Africa
throughout the 1890s. The Conservative and Unionist victory in
the 1895 elections filled her with dismay, particularly as it meant
the appointment of Joseph Chamberlain as Colonial Secretary.
'What an awful thing it seems to have Chamberlain at the Colonial
Office instead of good Lord Rippon,' she wrote to one of her
friends.[64] But she reserved her greatest hostility for Rhodes, whose
brutality and greed seemed to her to be endless and whose power
over members of the British Government was a great cause of
concern.[65] She believed that the Jameson Raid was planned by
Rhodes, and that 'Dr Jameson merely acted as his servant and
agent in making that wanton attack on the Transvaal'. In her view,
Chamberlain, Rhodes, and Jameson were all engaged in setting up
a conflict which was designed to result in war. When the war came,
however, Butler's views changed and she became a most outspoken
anti-Boer and supporter of the British cause. Her support was
stated in general terms rather than involving a rereading of the
events leading up to the war. Hence she opposed the British tradition of freedom to the Boer enslavement of the 'native races',
almost arguing that the British were fighting to abolish this slavery.
She insisted that her views were consistent with her long-held
beliefs about liberty and citizenship, arguing that the demand of
the Uitlanders for representation was parallel to the demand for
the vote being made by women.[66]

Butler was well aware that her position was not shared by others
in the abolitionist movement. 'I can count on the fingers of one
hand', she wrote to Millicent Fawcett, 'those in England (of our

[63] Henry Wilson to Miss Forsaith, 7 Jan. 1901, Butler Papers.
[64] Josephine Butler to Miss Forsaith, 11 July 1895, ibid.
[65] Josephine Butler to Stanley Butler, 20 Feb. 1895, ibid.
[66] Josephine E. Butler, *The Native Races and the War*, London, 1900.

abolitionist Federation) who are not strong pro-Boers; and our
Continental allies are much the same.'[67] But their hostility did not
deter her. There is no convincing explanation for Butler's change
of heart. Her grandson reports that on one trip to Europe, she was
angered by the criticisms of Britain she heard in Germany and felt
it necessary to defend her own country. But this hardly seems
adequate. The intensity, even vehemence with which she threw
herself into supporting the war almost makes one suspect that she
felt that the time had come to break with the abolitionist movement
and to recognize that she was no longer engaged in the same battles
as were her erstwhile followers.

The ironic aspect of this whole episode is that her stance on the
Boer War brought Butler into a close relationship with Millicent
Fawcett for the first time. Fawcett not only supported the war, but
was sent out by the Government to inspect the concentration camps
into which the British had herded Boer women and children. But,
unlike Butler, she had not expressed any earlier criticism of the
Government or of Rhodes and generally supported British imperial
expansion. During these years, she became one of Butler's close
allies. Their correspondence increased in frequency—and Butler's
letters certainly became more affectionate and confidential. Fawcett
in turn took it upon herself to ensure that Butler's central importance for the nineteenth-century women's movement should not be
forgotten, organizing the painting of her portrait and arranging
testimonials and expressions of support in the years just prior to
Butler's death.

II

What then are the distinctive features of Butler's feminism? One
can characterize it, easily enough, in terms which relate her very
closely to Davies and Cobbe. Butler shared their demand for an
end to the many legal, political, and economic restrictions which
women faced. As an advanced liberal, Butler followed through
the arguments which derived from liberal economic and political
theory more extensively than they did. In her earliest feminist
pamphlets, Butler stressed the economic question, arguing that it

[67] Josephine Butler to Millicent Fawcett, 20 June 1900, Butler Papers.

was the lack of access to employment which ensured and per-petuated women's subordination. As a consequence, she demanded an end to all Factory Acts and industrial legislation which applied to women, but not to men. In addition she sought legal and political reform: the end of the system of coverture and the laws which deprived married women of their property; the extension to women, whether married, unmarried, or widowed of the right to vote at parliamentary, local, and other elections on the same conditions which qualified men, and complete equality of civil and political rights between women and men.[68]

Butler combined these demands for an end to the restrictions on women with a very strong sense of the innate differences between women and men. Her views on the distinctive characteristics of women were very similar to those of Frances Cobbe. Like Cobbe, she believed that 'home is the nursery of all virtue' and that women were home-makers by instinct. She shared Cobbe's conviction that emancipation would not bring a diminution of the distinctive—and admirable—qualities of womanhood. Those who feared such an outcome did not understand the strength of Nature.

Every good quality, every virtue which we regard as distinctively feminine, will, under conditions of greater freedom, develop more freely ... It will always be in her nature to foster, to cherish, to take the part of the weak, to train, to guide, to have a care for individuals, to discern the small seeds of a great future, to warm and cherish those seeds into fulness of life. 'I serve', will always be one of her favourite mottos, even should the utmost freedom be accorded her in the choice of vocation.[69]

For her, as for Frances Cobbe, the inmates of orphanages and workhouses, to say nothing of the neglected children of the streets, were all in need of the care which only a woman could offer. 'It would be wise of the State', Butler insisted, 'to avail itself of this abundance of generous womanliness, of tender and wise mother-liness which lives in the hearts of thousands of women who are free

---

[68] Butler joined the Women's Franchise League when it was established in 1889. The League differed from the other suffrage societies in the nature of their demands. Where the other suffrage societies had by this time decided to campaign only for the vote for single women, the WFL refused to accept that married women should be excluded from this demand.

[69] Butler, *Education and Employment*, 18.

to bring their capacities to bear where they are most needed.'[70] Her veneration for this version of womanhood did not stop her demanding complete legal and political equality for women, but it did make her reject the idea that women should have the same education or even the same range of occupations as men. She disliked those advocates of women's rights who 'speak of women as if it were a compliment to them, or in any way true, to say that they are like men'[71] and she regarded Emily Davies as such a woman. Butler did not really want women's university education ever to approximate to that of men's—and she disliked the women who had received a college education, complaining of their want of 'grace'.[72]

But while one can establish these general features of Butler's feminism in this way, its central and defining characteristic, and the point which she always stressed when writing about herself, was her concern about the sexual double standard and the part it played in the oppression of women. In her preparedness to discuss this matter, Butler differed radically from both Davies and Cobbe, who attempted to avoid any reference to so unsavoury a question. Butler, too, had some difficulties in articulating this concern and she never found a wholly satisfactory way of analysing or discussing it or of integrating it into a general feminist theory.

It is in regard to the question of prostitution and the sexual double standard that one can see most clearly both the importance for Butler of her liberal political beliefs—and their limitations. In her autobiographical writings, Butler insisted that her horror at the sexual double standard was a dominating emotion from her early adulthood. But she was only able to make this concern public when she was called on to lead the Contagious Diseases agitation. Prior to this, it had been a private preoccupation. She was haunted by it in Oxford in the early 1850s, but rarely even entered into the discussions of it which occurred in her own home. Her concern about prostitutes and sexually victimized women suggested the avenue she should follow in Liverpool in her search to find others whose misery would help assuage her grief at the loss of her daughter. At this time she engaged in her own personal version of

[70] Ibid. 20.
[71] Ibid. 17.
[72] Josephine Butler to Stanley Butler, 17 June 1895, Butler Papers.

rescue work, helping some individuals directly and trying to offer some kind of spiritual solace to others.[73]

Butler's recollections serve, as they are intended to, to differentiate her interests, as a leading abolitionist, from those of many other mid-Victorian feminists whose primary concern was the plight of single middle-class women unable to earn a living or of married women who lost their legal identity and hence their right to own property on marriage. This insistence on the differences between her approach and that of the London-based women involved in campaigns to extend the education and the work of women and to obtain women's suffrage is quite reasonable, especially since many of these women did not support the Contagious Diseases agitation. But if one moves from Butler's later recollections to what she actually wrote and published in the late 1860s, one is less struck by these differences than by how very hard it was for her to incorporate her concern about prostitutes and the sexual double standard into her general discussions of the woman question.

In her first published pamphlet, *The Education and Employment of Women*, which appeared in 1868, Butler did not mention the problem of prostitution in any direct way. Her primary plea— for the recognition of the number of women forced to support themselves and hence of the need for better education and training for them—was very similar both in form and content to those which had been produced from the late 1850s by London-based feminists such as Barbara Bodichon and Bessie Raynor Parkes. Butler focused her attention on the two groups who were frequently written about at the time, governesses and seamstresses, and her insistence on the need for better education and training and for more work opportunities was a reiteration of arguments which were already familiar. Butler did discuss working-class women, pleading for a reduction in the many different kinds of prejudice which closed occupations to women or allowed them entry only under exceptionally arduous conditions. Trade unions were for her, as for Millicent Fawcett, a particular target for criticism—and she hoped they could be enlightened by well-meaning gentlemen! But Butler's actual subject in this pamphlet remains far removed from anything to do with prostitution. In a much-quoted sentence,

[73] Butler, *Memoir*, 59–71.

Butler hinted at her awareness of the connection between prostitution on the one hand and both the lack of other avenues of
employment and the very low pay which women had to bear on
the other—but only in a most oblique way. 'Economics', she wrote,
'lie at the very root of practical morality.'[74] But this statement was
given no expansion.

The lack of published references to the problem of prostitution
at this time does not mean that Butler later fabricated her early
concern. On the contrary, her correspondence shows clearly that
it was a major preoccupation. While she was writing her pamphlet
on women's employment, Butler received a letter from Frederick
Harrison explaining his ideas about the true role of women. Harrison was the leading English disciple of Auguste Comte and he
expounded Comte's views concerning the domestic and moral role
of women. This role was of central importance to the Comtists,
who believed that women should be worshipped as the embodiment
of humanity. To ensure that all women did carry out their domestic
role—and to protect them from anything as demeaning as wage
labour—Harrison proposed the closure of all industrial labour to
women.

Butler was sickened by his letter and appalled by his 'Satanic
theories'. She trembled all over while reading it but steeled herself
to reply to him in very direct terms. There were at that very
moment, she argued, some two and a half million unmarried
women in England who were supporting themselves by their own
labour. Harrison's suggestion would leave these women with 'the
alternative of starvation or prostitution'. Prostitution was not the
result of natural vice, she argued, so much as one of political and
social economy. And in turn, prostitution worked to lessen the
numbers both of men and women who married. Butler did not
believe that the Comtist ideal of having all women preside over a
family home was bad in itself, but it was absolutely cruel when
applied either to England or to France where demographic developments meant that vast numbers of women did not and could not
marry.[75]

At this point then, Butler expressed very clear views on prostitution in private, but she had not yet broken through the Victorian

[74] Butler, *Education and Employment*, 14.
[75] Josephine Butler to Frederick Harrison, 9 May 1868, Butler Papers.

taboos which prevented genteel women from discussing matters about sexual commerce in public . In 1869, in the long introduction she wrote to the collection of essays she edited on *Woman's Work and Woman's Culture*, Butler came closer to addressing her main concern. She had by now become very familiar with the statistics concerning women's employment and included a discussion of the Census figures for 1851 and 1861 which showed the extensive number of women who were dependent on their own earnings. The Census figures were horrifying enough, Butler argued, although they did not tell how many women received starvation wages.

Nor does the census include among those breadwinners the armies of women ... who are forced downwards to the paths of hell, by the pressures from above, through the shutting up of avenues to a livelihood by means of trade monopolies among men, and through the absence of any instruction or apprenticeship to qualify them for employment. Of this ... sorest of human griefs, we are never forgetful; no, not for a day ... The subject was thought too painful a one to be specially treated in a volume for general reading; therefore I think it the more needful to assert that these our fellow-women are not forgotten by us ... and ... *that there is no analogy whatever among men, however miserable certain classes of men may be, to the wholesale destruction which goes on from year to year among women.*[76]

But again, Butler did not explore this theme, pleading rather for better education, and for an understanding of true Christianity when it came to the question of the relationship between the sexes.

Butler's early writings display great unease and inexperience. The pleading tone and the reference to her own experience as a mother suggest a lack of self-assurance and a sense that she had not yet established a clear position or role for herself in relation to the women's movement. The start of the campaign against the Contagious Diseases Acts changed all that as Butler emerged very soon as a powerful leader, sure of her own abilities, of her command of her subject, and of her power over her followers. Her sense that this campaign was a sacred mission to which she had been called by God made her easily able to discuss many matters about which ladies were expected to be ignorant. It was moreover the case that

[76] Josephine Butler, ed., *Woman's Work and Woman's Culture*, London, 1869, p. xvi, italics in original.

the Contageous Diseases Acts allowed her to address the question of prostitution in terms of liberal theory and hence offered her a way of connecting her concern about the sexual double standard with her general concerns about civil liberties and about excessive government intervention in private life.

Most of Butler's early speeches expand and elaborate one of the arguments put forward in the 'Women's Protest against the Contagious Diseases Acts' published in the *Daily News* on 1 January 1870, namely, that the Acts were unjust 'because, so far as women are concerned, they remove every guarantee of personal security which the law has established and held sacred, and put their reputation, their freedom, and their persons absolutely in the power of the police'. Butler extended this line of argument into a general attack on the tendency to 'over-legislation', which she saw as 'the grand evil of the day'.[77] She was concerned about the tendency to central government regulation in place of local and municipal control over many community matters, including public health. She disliked the growing power of the executive and of ministers within government. She saw governments as usurping the power of Parliament through the 'modern fashion of the framing and issuing of orders or edicts independently of Parliament ... these orders being afterwards brought before Parliament for confirmation'. She was fiercely opposed to any attempt to legislate on questions of morality. The Contageous Diseases Acts were themselves an illustration of the growing tendency to over-legislate, to expand the powers of police and to interfere in the private lives of individuals.[78]

Butler gave this liberal approach a feminist slant by stressing her concern that legislative intervention was particularly harmful for women. The fact that women were not represented in Parliament made them particularly vulnerable to regulations which men would never impose on each other. When the women's suffrage movement first began in 1867, Butler had not joined it, seeing other questions as more pressing. The Contagious Diseases agitation, however, made her 'feel more and more anxious to get women's suffrage. My own observations have led me to feel and fear that we shall

[77] *Report of the Conference of the Association for the Defence of Personal Rights*, 14 Nov. 1871, Manchester, 1871, 24.
[78] See esp. Josephine E. Butler, *Government by Police*, London, 1879.

shortly be utterly swamped if we don't get it.'[79] This theme was a major one in Butler's correspondence in the early 1870s.

I feel more keenly than I ever did the great importance of our having votes, as a means of self preservation. We cannot always depend on the self-sacrificing efforts of noble men ... to right our wrongs, and now that the labourers are going to be enfranchised, our case becomes the worse; we shall be utterly sacrificed and lost, if we have no representation—if we become (tho' more than half the nation) the one unrepresented section under a government which will become more and more extended, more popular, more democratic, and yet wholly masculine. Woe is me! that people cannot see it.[80]

Initially then, the Contagious Diseases campaign combined in a very easy way Butler's great hostility to excessive government interference in the lives of individuals and her concern about the double standard in sexual morality. But in the course of the campaign, this connection became strained as she became more and more aware of the ways in which the Acts extended male control over women's bodies. In 1870 Butler toured the garrison towns of Kent, writing about the actual operation of the Contagious Diseases Acts in a series of letters to the *Shield*, the weekly paper put out by the National Association. These letters painted a vivid picture of the ways in which the Acts worked to establish new structures of male authority, which ensured men's unimpeded access to women's bodies. These structures gave individual men new power to humiliate women and Butler reported an incident in which a man chose to report to the police a woman with whom he had had a sexual relationship, thus ensuring that she was called before a magistrate, subjected to a public examination, and henceforth known in her neighbourhood as a prostitute. The power of police, magistrates, and doctors was a major theme in Butler's letters as she described this 'diabolical triple power'[81] and the way in which it created a whole network of men who were engaged in the systematic surveillance, degradation, and oppression of women. Butler voiced her views through several—extremely articulate—

[79] Josephine Butler to Miss Priestman, 18 Nov. 1873, Butler Papers.

[80] Josephine Butler to Mrs C. M. Wilson, 12 Nov. 1873, ibid. See also her letters to Henry Wilson, 24 Dec. 1872 and 14 June 1873 and her letter to Miss Priestman, 18 Nov. 1873.

[81] Josephine E. Butler, 'Letter to the Member of the Ladies' National Association', Aug. 1875, ibid.

prostitutes to whom she claimed to have spoken. 'It is men, men, only men, from the first to the last, that we have to do with!', declaimed one such prostitute.

To please a man I did wrong at first, then I was flung about from man to man, men police lay hands on us. By men, we are examined, handled, doctored and messed on with. In the hospital it is a man again who makes prayers and reads the bible for us. We are had up before magistrates who are men, and we never get out of the hands of men till we die.[82]

Butler's own additional comment is even more interesting: 'As she spoke, I thought "And it was a Parliament of men only who made this law which treats you as an outcast. Men alone meet in committee over it. Men alone are the executives." When men of all ranks thus band themselves together for an end deeply concerning women, and place themselves like a thick, impenetrable wall between woman and woman, and forbid the one class of women entrance into the presence of the other, the weak, the outraged class, it is time that women should arise and demand their most sacred rights in regard to their sisters.'[83]

In her subsequent letters, Butler dealt with other issues as well: the brutality of doctors; the extent to which examinations became a public event; the ways in which the Acts removed women from the street in order to locate them in brothels, which increased male control over prostitutes; the fact that the men involved in this whole process could switch roles—so that the man who was the magistrate one day was the client the day before. Butler shared the horror she had noted amongst prostitutes at the ways in which every aspect of their lives was determined by men. She personally could not bear 'to see an accused woman wholly in the hands of men and men alone, her life or death depending on the bias of a man'. A man such as Justice Stephen was particularly horrifying. Butler did not refer to his well-known views on the place of women, but to the fact that he was 'a coarse cynical fellow, who should be the last to cast a stone at a woman'.[84]

Butler's investigations in England were followed up by others in

[82] Josephine E. Butler, 'The Garrison Towns of Kent, Third Letter from Mrs Butler', *Shield*, 9 May 1870.

[83] Ibid.

[84] Josephine Butler to the Misses Priestman, fragment of letter, 5 Aug. 1889, Butler Papers.

France, Belgium, and Italy as she extended her concern about systems for the regulation of prostitution to cover Europe and the Empire. In the process, she was exposed to an extraordinary amount of information about the precise processes by which girls and women became prostitutes and the exact nature of the sexual acts they were required to perform. Some of Butler's insights into the implications and the ramifications of organized prostitution are extraordinary. She was herself fascinated by the vision of rampant female sexuality and of feminine evil which developed out of the whole regulatory system so that many of those who enslaved women were themselves enslaved by their sense of powerful and destructive femininity. It was especially when she visited Paris in the mid-1870s that this aspect of the question became clear to her.

We speak much of women, under the vicious system we oppose, being the slaves of men, and we realise all the tyranny and oppression which has reduced women to so abject a state; but when I went to Paris I began to see the picture reversed in a strange and awful way, and to understand how the men who had rivetted the slavery of women for such degrading ends had become, in a generation or two, themselves the greater slaves; not only the slaves of their own corrupted natures, but of the women whom they have maddened, hardened and stamped underfoot. Bowing down under the unrestrained dictates of their own lusts, they now bow down also before the tortured and fiendish womanhood which *they have created*.[85]

The operation of the Contagious Diseases Acts did not provide Butler with her first insight into the many ways in which men asserted their power and their control over women's bodies. Her own illnesses had done that, as she had had to submit to examination and interrogation by male doctors. 'O, if men knew what women have to endure, and how every good woman has prayed for the coming of a change, a change in this,' she wrote to her friend, Albert Rutson. 'How would any modest *man* endure to put himself into the hands of a woman medically as women have to do into the hands of men? ... believe me, the best and purest feelings of women have been torn and harrowed and shamefully wounded for centuries, just to please a wicked *custom*.' Butler commented on the fact that she had gained more from Elizabeth Garrett 'than

[85] Butler, *Personal Reminiscences*, 79. Emphasis in original.

from any other doctor ... *because* I was able to tell her so much more than I ever could or would *tell* to any *man*.'[86] Like Frances Cobbe, Butler dreaded the growing power of the medical profession in society and 'the superstitious reliance on medical opinion among the upper classes, from the Queen down to M.P.s'. The insistence by doctors that they be listened to on moral, sexual, and health matters made Butler feel that there was 'a deadly fight on the part of us women for our bodies' against medical outrage.[87]

Through the Contagious Diseases campaign, Butler came to recognize both the importance of female solidarity and of direct female support for herself. One of the notable points about the pamphlets, articles, and letters which she wrote in her capacity as leader of the Ladies' National Association is their stress on the importance of female solidarity and female activism. In 1875, for example, she wrote to the members of the Ladies' National Association to express her concern at the decline of female participation at meetings. It was her conviction that 'systematized prostitution will never be overthrown till it is attacked by women, and at the same time that it cannot resist the attack.'[88] It was necessary, not just that women work together on behalf of others who were directly subject to sexual exploitation, but also that they provide solidarity for others engaged in their cause.

Butler urged that, before any mixed meetings to discuss prostitution, a separate women's meeting should be held to pledge as many women as possible to attend the public meeting and to ensure a female presence on the platform. 'When this is not done, and a few women only are present, the trial to be encountered is much greater in the case of the brave women who do attend, and those who stay away are guilty of increasing for their sisters the trial, which would be almost unfelt if shared by a large number.'[89] These comments point to Butler's own awareness of the tensions evident within the abolitionist movement. Judith Walkowitz has explored the gender conflict within the overall movement for the repeal of the Contagious Diseases Acts, illustrating the way in which women

---

[86] Josephine Butler to Albert Rutson, 22 Feb. 1868, Butler Papers. Emphasis in original.
[87] See Josephine Butler to Mr Edmundson, 28 Mar. 1872, ibid.
[88] 'Letter to the Members of the Ladies' National Association', 1875, 5, ibid.
[89] Ibid. 8–9.

had to wage a double battle: their public fight to obtain the right of women to control their own persons was matched by a private struggle for recognition of their rights and authority within their own movement. Male supporters and organizers on many occasions actively discouraged the participation of women, especially when it came to policy formulation or to public appearances. Butler wrote to the executive of the Ladies' National Association, expressing her disquiet over the

tendency which I see among men to allow women to drop out of the foremost ranks in this crusade, the general tendency both at home and abroad to consider that our question having now attained the rank of a scientific and international question advocated by distinguished and learned men, it is less necessary that women should be the inspiring and even the guiding power.[90]

This tendency was evident amongst leaders of the campaign, and even amongst those who were Butler's close friends. Both Henry Wilson and James Stuart posed particular problems. Wilson, in his capacity as paid organizer, actively discouraged women from participating in meetings, while Stuart went so far as to attempt to take over and to determine the ways in which the Ladies' National Association expressed its views. In the 1890s Stuart suggested extensive alterations to a manifesto issued by the the Bristol branch of what had then become the Ladies International Association. Butler wrote to express her strong opposition.

It rather shocks me to see the Bristol ladies accepting so meekly the toning down of the *woman*'s manifesto by a *man*, however good a man. I am sure that if I had not assumed an assured, aggressive and defiant tone in 1869, when we were few and weak, our enemies would not have so quickly felt that there was something *vital* in our opposition. . . . Dear Mr Stuart used to council me to speak with moderation then, in 1869. 'You are *one* woman', he would say, 'you cannot speak for all women'. But other women echoed the defiance wonderfully. I have told Mrs Tanner I will not sign the Declaration unless some of the *weakening* is taken out.[91]

Butler's ideas about the importance of female involvement in the Contagious Diseases agitation had a strategic aspect as well. She

[90] Josephine Butler to the Ladies' National Association Executive, 11 Oct. 1877, ibid.

[91] Josephine Butler to Miss Forsaith, 31 Oct. 1896, ibid. Emphasis in original.

had a very strong sense of the dramatic impact which came from having 'pure' women, especially if they were elegantly clad and visibly genteel, publicly expressing their sorrow at the existing state of affairs. She placed great reliance, not just on prayers, but on the impact of prayer meetings held by women in or near Parliament. She was very taken by the American temperance tactic of having large groups of women praying outside saloons. The marshalling in public of genteel women was opposed by many men, but it had a profound impact on all who witnessed it.[92]

But the strategic question was only one aspect of a broader analysis of the need for sexual solidarity. Such solidarity already existed amongst men not only in relation to women's bodies but also in relation to their work. In the 1870s Butler collaborated with two of her fellow workers in the Contagious Diseases agitation, Elizabeth Wolstenholme Elmy and Emily Venturi, as well as two female factory workers, on a pamphlet opposing legislative restrictions on the industry of women.

The pamphlet was directed particularly at Mundella's proposed Amendments to the Factory Acts and at Sir John Lubbock's Shop Hours Regulation Bill, which would limit the hours of female shop assistants. It offered the standard objection to the inclusion of women in the category of 'children and young persons', the two groups who were seen as needing legislative protection because they were unable to act on their own behalf. Butler and her colleagues were concerned particularly to expose the sentimentality and the continuous appeal to a particular domestic notion of womanhood which was evident in the whole parliamentary debate on the question of women's employment. Although ostensibly concerned to improve the conditions of women, legislative interference in women's hours of work did not in fact offer any solution to the problems women faced. Reducing women's working hours, and hence their pay, would neither improve the conditions of factory work nor would it improve the health or the domestic comfort of women and their children. Such a proposal really reflected a concern, not with the interests of women, but with those of men. The Factory Acts Amendment Bill would not, Butler argued, reduce the daily labour of women from ten hours to nine.

[92] Josephine E. Butler, *Some Thoughts on the Present Aspect of the Crusade against the State Regulation of Vice*, Liverpool, 1874.

It 'merely provides for reducing the *paid* labour of women ... in order that the mother may employ it in unpaid labour at home'. The Act, they argued, seems to assume that a woman is so constructed that 'one hour (or more?) of unpaid household labour, added to nine hours of paid factory labour, will so relieve and refresh her as to humanise her otherwise inhuman toil'.[93]

It is not difficult to show the extent and the nature of Butler's critique of masculinity as it developed through the Contagious Diseases agitation. It is evident in a vast number of her letters, speeches, addresses to the Ladies' National Association and reports to the *Shield*. But the difficulty posed for later historians is that Butler herself was reluctant to accept the implications of this critique or to integrate it into a general approach to the woman question. Although this critique was very prominent during the time that Butler was actually investigating the working of the Contagious Diseases Acts, when she stopped visiting the towns in which the Acts were in force, it disappeared from many of her speeches.

Increasingly through the 1870s, Butler appealed to large general audiences of women speaking as a Christian and as a mother to others charged to care for and to protect the innocence of their children. Hence she spoke as a rescue worker and as a moral and religious reformer, but without any reference to the sexual politics which she explored in the early numbers of the *Shield* and which she continued to address in her many letters to the Ladies' National Association. Once the Contagious Diseases Acts were repealed, she did her best to forget all about her earlier critique of masculinity. In her *Personal Reminiscences of a Great Crusade* written in the 1890s, she stressed the universality of her concern in terms which diminish the specifically female or feminist involvement. Her crusade was not in any way a sex war.

I am anxious to make my readers clearly understand that our early conflict in this cause was—at least for myself and the considerable group of firm and enlightened women with whom I had the happiness to work—much less of a simple women's war against man's injustice than it is supposed to have been. It was wider than that. It was as a citizen of a free country

---

[93] Josephine E. Butler *et al.*, *Legislative Restrictions on the Industry of Women, Considered from the Women's Point of View*, London, n.d., 8.

first, and as a woman secondly, that I felt impelled to come forward in defence of the right.[94]

She thus placed great emphasis on the way in which this crusade awakened sympathy amongst women for their less fortunate sisters and 'helped to conjure up also a great army of good and honourable men ... who ... soon became aware that they were fighting also for themselves, their own liberties and their own honour'.

In her *Personal Reminiscences of a Great Crusade*, Butler played down very considerably the work of the Ladies National Association, concentrating far more on male parliamentary supporters, journalists, etc. Thus while it includes detailed descriptions of some cruel and brutal men, particularly those involved in policing prostitutes, it offers, as a contrast, noble and dedicated and generous men such as James Stansfeld, to whom the book is dedicated. There is little here about the need for women to work together and nothing about Butler's horror at the way in which, through the regulation of prostitution, men took it upon themselves to control every aspect of the lives of the women who fell under these regulations.

Butler's ideas on male sexuality and on masculinity tended to be expressed either in private correspondence or the newsletters, speeches, and papers which she wrote specifically for the Ladies' National Association. They were ideas which she expressed to select male friends and to female friends and supporters—they were not for general consumption. Moreover, they were not ideas which she wanted to extend or develop in any way. Her own close relationships with men—as daughter, wife, and mother—did not predispose her to the further extension of a critique of masculinity which would undermine any possibility of heterosexual harmony. Butler was not critical of marriage or of family life *per se*. She sought a reform in the laws pertaining to married women's property, and she believed that marriage should be an equal partnership. But she did not believe that, in itself, marriage or family life contributed to women's oppression. Hence her critique of masculinity was confined to exploring the ways it operated in regard to illicit sex.

Butler's return in her later years to the liberal critique of the Contagious Diseases Acts and to the whole question of the regu-

---

[94] Butler, *Personal Reminiscences*, 42.

lation or the policing of prostitutes is only too easy to understand in the light of the alternatives available to her. The end of the Contagious Diseases Acts did not, of course, bring the end either of prostitution or of the double standard in sexual morality in England. As Butler had herself said, these changes required a major change in the economic circumstances of women and a great moral transformation in the behaviour and the outlook of men.

Throughout the 1870s she bemoaned the lack of religious or moral concern within society at large and pointed to the need for a great moral revival. This was part and parcel of her insistence that women be the leading figures in the Contagious Diseases agitation. Men, she argued, could not understand the wider implications of the regulation of prostitution, nor did they see the driving force in the campaign for it to end. Many men who had opposed the Contagious Diseases Acts as cruel and illegal, had deserted the campaign when they understood 'the thoroughness of our crusade, and that it is directed not only against a chance cruel result of vice, but against the tacit permission—the indisputable right, as some have learned to regard it—to be impure at all. The touchstone of the central principle of our movement is too severe a test for such men, and they fall away.'[95] Thus Butler herself used the language of social purity to expound her own sense of the change that was needed to wipe out prostitution and the double moral standard.

But the great upsurge of moral fervour and of activity to curb sexual licence and promote social purity, which occurred in the mid-1880s, did not bring the changes which Butler sought. She welcomed certain aspects of the new moral fervour which emerged after W. T. Stead had shocked England by revealing the existence and the extent of child prostitution in 1885. Her own recognition of the need for some form of action or intervention within the sphere of sexual morality was demonstrated by the fact that she became a member of the National Vigilance Association for the Repression of Criminal Vice and Immorality which was established in 1886.

The National Vigilance Association set up local committees with a large co-ordinating body which had as its objectives: the lobbying of Parliament in order to amend legislation; the co-ordination of

---

[95] Josephine E. Butler, *Sursum Corda: Annual Address to the Ladies' National Association*, Liverpool, 1891.

rescue and prevention work amongst prostitutes; the protection of young girls and the prosecution of offenders; and generally the stimulation and maintenance of a healthy public opinion on the subject of public morality. The National Vigilance Association has been very harshly treated by most recent historians—and this is not surprising. Its attacks on the literary works of Rabelais, Balzac, and Zola, which extended to the successful prosecution of their English distributors, along with its hostility to birth control, its support for legislation which gave police and welfare workers much wider powers in regard to the removal of children from mothers deemed unsuitable or unfit, and its attempts to remove prostitutes from the streets all combine to make it a most unappealing organization to an essentially libertarian age. At the same time, the involvement of enormous numbers of feminists in the National Vigilance Association demonstrates the extent to which Victorian feminists believed both that women needed to be protected from male sexual licence and that stricter moral standards would benefit women. Butler herself joined the Association and remained a member of it for some eight or nine years. She sat on its council for some of those years, despite her growing reservations about it.

Butler's reservations about the National Vigilance Association centred on their tendency to attack individuals for their immorality. She disliked their tendency to harass prostitutes or their clients, arguing that it was not the individual behaviour of men and women but the actual organization of prostitution which had to be attacked. Moreover, while Butler insisted in a general way on the need to make men adhere to the same sexual and moral standards as women, she was unable to feel the wrath for male transgressors expressed by others who shared her desire to see a general improvement in moral standards. On the contrary, Butler expressed enormous sympathy with many individual men who had engaged in immoral activities, as indeed she did with many prostitutes. When the social purity enthusiasts of the 1880s expressed their horror at the scandalous private lives of Parnell and Sir Charles Dilke and sought to have them excluded from public life, Butler was loath to add her name to the memorials she was sent, feeling pity for them rather than anger. It is hard to resist the thought that her own experiences were important here.

Although irrefutable evidence for this is not available, it does seem that some at least of Butler's male friends fell in love with her. This certainly seems to have been the case with both Albert Rutson and James Stuart. Rutson nurtured and cared for her through the depressing years which followed the death of her daughter and which were dominated by undiagnosable ill health, while Stuart devoted much of his life to working for her and her cause and took her family as his own. While not wanting to suggest either that Butler was ever unfaithful, or that her marriage was in any way an unhappy or inadequate one, she clearly responded to masculine sympathy and affection. And it does at least seem likely that the complex web of emotional entanglements in which she lived and worked gave her sympathetic insights into the ease with which others transgressed moral, sexual, and social norms. Unlike Millicent Fawcett, she tended to regard individual sinners as weak rather than evil and to pity rather than to castigate them. Her sympathies even extended to include Oscar Wilde. Her letters to her son during 1895 suggest that she was haunted by the horror he would have to endure in Reading Gaol.

I am *so sorry* for Oscar Wilde. I dare confess it to you. Most people are shocked at one feeling for him. It is such a complete rush down to perdition. What must solitary confinement be to such a man? He who loved praise and was much flattered by a certain set has now to sit and brood over the general loathing and contempt which has been poured upon him. I long to be allowed to write him a letter in prison.... I hope they will treat him mercifully.... As you say there are others worse than he, and 'society' seems lately very diseased in this way. So it is well there should be a sharp awakening—but O! I pity the criminal on whose head society's vials of wrath are poured.... I pray for him constantly—that God will tell him that *He* does not despise him.[96]

But personal sympathy was only one of the issues here. It was augmented by her whole approach to prostitution and to sexual immorality. For Butler, as for some recent feminist theorists, the central problem of prostitution was not so much the reason why women become prostitutes, although she did address this question. Rather she was concerned with the reasons why the male demand for prostitution existed at all. Where twentieth-century writers such as Carole Pateman see this as part of the sexual contract, the

---

[96] Josephine Butler to Stanley Butler, 4 June 1895, Butler Papers.

exercise of the law of male sex-right and one way in which men ensure their access to women's bodies, Butler looked at it in moral terms as a problem of controlling male lust.[97] Hence she sought a moral transformation to end it. But the transformation she sought was clearly not going to emerge through the surveillance activities of the National Vigilance Association. Indeed, it was much closer to the kind of transformation sought by those fighting to abolish negro slavery. The moral fervour of liberal reform campaigns was the kind with which Butler identified rather than that of the social purity movement. It is significant that despite her own membership of the National Vigilance Association, Butler was adamant that her own Ladies' National Association should not ever become a mere rescue society, but that it should keep its essentially political orientation. But the repeal of the Contagious Diseases Acts left her without a target or a rallying cry around which to organize in England. Eventually, in the mid-1890s, Butler felt unable to tolerate the increasingly interventionist approach of the National Vigilance Association or its attempts to regulate morality by legislation, and she resigned. But this resignation left her with no path to follow in England.

Ultimately, Butler faced an insoluble dilemma. On the one hand, there was this difficulty of integrating a critique of masculinity and male sexual power within a liberal equal rights tradition which took no account of gender. On the other, there was the problem of how to attack the sexual double standard or to organize a campaign around prostitution which did not either end up as a form of rescue work or involve interference in the lives of individuals which was unwarranted and, in Butler's own view, cruel and unacceptable.

Butler's awareness of this problem is indicated by the redirection of her activities, from as early as the mid-1870s, away from England and towards the broader question of the regulation of prostitution throughout Europe and the Empire. She was a moving force behind the formation of the British, Continental, and General Federation for the Abolition of Government Regulation of Prostitution which was established in 1875 and of which she became the secretary. Through much of the 1870s and 1880s, it is evident that she was as much concerned about the regulation of prostitution in France, Belgium, and Italy and about the white slave trade as she was about

[97] Carole Pateman, *The Sexual Contract*, Oxford, 1988, 194–5 and *passim*.

the Contagious Diseases Acts. In the 1880s and 1890s, her focus moved to include India as she became a leader in the campaign to end the organization of prostitution through the Cantonment Acts. When the Contagious Diseases Acts were finally abolished, and the question of what should happen to the Ladies' National Association came to the fore, she suggested changing its name to the 'Ladies' International Association' which would work through parliamentary pressure for the colonies as well as 'lending our aid, financially, a little yearly, and personally active when possible, for the abolition of the Police des Mœurs in the near neighbouring countries of Europe and everywhere'.[98]

Butler's constantly shifting focus has been seen as a sign of restlessness and even of instability. But this reading misses the essential point, which was the impossibility for her of fighting against prostitution unless she could do so through a political framework which attacked the legal systems regulating prostitution. Without this, it was all too easy for prostitutes themselves to become the targets and the victims of purity campaigns. Butler's dilemma was not the result of her own lack of theoretical breadth or of her own limitations. What she faced was the insoluble problem which confronts all feminists who live in and are part of a heterosexual world, who participate in national politics, and who seek alliances and joint actions from their sympathetic male colleagues in their concerns about the oppression of women —but who cannot avoid coming to the conclusion that the very organization of heterosexuality involves the oppression of women. Faced with this problem, Butler turned again to religion. Her grandson, who was very close to her in her last years, was clearly embarrassed about the intensity of her belief that a great religious cataclysm was imminent and that this would bring a new world, or at least a new world order. But this idea is only too easily understandable. Butler had always sought to resolve difference and conflict through prayer and through her belief in the transforming powers of Christ, and this was the only possible way she could harmonize her simultaneous desire for sexual harmony with her beliefs in the dangers posed to women by male sexuality. She followed the path of many religious reformers, seeking a great religious transformation, for

[98] Josephine Butler to Miss Priestman, 7 May 1886, Butler Papers.

without it, the cause, to which she had devoted so much of her life, would be lost.

6

Millicent Garrett Fawcett

MILLICENT GARRETT FAWCETT was the only Victorian feminist who lived to celebrate the enfranchisement of women in 1928.[1] Her own immeasurable contribution to this cause was formally recognized in 1924, when she was made a Grand Dame Cross of the Order of the British Empire and it was emphasized, albeit posthumously, in the memorial in Westminster Abbey which stated that she had 'won citizenship for women'.[2] As this makes clear, Fawcett's activity spanned several successive stages within the women's movement. It was not exceptional longevity, but rather the fact that she had become involved in the women's movement at so early an age which accounted for this.[3] Fawcett was a very young member of the first Women's Suffrage Committee in London in 1867. Thirty years later, when the various suffrage societies amalgamated, she became President of the resulting National Union of Women's Suffrage Societies and remained in that position until 1918 when she resigned. Although no longer the

[1] Millicent Garrett Fawcett (1847–1929). For biographical details, see Millicent Fawcett, *What I Remember*, London, 1925 (repr. Westport, 1976); Ray Strachey, *Millicent Garrett Fawcett*, London, 1931.

[2] Ann Oakley, 'Millicent Garrett Fawcett: Duty and Determination', in *Feminist Theorists: Three Centuries of Women's Intellectual Traditions*, ed. Dale Spender, London, 1983.

[3] Emily Davies lived to see the partial enfranchisement of women in 1918, as she died in 1921 at the age of 91. Fawcett was 82 when she died, the same age as Frances Cobbe. Josephine Butler died when she was 78.

suffrage leader, she remained a prominent suffrage campaigner throughout the 1920s.

Despite her enormous importance within the women's movement, Millicent Fawcett has been the subject of remarkably little scholarly attention. Her biography was written shortly after her death by her friend and colleague, Ray Strachey, and is only now in the process of being revised.[4] She figures necessarily within most studies of the women's suffrage movement, but her role has often been played down, in contrast with the dynamic actions of the Pankhursts and the Women's Social and Political Union. It is only very recently that the magnitude of Fawcett's achievements in regard to the National Union of Women's Suffrage Societies has even begun to be recognized.[5] But it still remains the case that her wide range of published writings on every aspect of the woman question, her interest and participation in the education campaigns and in debates about every aspect of women's work, and her intense involvement in the work of the National Vigilance Association await detailed analysis.

Although not the subject of extensive detailed research, Fawcett plays an important role in a number of general interpretations of nineteenth-century feminism. For many writers, Millicent Fawcett exemplifies Victorian bourgeois or liberal feminism, in her outlook, her attitudes and her approach. The aspects of Fawcett which are important here are her emphasis on the importance of political and legal change, her moderation, her lack of any radical social and economic criticism, and her apparent opposition to the campaign to oppose the Contagious Diseases Acts.[6] Her ideas on the woman question are almost invariably seen as an extension of the liberal

---

[4] David Rubinstein, *Millicent Garrett Fawcett*, forthcoming.

[5] See Leslie P. Hume, *The National Union of Women's Suffrage Societies*, New York, 1982; Sandra Holton, *Feminism and Democracy: Women's Suffrage and Reform Politics in Britain, 1900–1918*, Cambridge, 1986; and Jill Liddington and Jill Norris, *One Hand Tied Behind Us: The Rise of the Women's Suffrage Movement*, London, 1978.

[6] See Olive Banks, *Faces of Feminism: A Study of Feminism as a Social Movement*, Oxford, 1986, 66; Constance Rover, *Women's Suffrage and Party Politics in Britain, 1866–1914*, London, 1967, 57–8; T. Davis *et al.*, 'The Public Face of Feminism: Early Twentieth Century Writing on Women's Suffrage', in *Making Histories: Studies in History Writing and Politics*, ed. R. Johnson *et al.*, Birmingham, 1983, 309.

ideas on political economy which she shared with her husband, Henry Fawcett.[7]

The picture of Fawcett as a moderate and pragmatic campaigner is supported by her overall style. While she was more inclined than Emily Davies to take to the platform, and wrote essays and speeches with enormous facility, Fawcett was also a skilled committee woman well able to deal with all the grind and daily labour of committee work. Unlike Davies, she did not particularly enjoy it— indeed, when she resigned as president of the National Union of Women's Suffrage Societies in 1918, she made clear her relief at not having to attend another meeting. She shared something of Davies's method, making careful notes of meetings and discussions, and was sometimes quite as cautious and legalistic as Davies, insisting that witnesses be present if she was involved in contentious discussions. She was not a committee woman in the way that Davies was. She did not work committees in quite the way Davies did, to ensure that their membership, agendas, and programmes reflected her views, choosing instead to make direct statements to meetings or in the press. But at the same time, she neither had, nor aspired to, the inspirational qualities of Butler. Fawcett's speeches and articles tend to a matter-of-factness, enlivened quite often by humour and by a telling turn of phrase. While never subject to the kind of devotion inspired either by Butler or by the Pankhursts, Fawcett was none the less enormously liked and admired by many of her followers who saw her, as she would have liked to be seen, as a great political leader.

But while Fawcett did not ever seek to emulate Butler and rejected her approach to the Contagious Diseases Acts, a close reading of Fawcett's writings and of her political involvements cannot sustain the view of her simply as a liberal pragmatist. This view of her can certainly be supported if one looks only at her economic writings and her arguments and activities in the suffrage campaign. But it becomes harder to sustain if one looks beyond her suffrage writing: at her interest in the social purity movement and at her concern to protect young girls from sexual exploitation.[8]

[7] See e.g. Dale Spender, *Women of Ideas and What Men Have Done to Them*, London, 1983, 354–5.

[8] For a brief discussion of Fawcett's involvement in the social purity campaigns, see Sheila Jeffries, *The Spinster and her Enemies: Feminism and Sexuality 1880–1930*, London, 1985, 74–5.

Incorporating this aspect of Fawcett's work into a general assessment of her does not immediately produce a radically different version of her ideas. But it does point to a number of tensions and conflicts in her outlook and, by doing so, shatters the idea that she can simply be seen as a Victorian liberal feminist. Her commitment to liberal principles was profound and it was one which she frequently acknowledged. But alongside this, she had an equally profound concern about suffering womanhood, which could not always be contained or expressed within the terms of liberalism. It found expression in far more explosive ways, through attacks on men who seduced or attempted to seduce and then abandon young women, and in her fierce attempts to raise the general moral standard in ways which would protect women and enhance their overall status. Thus while Fawcett engaged in careful political campaigning all her life, from time to time the even tenor of her activity was interrupted by passionate outbursts, which threatened to damage those very moderate campaigns to which she devoted so much of her time.

That such tensions exist within Fawcett's ideas about and approach to the woman question is immediately evident to anyone who looks beyond her suffrage work and takes note of her involvement in the campaigns directed at the double standard in sexual morality. Edward Bristow deals only cursorily with Fawcett in his study of social purity movements, but notes that while she was a moderate on the suffrage question, she became a militant in the social purity movement in 1885.[9] In a much more sympathetic treatment of Fawcett, Ann Oakley has recently commented on the complexity and inaccessibility of her moral values and on the fact that her behaviour occasionally appears hard to understand. She cites as an example of this the Cust affair—Fawcett's personal campaign to prevent the parliamentary candidature of a man whom she believed to have seduced and then abandoned a young girl when she became pregnant.[10]

Oakley is right to point to the importance of this episode. But she is incorrect, in my view, to see this as the only exception to the

[9] Edward J. Bristow, *Vice and Vigilance: Social Purity Campaigns in England, 1700–1900*, Dublin, 1977, 121.

[10] Oakley, 'Millicent Garrett Fawcett', 194; see also Susan Kingsley Kent, *Sex and Suffrage in Britain, 1860–1914*, Princeton, NJ, 1987, 153–5.

rule of Fawcett's 'single-minded and life-long devotion to the suffrage cause'.[11] It seems to me that this episode requires more analysis than it has been given and that taken together with Faw- cett's involvement in the National Vigilance Association, it offers some very important insights into the whole question of sexual exploitation within her feminism.

It was only through her connection with the National Vigilance Association in the 1880s and 1890s that Fawcett was able to express her views on the sexual oppression of women and to channel them into particular campaigns. But the intensity of Fawcett's involvement in these campaigns demonstrates the inadequacies of liberalism in solving all the problems of women's oppression. It was impossible to integrate the problem of the sexual oppression of women into a framework established in relation to a form of politics which assumed that humanity was masculine and which did not have any analysis of sexual difference or sexual power. For most of her life, Fawcett accepted this limitation, assuming that once women had the vote, they would be able somehow to alter their overall situation. But from time to time, the limitations in this approach became obvious and she sought other means of raising moral standards in order to protect women from sexual exploitation—and to punish the men who exploited them. In the end then, what Fawcett demonstrates is the impossibility of finding in liberalism a complete approach to feminism—even for one as dedicated to liberal principles as Fawcett herself was.

I

Millicent Garrett Fawcett was the seventh of the ten children of Newson Garrett, and of his wife, Louise Dunnell.[12] By the time of Millicent's birth, Newson Garrett was a very successful middle- class business man. He had a malting business, dealt as a merchant in corn and coal, owned a brickyard, and built both houses and ships. The family was based in Suffolk where they had two homes:

---

[11] Oakley, 'Millicent Garrett Fawcett', 194.

[12] Millicent was the eighth child born to her mother but the third Garrett baby died very young. Hence, as she says in her autobiography, she was never sure whether to call herself the seventh child or the eighth; Fawcett, *What I Remember*, 9.

one in Snape, where the malting works required Newson in the winter, and one in Aldeburgh where they spent the summer. Newson Garrett was a largely self-made man, with little education but boundless energy. His first start in business was given him by his wife's father who lent him some of the capital to establish himself as a merchant. But after this, his successes—and occasional failures—were all attributable to his own effort. Thus all the Garretts grew up, as Jo Manton has pointed out, 'in an atmosphere of triumphant economic pioneering', which contributed to their belief in the merits of free enterprise, and to their relative lack of sympathy with the poor and the unfortunate.[13]

In her autobiography, Millicent Fawcett followed the same pattern as Josephine Butler, in turning to her family of origin in order to explain her later activities and ideas. Unlike Butler, she lacked a parent who could be presented heroically or who could assume the role of a political model. But her efforts in this direction centred absolutely on her father. He was a 'man of the people', admired and liked by the local fishermen with whom he maintained close contact.[14] Despite his wealth, he and his family identified with the local community and not with the few aristocratic families who lived in Aldeburgh. Newson Garrett was also public-spirited and an excellent employer. His commendable public life was well balanced by his familial role and Fawcett presents him as a man of warmth and vitality, affectionate to his family and closely involved with all the developments in his children's lives. Temperamentally, he was 'generous, daring, impulsive and impatient, and I am afraid I must add, quarrelsome'. But Millicent Fawcett deals very lightly with this flaw, suggesting to the reader that her father's frequent quarrels simply added a little spice to life.[15]

By contrast with this detailed picture of her father, Millicent is very sparing of references to her mother. Nothing is said of her mother's background or parentage: indeed she is not even named. But the brief treatment of her makes it clear that Fawcett found her mother's religion, her devout Evangelicalism and Sabbatarianism, extremely uncongenial. The intensity of Mrs Garrett's religious faith was apparently acknowledged within the wider community

[13] Jo Manton, *Elizabeth Garrett Anderson*, London, 1965, 28.
[14] Fawcett, *What I Remember*, 10–11.
[15] Ibid. 30.

of Aldeburgh, but made no impact on her family. Where Josephine Butler's family imbibed a great love of the Bible from John Grey's reading and discussion of it, The Garretts were treated to a weekly session during which Newson Garrett raced through some passages, turning over several pages at a time to speed up the proceedings. Eventually his wife lost patience with this travesty and so even this form of domestic religious observance came to an end. The family continued to attend the local church, unless Newson Garrett was engaged in one of his periodic battles with the vicar, in which case they went to the local chapel! But Millicent felt that she gained no insight into religion until her late teens when she attended some of the services of F. D. Maurice, who 'awakened in me new thoughts and, I hope, partially at all events, new reverences'.[16]

Alongside her mother's uncomfortable religious views, Fawcett adds another quality which inhibited the possibility of closeness between mother and daughter: namely her mother's extreme conservatism on political questions. Newson Garrett, too, saw himself as a Conservative, but in this he was mistaken.

My father, until he was past middle life, believed himself to be a Conservative, but he was not in the least a Conservative in temperament. Everything new appealed to him, rather as it did to the Athenians of old.... About the early 'sixties, it occurred to him that he was not a Conservative and he wrote to Sir Fitzroy Kelly, then M.P. for East Suffolk, for whom he had hitherto voted, explaining that he had changed his politics and should henceforth support the Liberal Party.[17]

But there was no mistake in regard to his wife and she sympathized neither with her daughters' approach to national politics nor with the involvement in the women's movement which was important to so many of them.

Fawcett's girlhood was similar to that of many in her social class. She and her sisters began their education with governesses at home, enjoying their large family circle and the local community. Their father taught them all to ride and took them with him as he went around the countryside. As country children, they were given the

[16] Fawcett, *What I Remember*, 45. In Fawcett's novel, *Janet Doncaster*, Janet's mother is devoutly religious, but so narrow and rigid in her outlook as to be quite unable to sympathize with, support, or even acknowledge the true nature of her daughter.

[17] Fawcett, *What I Remember*, 32.

kind of physical freedom experienced by both Butler and Cobbe and were allowed to wander alone by the sea-shore and to explore their local area. As a result, the Garretts grew up as active, energetic, and healthy women, all of whom enjoyed physical exercise. Millicent was always an active walker and forsook mountaineering in later years only because her blind husband was so anxious about her safety.[18]

In their teens, all the Garrett girls were sent to Miss Browning's school at Blackheath. Although this was a small private school, working without the benefit of external inspection or examinations, Millicent regarded it as offering an excellent education. She seems particularly to have admired Miss Browning's refusal to teach—or to let the girls practise—needlework and her emphasis on intellectual development rather than on accomplishments. To her great regret, she was forced to leave school earlier than she had anticipated: financial problems experienced by her father necessitated a reduction in the family's expenditure when Millicent was just 16. She continued to read and to pursue her interests at home, but private study did not supply the place of a formal education. Her sister Elizabeth had thought that Millicent would take the Cambridge University Local Examinations, but this did not occur.[19]

After leaving school, Millicent spent a lot of time in London, staying with her eldest sister, Louise Smith. Louie, as she was affectionately called, was herself a radical liberal, friendly with other advanced liberals and with a number of people involved in the early stages of the women's movement. It was she who took Millicent to the party at Aubrey House, the home of Clementia and Peter Taylor, where Millicent both met her future husband, Henry Fawcett, and found her main area of feminist activity, the suffrage campaign.

For Fawcett, as for Josephine Butler, the question of an independent occupation had hardly even been raised when she married. Fawcett was just 20 in 1867 when this occurred. She had met Henry Fawcett the year before and he proposed to her shortly afterwards. Although Millicent had not yet become deeply involved

---

[18] Strachey, *Millicent Garrett Fawcett*, 67.
[19] Elizabeth Garrett to Emily Davies, 3 Oct. 1861, Davies, 'Family Chronicle', fo. 232.

in the women's movement by this time, the marriage in itself nearly became a feminist issue. Millicent's older sister, Elizabeth, opposed it, possibly because Henry Fawcett had proposed to her just one year earlier! To support her opposition, Elizabeth suggested that she would try to obtain for Millicent 'Mme Bodichon's, Miss Crowe's and others' opinions of Mr Fawcett'.[20] As Fawcett had also proposed to Bessie Raynor Parkes, it is likely that the opinions of him expressed by this group would have been less than favourable.[21] Millicent, however, had no inclination to accept the advice of an older generation of feminists. 'I don't know Mme Bodichon,' she replied to Elizabeth,'—if I did, of course I cannot say what weight her opinions might have with me; but at present, judging from Dr Bodichon's appearance, I should say that it was improbable that we should agree in the choice of husbands.'[22]

Millicent Fawcett's first introduction to the organized women's movement came shortly after her marriage when, in 1867, Clementia Taylor invited her to attend a meeting of the London National Society for Women's Suffrage, of which she was secretary.[23] Millicent Fawcett had, of course, been aware of the women's movement for many years before becoming directly involved in it. She had long been a spectator of the battle her sister Elizabeth was waging in order to gain a medical education. Their father, Newson Garrett, had actively supported his daughter, throwing his weight behind her attempt to get London University to change its Charter and to admit women as students. Elizabeth Garrett had been quite friendly with the Langham Place Circle and was a very close friend of Emily Davies. The two older women apparently had frequent discussions about the women's movement in front of the younger Garrett sisters, in the course of which

[20] Strachey, *Millicent Garrett Fawcett*, 26.

[21] David Rubinstein, unpublished paper, 'Victorian Feminists: Henry and Millicent Garrett Fawcett'. I am grateful to David Rubinstein for giving me a copy of this paper.

[22] Millicent Garrett to Louie Smith, 24 Oct. 1866, quoted in Strachey, *Millicent Garrett Fawcett*, 27.

[23] Clementia Taylor was the first secretary of the London National Society for Woman's Suffrage. The wife of Peter Alfred Taylor, she was, like her husband, a radical liberal—a member of the National Vigilance Association for the Defence of Personal Rights and later a member of the Women's Franchise League. Her home, Aubrey House, was a central meeting place for feminists and other liberal and radical political activists and intellectuals throughout the 1860s and 1870s.

Millicent's role as the suffrage leader was already suggested. Although the younger Garretts were not particularly filled with affection for Emily Davies, most of them followed the lead of their elder sister and became involved either in the women's movement or in local government and school boards.[24]

Fawcett's early involvement in the women's movement was rather different in kind from that of both Davies and Cobbe. For both of them, the social aspects of feminist involvement were very important. As we have seen, Davies found in it a full-time occupation and a series of interests which she shared with close women friends. Cobbe never had this level of involvement. But for her, too, feminist interest was closely involved with the philanthropic work she had been engaged in with other women and she too worked alongside close women friends. When she entered into suffrage work and when she withdrew from it, she did so in the company of Mary Lloyd and of another close friend, Miss Hampson.

Fawcett's experience was entirely different. She began her suffrage work as a newly married woman who was assuming not only domestic responsibilities, but also the care and assistance of a blind husband. Where Davies and Cobbe had both been in their late thirties when they turned to this new field, Fawcett was just 20 and hence had no experience of independent adult life. Thus when she was barely 20, Millicent Fawcett suddenly found herself no longer a young girl living in a parental home, but rather a wife who had an unusually large set of tasks. She had to set up and run the two homes necessitated by the fact that her husband was both a Member of Parliament and the Professor of Political Economy at Cambridge and to organize his and her own social life.[25]

Millicent Fawcett's life was unusual, not least in the fact that her education recommenced after marriage. Her new life called for and enabled her to show her enormous competence and somewhat formidable energy. In addition to a substantial range of domestic and familial tasks, she assisted her husband in much of his work. The fact that Henry Fawcett was blind meant that he needed

---

[24] See Patricia Hollis, *Ladies Elect: Women in English Local Government 1865–1914*, Oxford, 1987, 88–9.

[25] See Strachey, *Millicent Garrett Fawcett*, 31–41.

constant attendance and Millicent acted for some time as his secretary and amanuensis. In the process, she gained a solid grounding in political economy. Indeed, by 1871 she was recognized
as the most eminent female political economist in England and
was suggested as a possible member of the Political Economy
Club.[26] At the same time, she was in the process of becoming
prominent as a speaker, a writer, and a campaigner in the women's
movement.

The Fawcett marriage was apparently a very happy one. In her
autobiography Millicent conveys a strong sense of the mutual
affection and shared interests between herself and her husband,
and this view is amplified in Ray Strachey's biography.[27] Both
these works are notable for their reticence and their concern about
decorum, but there is no particular reason to disbelieve their
accounts. The Fawcetts shared an enormous number of interests
as well as holding very similar values and political views. They
enjoyed the same activities and, to an extent unusual amongst
Victorians, engaged in social life together. Millicent seems to have
been welcomed into Henry's social circle and to have established
her own close ties with many of his friends.

The novel *Janet Doncaster*, which Millicent wrote in the early
1870s, suggests that she regarded her marriage as an ideal one. The
novel contains a number of autobiographical references, in the
narrow religiosity of Janet's mother and, apparently, in the character of Janet herself. As we shall see, the central issue is the problem
of marriage, especially the confinement of women to unhappy
marriages. But the interesting point here is the way in which Janet's
husband, a drunk and dissolute member of the gentry, is contrasted
with the man she really loves, a young Cambridge tutor, who
understands Janet, sympathizes with her aims, and assists in her
intellectual development. Ultimately Janet is able to marry this
young man and, or so we are led to believe, comes to realize the
full possibilities of a happy and companionate marriage.[28]

A number of Henry's parliamentary colleagues commented on
the pretty sight the Fawcetts made, with the youthful and attractive

---

[26] Rubinstein, 'Victorian Feminists', 8.

[27] Fawcett, *What I Remember, passim*; Strachey, *Millicent Garrett Fawcett*,
101.

[28] Millicent Garrett Fawcett, *Janet Doncaster*, London, 1875.

Millicent described as 'a very nice attractive ladylike little person', by Gladstone's secretary, leading her tall, fair-haired blind husband.[29] Such a vision could not but appeal to the Victorian taste for womanly self-sacrifice. Like her older sister Elizabeth, Millicent was an ideal public representative of Victorian feminism, combining a pretty face and a very feminine appearance with an extraordinary strength of mind. This image of the ideal devoted couple did not quite extend into one of an ideal family. Within two years of their marriage, the Fawcetts had their only child, a daughter. There is no extant information to explain why there should have been only one child. The advent of Philippa did not, however, end Millicent Fawcett's public activities. She continued to give public lectures, to address meetings, and to campaign for the suffrage and for the higher education of women. This led to a series of allegations about her lack of attention to her daughter. Indeed, as one of Henry's friends wrote, it was widely believed in London that Philippa had been boarded out since birth as Millicent had absolutely refused to undertake her early education or to supervise her care.[30] In fact, of course, Philippa remained at home throughout her childhood. Like most other children of her class, she was attended by a nanny and thus did not materially reduce the amount of time Millicent devoted to other activities. As in many middle-class families, Philippa had her regular time with her parents, coming into the drawing-room every afternoon for her hour with them. Hence the suggestion that Philippa was neglected presumably arose from the fact that her mother was associated with the women's movement—and hence with demanding rights for women which were often seen as denying their traditional familial role and responsibilities.

Fawcett's relationship with her only daughter remains very much a closed book. In fact her major period of feminist activity did not really begin until after Henry Fawcett's death in the mid-1880s. She gave many speeches and wrote a number of articles prior to that, but she only emerged as the leader of the suffrage movement after it. It is thus possible that she supervised her daughter's upbringing quite closely. But there is simply no way to tell. There seems to have been little tension between them—and Philippa

[29] Rubinstein, 'Victorian Feminists', 3.
[30] Strachey, *Millicent Garrett Fawcett*, 62.

certainly did not rebel against her mother. On the contrary, she became one of the stars of the movement for the higher education of women by coming out above Senior Wrangler in her final examinations in 1887. Her result was the best that any women had yet achieved and was followed by great rejoicing. Millicent herself was not present when the results were announced. She 'felt too keenly about what was going to happen to dare to be present'.[31] Newson Garrett was there, however, and Millicent rushed to Cambridge as soon as she heard to join in the celebrations. Philippa's success led to a renewal of the attempt to persuade Cambridge to admit women to degrees as well as access to examinations—but this endeavour was unsuccessful. After she left Cambridge, Philippa became a very active suffragist, distributing pamphlets, raising money and helping to arrange suffrage meetings. She went on to a career in the Civil Service in the Education Department.

Like so many Victorian feminists, Millicent Fawcett found in her husband a very supportive partner. As we have seen, Henry Fawcett combined a taste for feminists with an interest in the 'woman question'. Having been accepted by Millicent, however, his interest and attention apparently remained fixed on her. He was a most useful husband, providing a training not only in political economy, but in reading and understanding government blue books, legislation, and parliamentary procedures. His interest in and sympathy with the women's movement seem to have been extended under Millicent's influence so that he became not only a most important parliamentary spokesman for the cause, but also used the power available to him as Postmaster General in the early 1880s to expand the range of clerical work open to women.[32]

Marriage did not loosen Millicent Fawcett's ties with her family of origin. She remained close to her sisters Agnes and Elizabeth and to her brother Sam. She and Henry visited her parents regularly and offered hospitality to any Garretts visiting London or Cambridge. The shared commitment to feminism amongst the Garrett sisters did not, however, prevent great tension and distress. Indeed, differences of opinion on questions pertaining to the women's movement were sometimes the cause of this tension. This was certainly the case with the Contagious Diseases agitation.

[31] Fawcett, *What I Remember*, 140.
[32] Ibid. 108–9.

When opposition to the Acts was mobilized in the late 1860s, and especially after the formation of the Ladies' National Association, Millicent was in a great quandary. Her husband opposed the Acts and sympathized with the agitation, but felt that he and Millicent should remain aloof from it, concentrating their energies on the suffrage campaign. Her sister Agnes, who had by now set up a home and an interior decorating business with their cousin, Rhoda Garrett, strongly supported the agitation and Rhoda became a well-known speaker in its defence. Elizabeth Garrett held an entirely different view: not only did she oppose the Contagious Diseases agitation but she publicly supported the Acts, seeing them as a necessary public health measure.[33] This stance lost Elizabeth Garrett the friendship of many feminists. It did not end her relationship with Millicent, who ultimately followed her husband's counsel and kept silent about the Acts, but it certainly caused great discomfort.

Their disagreement over the Contagious Diseases Acts was the first of a series of conflicts between these two sisters concerning the women's movement. In the mid-1880s, Elizabeth disapproved of the support which Millicent gave to W. T. Stead in his campaign against the sexual exploitation of young girls. In the early twentieth century, the tables were turned and it was Millicent's turn to disapprove of the support Elizabeth gave to the militants, even in the years after 1908, when Millicent had decided that any co-operation with them was impossible. But the sisters managed to combine affection with disagreement and their relationship continued unabated. In the end Elizabeth was converted to Millicent's position on the suffrage agitation and she ended her connection with the Women's Social and Political Union in 1911.

These relationships with her family of origin continued throughout Millicent's marriage, becoming even more important in her widowhood. Henry Fawcett died quite suddenly in 1884 leaving Millicent a widow at the age of 37. Her family was a major support in her bereavement. Shortly after Henry's death, Millicent and her daughter moved into the home of Agnes Garrett in Gower Street. Agnes had recently suffered the loss of her cousin and companion, Rhoda, and hence she, like Millicent, was seeking both a new domestic arrangement and companionship. Thereafter the two

---

[33] Manton, *Elizabeth Garrett Anderson*, 179–82.

sisters seem to have been very close and to have shared a great deal. As with all the other aspects of Millicent Fawcett's personal life, this relationship is not in any way documented. Thus the idea that they remained close companions is suggested by the way they travelled, entertained, and went out together rather than by any more direct evidence. Agnes Garrett seems to have shared Millicent's enjoyment of music and Millicent commented on her regrets when Agnes did not attend concerts which she found particularly moving or enjoyable. In their later years, the two sisters holidayed together sometimes in England and sometimes abroad.

Agnes was not the only woman to whom Fawcett was close. Early in her widowhood, she met and became very friendly with a neighbour, Dr Jane Walker. Those holidays which Millicent did not spend with Agnes were spent with her, and both Dr Walker and Agnes accompanied Millicent to St Andrews University in January 1899, when she was awarded an honorary degree. Millicent Fawcett saw Jane Walker frequently and corresponded with her constantly when either was out of London. Many of the letters quoted by Ray Strachey and dealing with the last forty odd years of Millicent's life were written to Jane Walker. As one would expect, it is not really possible to gauge the emotional content of the relationship from these, but they demonstrate both that Fawcett wrote entertaining letters—and that she was accustomed to detailing her daily activities to this particular friend.

In the years after Henry Fawcett's death, even more than in those preceding it, discussion of Millicent Fawcett concentrates on her public life. Her extreme reticence and the lack of any known collection of intimate or revealing letters prevents one from dealing with her personal life, while there is abundant material concerning her public activities. It was in these years that she really emerged as a major figure in British public life not only as the leading suffragist, but also through her involvement in the Home Rule controversy and later in the Boer War. Her activities in these last two can easily be traced through newspaper reports of her speeches and appearances or from her own papers which include extensive correspondence on all her public engagements.

It was in the years immediately after Henry Fawcett's death that one can see most clearly the contrasting and even contradictory impulses in Millicent Fawcett's activity. On the one hand, she was engaged in a continuation of the interests she had shared with her husband by advocating his views on the question of Ireland. But at this very time, she took up other questions which he would never have countenanced. Thus in 1885, the year following his death, she catapulted herself into the midst of the furore created by W. T. Stead's series of articles, 'The Maiden Tribute of Modern Babylon'. In Strachey's view, the publication of Stead's articles 'brought back all her old fighting spirit with even more intensity and strength than of old'.[34]

Fawcett was but one of many who were galvanized into action by the Stead articles and who became a staunch supporter of social purity issues in the mid-1880s.[35] In August of 1885, Fawcett joined Josephine Butler, Ellice Hopkins, James Stansfeld, James Stuart, and a number of others in becoming a founder member of the National Vigilance Association. As we have seen, the National Vigilance Association was the spearhead of a new and militant campaign to raise the level of morality in all areas of life. Fawcett served on its Executive for many years, resigning only in 1926.[36] Although a member of the National Vigilance Association for 30 years, Fawcett was active mostly during the late 1880s and the 1890s when she chaired the Preventive and Rescue Sub-Committee.

At the very time that Millicent Fawcett was engaging in sexual campaigns which Henry Fawcett would have strongly discouraged, she was also devoting a great deal of energy to the exposition of his views in regard to the question of Ireland. The Irish question dominated British politics for most of the 1880s and 1890s. Henry Fawcett had always been deeply interested in Irish affairs and strongly committed to the notion that Ireland was part of the United Kingdom. He had opposed any suggestion of Irish Home Rule during his lifetime and Millicent shared this view. She also shared her husband's critical view of Gladstone and his opposition to many of the policies of the Liberal Party. Finally, when Gladstone announced his conversion to Home Rule, Millicent

---

[34] Strachey, *Millicent Garrett Fawcett*, 107.

[35] See Bristow, *Vice and Vigilance*, 120–5; and Deborah Gorham, 'The "Maiden Tribute of Modern Babylon" Re-examined: Child Prostitution and the Idea of Childhood in Late Victorian England', *Victorian Studies*, 21 (1978), 353–79.

[36] She is listed as a member of the Executive in the *Vigilance Record* until this year.

Fawcett felt she could no longer support the party which he led. She became a Liberal Unionist and was very active both in the Women's Liberal Unionist Association and in the general campaign to gain adherence to the Liberal Unionist position. In 1888 and 1889, Millicent Fawcett toured the country, insisting that Gladstone's conversion to Home Rule was a capitulation made in the face of violence and intimidation in Ireland, and in order to ensure the support of Irish Members to buttress his dwindling majority in Parliament. In her view, Gladstone's position was indefensible, based on no ascertainable principle and absolutely contrary to the interests of the British Empire and of the Irish themselves.[37] In some ways she seemed to be attempting to replace her husband by recalling his views at many of the large public meetings addressed by the Liberal Unionist leaders. It was in the course of this agitation that Fawcett really became a major national figure, featuring on platforms alongside Lord Derby or Lord Hartington and often giving speeches, which were given at least as much press coverage as theirs.[38]

Although Fawcett was active in support of the Liberal Unionists in the late 1880s and the 1890s, their views were not congenial to her. She did not share the conservative political views of many fellow Unionists and she found their opposition both to women's suffrage and to the participation of women in political debate insufferable.[39] Ray Strachey sees her involvement with the Liberal Unionists at this time as something Fawcett maintained in part out of loyalty to Henry and in part because, at a time when the suffrage movement was in the doldrums, it offered her a way to expand her own hold on political events and her influence on public opinion.[40] Others have suggested that it points to a growing conservatism in Fawcett's own political outlook.[41] Either way, it is clear that Unionism did not express all Fawcett's political beliefs and she formally severed her ties with them when, having joined with the Conservative Party, the Unionists rejected free trade in favour of a protectionist policy. Whatever she might think of the Liberal

[37] For her views on Ireland, see Strachey, *Millicent Garrett Fawcett*, 125–31.

[38] See e.g. reports of her speeches at Nottingham, *The Times*, 19 Sept. 1888, 19; Birmingham, *The Times*, 27 Apr. 1889, 7; Cork, *The Times*, 17 May 1889.

[39] Strachey, *Millicent Garrett Fawcett*, 129–30.

[40] Ibid. 130.

[41] Conversations with David Rubinstein.

Party, she never abandoned the basic principles of mid-nineteenth century economic liberalism and regarded protectionism as anathema.

As we shall see, Fawcett's involvement was not always welcomed by her new Conservative and Unionist allies, especially when she tried to get them to endorse her views on sexual morality and social purity and ran a single-handed campaign to make them reject as their candidate for North Manchester Harry Cust, a young man with a questionable sense of sexual morality. Fawcett mounted an extensive battle against Cust, and through him against the double standard in sexual morality—and she did so against all the advice of her friends and supporters within the women's movement and in the face of their insistence that she was thereby harming the cause she had served so long.

After the Cust affair, Fawcett did not embark on any other sexual campaigns. Within a few years, she was caught up first in national politics and then in a renewal of the suffrage campaign in ways which did not leave much free time. As the height of the Home Rule controversy passed, there was a new issue of concern: the Boer War, which began in 1899. Fawcett's public renown by this time is clearly demonstrated in the fact that she was chosen to head a commission of women who were to inquire into and to report on the conditions of the concentration camps set up by the British for Boer women and children. The fact that Fawcett was a staunch defender of the British involvement in the war and that she was a prominent Unionist obviously made her particularly suited to this task in the eyes of the Government. But it was the first time that such a commission had been headed or staffed entirely by women and it did suggest a new sense of their public and political role.

In this role, and in the report that the commission issued in 1902, one can see Fawcett in all her complexity. On the one hand, her lack of compassion for Boer women and their children is very evident. The Boer women are pictured as ignorant peasants, whose superstitious practices and lack of knowledge about health and hygiene is seen as a major contributing factor to the high rate of infant mortality within the camps.[42] Fawcett never questioned the

[42] 'Report on the Concentration Camps in South Africa by the Committee of Ladies appointed by the Secretary of State for War containing Reports on the

need for the camps in terms of British military strategy, and took no cognizance of the stress or demoralization faced by the Boer women in their harsh new circumstances.[43] But the report is none the less an impressive one, outspoken in its criticism of the military authorities and of the camp administration, pointing to the complete lack of forethought about the needs of the inmates in the position and design of the camps and castigating many named individuals for their brutality and incompetence. It contained a large number of recommendations for improving the location, the design, and the management of the camps, which were in fact carried out, reducing the mortality rates within the camps considerably. Despite Fawcett's own very blatant political sympathies, the report was a remarkably careful and well-documented one and it continues to be used as a means of ascertaining the actual condition of the camps.[44] Fawcett's own beliefs about the justice of the war and her pronounced anti-Boer feelings did not then blind her to the incompetence of the British or to some of the injustices they inflicted on their foes.

But despite her prominence on the political scene, Fawcett was increasingly out of sympathy with the dominant political parties. Her breach with the Liberal Party continued, but even the Unionists were adopting policies she could not accept. She worked with them until 1903, the year of Chamberlain's protectionist campaign. As a fervent free-trader from her earliest years, Fawcett simply could not accept this policy. In subsequent years, she lived without any party affiliation. The political framework with which she was both comfortable and familiar was that which obtained from the 1850s to the 1880s and 1890s. In the years after that, she made shifts and alliances according to particular issues and interests. But while actively engaged in it, she was increasingly out of sympathy with the main direction of political debate. In the late 1920s Fawcett made her own position very clear. Her friends and supporters had attempted since the end of the war to obtain some formal

Camps in Natal, the Orange River Colony and the Transvaal', London, 1902. Fawcett's own copy of the report, containing many photographs, is in the Fawcett Library.

[43] Ibid. 2–10, see also Strachey, *Millicent Garrett Fawcett*, 185–90; Fawcett, *What I Remember*, 167–70.

[44] See e.g. S. B. Spies, *Methods of Barbarism: Robertson and Kitchener and Civilians in the Boer Republic: January 1900–May 1902*, Cape Town, 1976, 254–67.

recognition of her work and there was widespread criticism when she was not included in Baldwin's New Year's Honours list in 1924. Fawcett herself insisted that she had not the slightest claim on Baldwin or on any other party leader.

I have not belonged to any political party since I left the Liberal Unionists when they took up Protection (then called tariff reform). My work has been wholly outside Party lines to endeavour to influence public opinion, and therefore all Parties, not by force but by reason, experience, and common sense, that the whole community would benefit by raising the political, educational, professional and industrial status of women. When I was hard at work as President of the National Union of Women's Suffrage Societies, I used to tell my friends that I was specially fitted to fill a non-Party post, for I could not be a Conservative because I was not a Protectionist, nor a Liberal because I was not a Home-Ruler, nor a member of the Labour Party because I was not a Socialist.[45]

Fawcett's sense of being outside the national political debate was not as hard to bear as it might have been because it coincided with her renewed sense of the importance of women's suffrage. Her resurgence of interest was echoed elsewhere. The expansion in interest in suffrage amongst working women in the North of England and the establishment of the Women's Social and Political Union set the stage for a new round of suffrage agitation. Fawcett's outstanding qualities as a leader are evident in her response to these developments: in the way in which she welcomed new approaches and new suffrage groups, and accepted the need for change and adaptation within her own society to meet new conditions.[46] She presided over an enormous expansion in the size and importance of the suffrage movement. She succeeded in making the National Union of Women's Suffrage Societies, of which she was president, not only a large and well-organized body, but one which did train a generation of women in the ways and the practices of political life.

The years leading up to the First World War were extraordinarily busy ones for Fawcett, involving an endless round of meetings, speeches, demonstrations, and correspondence. Her humour never

---

[45] *The Vote*, 22 Feb. 1924, 62. See also Strachey, *Millicent Garrett Fawcett*, 152.

[46] This view of Fawcett is endorsed in a number of recent studies. See e.g. Liddington and Norris, *One Hand Tied Behind Us*, 13; Holton, *Feminism and Democracy*, 32.

deserted her: she welcomed the establishment of the Anti-Suffrage League in 1908 on the basis that, by providing a new target, it enabled her to continue her work with renewed energy.[47] She was very closely involved in the attempts made by H. N. Brailsford and the Conciliation Committee to produce a bill which would allow a limited measure of female suffrage as a first stage to full adult suffrage.[48] There was also much concern within the National Union of Women's Suffrage Societies about the strategy it should adopt and about its relationship to other parties. The failure of the Conciliation Committee and the evidence this provided of the absolute intransigence of Asquith on the question of women's suffrage led to a new alliance between the National Union of Women's Suffrage Societies and the Labour Party. Although Fawcett did not initiate this particular move, she gave it her whole-hearted support.[49] She defended and explained the establishment of the Electoral Fighting Fund which was set up to assist Labour candidates and she was herself the president of the Fund.

Fawcett's position on the relationship between the Labour Party and the National Union of Women's Suffrage Societies was different from that of some of her supporters. For many of her supporters, this alliance pointed to the changing outlook of the National Union of Women's Suffrage Societies. It expressed their interest and involvement in the Labour Movement. For Fawcett, by contrast, the new policy did not end the basically non-party nature of the National Union of Women's Suffrage Societies. She agreed to support Labour Party candidates only because theirs was the only party which had formally endorsed women's suffrage. This support did not entail an overall agreement with the Labour Party platform and it was equally available to any other party which expressed itself unequivocally in support of women's suffrage.

For all her merits as a leader, and for all the skill which her followers and supporters acknowledged, Fawcett was becoming

[47] Strachey, *Millicent Garrett Fawcett*, 233–7.
[48] See F. M. Leventhal, *The Last Dissenter: H. N. Brailsford and His World*, Oxford, 1985; and Holton, *Feminism and Democracy*, 69–75.
[49] For a discussion of the suffrage–Labour alliance and the establishment of the Electoral Fighting Fund, see Holton, *Feminism and Democracy*, 76–115. Fawcett's views were expressed in a piece entitled 'Be Thou Strong', *The Common Cause*, 23 May 1912, 100. See also 'The New Policy Declared', *The Common Cause*, 14 Mar. 1913, 833, 839.

more and more out of step with the thinking of a younger generation of feminists. She held out until the end of the War, but resigned her position as president of the National Union of Women's Suffrage Societies shortly after it—and with evident relief.

Like Davies, Fawcett turned more closely to her family of origin in these last years, travelling and enjoying London, constantly accompanied by her sister Agnes. Fawcett, too, was unable to accommodate some of the shifts within the suffrage movement, feeling compelled to resign from the Board of Directors of the *Woman's Leader*, which was effectively the paper of the National Union of Societies for Equal Citizenship, when in 1925 the Union committed itself to the support of family allowances and mothers' pensions under the leadership of its president, Eleanor Rathbone. But while resigning from the paper, Fawcett remained on friendly terms with Eleanor Rathbone and continued to participate in some of the activities of the National Union: one of her last public engagements was a luncheon given by the National Union in honour of the new women Members of Parliament.[51]

Fawcett's role in the women's movement was acknowledged not only by friends and colleagues, but by the state through the award to her of Dame Grand Cross Order of the British Empire in 1924—which was a source of greater pleasure to her than she had quite expected! She lived not only to see the complete introduction of women's suffrage, but also to have an eightieth birthday which was

[50] Strachey, *Millicent Garrett Fawcett*, 335.

[51] Cited in Mary Stocks, *Eleanor Rathbone*, London, 1949, 118. Fawcett's continued friendship with Rathbone, despite this fundamental political difference was in marked contrast to her attitude to those members of the executive committee of the NUWSS who resigned over their pacifism and refusal to support the war effort. Although Kathleen Courtney and Catherine Marshall had worked with her for close on ten years, they were cast out for ever when they opposed her during the War. Both women were grieved by their break with Fawcett and sought to re-establish some form of contact with her after the first measure of women's suffrage was achieved in 1918, but Fawcett refused to have anything to do with them. Kathleen Courtney proposed a Suffrage dinner for all those who had been active in the cause, but gave up the idea when Millicent Fawcett refused to have anything to do with it. 'Isn't it strange', Courtney wrote to Catherine Marshall, 'that in the midst of her victory she should be so vindictive? ... In reply to a letter of congratulations, she sent me a *duplicated* post-card of the most formal kind, which she had addressed and signed with her full name. That was obviously intended, I suppose, to make it clear that she did not wish to receive letters of the kind from me.' Letter from Kathleen Courtney to Catherine Marshall, 5 Mar. 1918, Marshall Papers, Cumbria County Record Office.

celebrated as a major event within the women's movement. She died in August 1929 quite suddenly—and only a matter of weeks after she had had the great pleasure of celebrating the granting of women's suffrage.

II

Despite the frequent dismissal of Fawcett as one who merely applied liberal ideas to women, her feminism is considerably more complex than that. Unlike the other feminists in this study, it does not centre on one particular view or set of beliefs. If one looks carefully at Fawcett's writings and at her life, one can see two distinct sets of concerns which bear an uneasy relationship to each other. On the one hand, there is the great body of her essays and speeches, and of her work in the suffrage, education, and medical campaigns, all directed towards gaining legal and political equality for women as well as access to the public sphere, and full recognition of their contribution to society at every level. On the other hand, there is Fawcett's autobiography, her novel, and her discussions and campaigns directed towards purity, all of which centre on the sexual exploitation and victimization of women and on their imprisonment within marriage. The main problem for anyone wishing to understand Fawcett's feminism, is how to bring these two sets of concerns together.

No discussion of Fawcett can ignore or underestimate the importance to her of certain liberal principles. Although critical of the Liberal Party, she criticized it because it had 'acted in direct opposition to the principles of Liberalism'.[52] Thus even after she had ceased to have any direct affiliation with the Liberal Party in the late 1880s, Fawcett's accounts of the women's movement continued to emphasize its relationship to the broader political and social currents which had brought liberalism in their train. The whole movement for the emancipation of women, she argued,

must be regarded as one of the results of the upheaval of the human mind of which the French Revolution was the most portentous manifestation. The awakening of the democratic spirit, the rebellion against authority, the

[52] Strachey, *Millicent Garrett Fawcett*, 122.

proclamation of the rights of man, were almost necessarily accompanied by the growth of a new ideal concerning the position of women.[53]

In her first major work, *The Essays on Social and Political Subjects*, which she wrote with her husband, Millicent Fawcett was concerned primarily with the explication of liberal principles and with their application to a series of social questions, most of them involving the situation of women. Fawcett's emphasis on the importance of liberalism as providing the foundation for feminism was also evident in the prominent role she ascribed to J. S. Mill within the women's movement. Although Mill had made some very negative comments about Millicent Fawcett, there is never any suggestion that she had reservations about him. As we have seen, she went so far as to attribute the actual development of a women's suffrage movement 'to the life-long advocacy and guidance of the late J. S. Mill'.[54] Fawcett followed Mill in a number of arguments. Like him, she argued that the legal and political restrictions which women faced were the 'survivals from a state of society that has passed away', and that the real task of the women's movement was that of 'improving the lot of women, both as regards law and custom, so as to bring it into accord with the needs of the present time'.[55] Similarly, she argued that much of what passed as women's nature was an eminently artificial thing which resulted from their essentially unnatural existence.

Like most other mid-Victorian feminists, Fawcett appealed directly to liberal economic theory in her discussion of the economic and social problems women faced. In her view, the economic sufferings of women derived from artificial restrictions and barriers which prevented their entering many trades and occupations. What she sought was an end to these restrictions. Women, she insisted, were not seeking any special privileges, but merely 'a fair field and no favour'. To those who feared that women would overstock the employment market or enter into occupations for which they were unsuited, Fawcett replied that a free market would prevent this from occurring. The very demand that women be freed from the

---

[53] Millicent Garrett Fawcett, 'The Women's Suffrage Movement', in *The Woman Question in Europe*, ed. Theodore Stanton, London, 1888, 2.

[54] Ibid. 3–4.

[55] Millicent Garrett Fawcett, 'The Uses of Higher Education to Women', *Contemporary Review*, 50 (1886), 724–5.

artificial restrictions which closed most employments to them was, she insisted, 'really only a phase of the free trade argument'.

Free-traders urge that all artificial restrictions upon commerce should be removed, because that is the only way of insuring that each country and each locality will occupy itself with that industry for which it has the greatest natural advantages. In like manner, we say, remove the artificial restrictions which debar women from higher education and from remunerative employment ... and the play of natural forces will drive them into those occupations for which they have some natural advantages as individuals.[56]

Although all her other arguments were in line with his, in one important respect, Fawcett's appeal to the free market as a way of allocating women to appropriate occupations differed from Mill's. Although insisting on the need for women to have opportunities for employment and activity outside marriage, the emphasis throughout *The Subjection of Women* was placed on marriage and on married women who would always be the majority amongst their sex. Mill took great pains to insist that the reforms he was urging would not in any way reduce the likelihood of women marrying—he was seeking rather to raise the tone of marriage and to increase the moral benefits to and the happiness of both women and men within marriage. Fawcett, too, accepted that most women would marry, but she was far more concerned than Mill to insist that many women were not suited to marriage and that such women were often 'the noblest and best' amongst their sex, and only able to carry out their work because they were unencumbered by marital and familial obligations.

Where Mill tended to see unmarried women as ones who had not had the opportunity of marriage, Fawcett emphasized the active choice exercised by some women who recognized their own lack of fitness or inclination for marriage. Some women, she argued, sought to develop their talents and abilities in other directions. Fawcett attacked those who referred to unmarried women as superfluous, pointing always to what had been achieved by single women like Harriet Martineau, Florence Nightingale, and Mary Carpenter. She clearly enjoyed being able to claim that she was 'a

[56] Millicent Garrett Fawcett, 'The Future of English Women: A Reply', *Nineteenth Century*, 4 (1878), 352.

humble follower of St. Paul and believe that it is best for some people to pass through life unmarried'.[57] Unlike Mill, she was always at great pains to emphasize the immense importance of the social, intellectual, and literary contribution which women, many of them single, had already made.

Although arguing that not all women were suited to be wives and mothers, Fawcett did not in any way reject the idea that there were fundamental differences between women and men which derived from maternity.

The motherhood of women, either actual or potential, is one of those great facts of everyday life which we must never lose sight of. To women as mothers, is given the charge of the home and the care of children. Women are, therefore, by nature as well as by occupation and training, more accustomed than men to concentrate their minds on the home and domestic side of things.[58]

Like Butler and Cobbe, she placed a particularly high value on the nurturing qualities which made up womanliness, urging her followers to ensure that they did not give up 'your love of children, your care for the sick, your gentleness, your self-control, your obedience to conscience and duty, for all these things are terribly wanted in politics'. Fawcett followed a common line of argument in the nineteenth century, by insisting that it was as much the differences between men and women as their similarities which made it necessary that they be enfranchised. First of all women needed to be able to defend and protect their own interests. Men had shown no particular inclination to protect women against the various forms of sexual and social exploitation to which they were particularly vulnerable and women had to do this for themselves. Secondly, it was desirable that the particular qualities and forms of experience which women had as a result of their domestic tasks should be evident within government. Like Butler, Fawcett argued that increasing independence and strength would only serve 'to strengthen their true native womanliness'. She went even further in her insistence that the moves to open educational institutions and the professions to women had been accompanied by a

[57] Ibid. 351.
[58] Millicent Garrett Fawcett, 'Home and Politics: An Address delivered at Toynbee Hall and Elsewhere', Central and East of England Society for Women's Suffrage, n.d., 3.

'reconquering of their own sphere'. Even the 'new-born zeal for needlework and cookery' could be seen 'as an offshoot of the "women's rights" movement'.[59]

But while Fawcett insisted both on the intrinsic and irremovable differences between the sexes and on the importance of womanliness, her approach to these questions differed somewhat from those of Butler and of Frances Cobbe. For one thing, Fawcett addressed these questions mostly in the late 1880s and 1890s, when opposition to the women's movement had been mobilized—and usually in response to an attack on the movement and its objectives which had been couched in terms of the threat they posed to 'womanliness'. There is little reference to this quality in her earliest writings. When discussing the education of women in the late 1860s, for example, Fawcett insisted constantly on the need for women to be given the same education as men, in order that they be equally equipped to deal with whatever situation they should face. The emphasis here was on equality and freedom of choice for women. There was no reference to the importance of having women bring their particular qualities to bear on medicine and on whatever else they took up.[60] Moreover, although not averse to detailing the achievements and the merits of well-known women philanthropists, Fawcett was not herself a philanthropist and did not ever suggest that this activity would be congenial to all women. Thus while elaborating on the ways in which women's traditional tasks could be expanded and taken into the public sphere, Fawcett did not confine women's role to this. When discussing what educated single women could do, she was necessarily confined to the careers which were already open to women, particularly medicine and teaching. But she stressed in both the fact that they offered 'work worthy of a rational human being' and that they allowed a woman to earn a reasonable living.

Fawcett saw educated women as having an important public role to fulfil, but the one she advocated most earnestly was that of supporting the work of the women's movement by engaging in the fight against the continuing legal and social injustices women faced. She shared with Emily Davies a sense that the full range of women's

[59] Millicent Garrett Fawcett, 'The Future of Englishwomen', 354.

[60] See e.g. Millicent Garrett Fawcett, 'The Medical and General Education of Women', *Fortnightly Review*, 4 (1868), 554–71.

abilities and inclinations would not be known until they were properly educated and given the chance to see what they could do—and that they could take their womanliness and apply it to any situation. Thus throughout Fawcett's writings, one can see a careful balance between the ideas of sexual equality and those of sexual difference. In the early years, equality was given greater emphasis. By the 1880s and 1890s, sexual difference and the importance of preserving it came rather more to the fore. But for all her later stress on the importance of womanliness, Fawcett's definition of it could be extremely broad. She included qualities such as thoroughness, ability to carry out any task required and courage, quite as often as she did nurturance.[61] It is significant that Joan of Arc was one of Fawcett's favourite heroines, demonstrating an enthusiasm for the militant rather than for the domestic woman.[62]

While enjoining her followers not to give up their womanliness, Fawcett did not see this quality as a basis in itself for political or social action. Just as she did not see philanthropy as the automatic resort of women, so too she did not seek to establish particular forms of organization or campaigning which were suited to women or drew on their particular qualities. On the contrary, she sought to become and to make others into efficient and competent political campaigners, with a clear understanding of how the political world worked and an equally clear ability to manage it. Womanliness, for her as for Davies, encompassed decorum, propriety, and the 'domestic virtues' as well as 'pity and gentleness, purity and compassion'.[63] It was an integral part of being a female. As such, it needed to be accepted and developed, but it was never for her, as it was for Butler, the basis of female activity nor could it set limits on what women would become.

Fawcett's ideas on sexual difference were quite compatible with her espousal of liberal economic ideas. Indeed, as we have seen, they provided a necessary basis for the application of these ideas to women. It was only the existence of sexual difference which could ensure that, once existing legal and social restrictions were

[61] See e.g. Millicent Garrett Fawcett, 'Old Ideals of Woman', *Woman's Signal*, 7 May 1896, 295.
[62] Strachey, *Millicent Garrett Fawcett*, 179–80. See also Millicent Garrett Fawcett, *Five Famous French Women*, London, 1908; and Millicent Garrett Fawcett, *Joan of Arc*, NUWSS, London, 1912.
[63] Fawcett, 'The Uses of Higher Education to Women', 725.

removed, women would continue to undertake their traditional domestic tasks and would seek appropriate forms of employment. Thus, right from the start, Fawcett devoted her attention to insisting on the need to remove from women those political, legal, and social restrictions which bound them in subjection, and denied both their adult status and their full intellectual and personal development.

This summary of Fawcett's feminism fits very neatly into the accepted view of her, as indeed it fits very easily into the framework of Victorian liberal feminism generally. But it does not encompass all her concerns, nor does it offer any explanation as to why Fawcett herself became a feminist or entered into the women's movement. Fawcett attempted to provide such an explanation in her autobiography. Entitled *What I Remember*, Fawcett's autobiography followed the standard pattern of Victorian feminists. It was not intended to offer any startling revelations, but rather to be part of her wider propaganda for the women's movement by explaining her own particular involvement within it. The chapter entitled 'Early Suffrage Work: Sowing Seed', however, begins in a rather surprising and dramatic fashion. It describes an incident in a biography of Abraham Lincoln concerning his visit to a New Orleans slave market. While there, 'he saw a young mulatto girl exposed naked before the buyers and handled by them as if she were an animal.... one of his companions declared that Lincoln burst out "My God, boys, let us get away from this. If ever I get a chance to hit that thing, I'll hit it hard." '[64] Fawcett of course disclaims any intent to compare herself with Lincoln or to liken 'the legal and social subjection of women in England in the nineteenth century with the gross horrors of the slave trade in its most terrible aspect'. But the powerful image of the slave girl remains.

It is followed, and in some ways reinforced, by her recounting of one of the 'small accidentally heard conversations' which moved her to devote herself to gaining political and social equality for women. The conversation occurred at her parents' home while she and two guests were waiting for a dance to begin.

My two companions were talking, and presently took up the subject of the failure of a recent marriage in our immediate circle. The young

[64] Fawcett, *What I Remember*, 116.

husband and wife were estranged, and no one exactly knew the reason why; after pursuing this interesting theme for some time, one said to the other, 'I cannot see what she has to complain of. *Look how he dresses her!*' I fumed inwardly, but said nothing. I thought I would like to make that sort of talk impossible. I kept on thinking about it, and the shame and degradation of it, which seemed to be accepted by my companions as a matter of course. I did not know anything at that time about 'kept women', but 'Look how he dresses her' was of its essence.[65]

Fawcett's account of her early interest in the suffrage movement was, of course, written many decades after the events and conversations which are described. It is thus possible that the concern about sexual exploitation and degradation which it contains was the product of later experience rather than the precipitating factor in her involvement in the women's movement. Either way, it seems clear that these issues played an important part in her overall concern about women. The problem that she faced was how to integrate them into her writings and her feminist activities.

Where Josephine Butler found in the opposition to centralized government, which she shared with other provincial liberals, the connecting link which enabled her to articulate her views about and to campaign against prostitution, the kind of liberalism with which Fawcett came into contact had the reverse effect. Millicent Fawcett's real introduction to liberalism came from Henry Fawcett and from his friend and colleague, J. S. Mill. For both of them, the situation of women was entirely explained in terms of liberal political theory. Women had so long been denied political and legal rights that this situation and all its consequences appeared natural. The ending of existing restrictions and the provision of legal and political rights, including full access to education and employment, would, in their view, end all the other forms of injustice from which women suffered. Mill was by no means unaware of or insensitive to the problems of domestic violence or of the sexual subordination of women, both in and out of marriage. But he believed that once women gained full citizenship, they would not only affect the legislative process, but would also benefit from a general rise in status both within their families and in the community as a whole. Thus he saw any campaigns specifically directed at these sexual questions as of lesser importance than the suffrage. Moreover, once

[65] Ibid. 117. Italics in the original.

enfranchised, women would be able to deal properly with problems such as prostitution and domestic violence.

In her early years as a feminist campaigner, Millicent Fawcett accepted Mill's views. It was as a result of this that she refrained from taking any part in the Contagious Diseases agitation. Far from opposing that agitation, she supported it—but she was persuaded to remain aloof from it. Ray Strachey insists that this was a very painful decision for Fawcett, taken only after considerable internal struggle.[66] As Fawcett's friend and defender, one might expect Strachey to present her as sympathetic to a cause which later feminists regarded as enormously important. But there is other evidence that supports this view. In the early 1870s John Stuart Mill was the president of the London National Society for Women's Suffrage, while Millicent Fawcett was a member of its executive committee. Mill was absolutely adamant that this Society remain completely separate both from the Contagious Diseases agitation and from any other suffrage societies that supported this agitation.[67] He had some difficulties in enforcing his views: a number of members of the executive committee were sympathetic to the Contagious Diseases agitation—and hostile to the somewhat questionable means which Mill and Helen Taylor used to gain support. Fawcett was listed by Mill in the column headed 'hostile' to his views. Mill was in Avignon while all the debate within the London National Society for Women's Suffrage was going on, but he sent his instructions and discussed his ideas in letters to George Croom Robertson, who was a member of the executive committee. In one of these letters, he set out his views about Millicent Fawcett. He hoped that she could be moved from the column headed 'hostile' to the next one which was 'uncertain':

I do not think she could ever be more than uncertain. But we should much rejoice if she can be brought right. She is quite public spirited and is a recent convert to the C.D.A. movement, which I do not think her husband sympathizes in. All this is favourable; but on the other hand, she has a prosaic literal way of looking at things, and is apt to be, as I dare say you have noticed Mr Fawcett also is, a little doctrinaire—to see a principle in its full force, and not to see the opposing principles by which it might be

---

[66] Strachey, *Millicent Garrett Fawcett*, 52–3.

[67] For a discussion of this, see B. Caine, 'John Stuart Mill and the English Women's Movement', *Historical Studies*, 18 (1978), 52–67.

qualified, hence she may at any time fancy that consistency demands what I think foolish conduct.[68]

Mill's general assessment of Fawcett was not without insight—although a later comment was rather wide of the mark. When it appeared that Fawcett might not shift her stance, he insisted that she was quite dispensable, having 'neither a speculative nor an organising intelligence, and therefore, even supposing she were twice her present age, she is quite unfit to be a leader, though an excellent guerilla partisan'.[69] It is certainly hard to square this with Fawcett's later career, but it does serve to emphasize Mill's concern that she could not be brought to accept his view. Millicent Fawcett was, as we have seen, subject to other pressures as well. Her sisters pulled in quite contrary directions, as Rhoda and Agnes Garrett both participated in the Contagious Diseases agitation while Elizabeth publicly supported the Acts themselves.

Ultimately Millicent did fall into line behind Mill and Henry Fawcett, refraining from any comment on the Contagious Diseases agitation and devoting her energies to the suffrage campaign. Unlike Mill, however, she never criticized the motives, the abilities or the conduct of those who combined their suffrage work with the campaign to abolish the Contagious Diseases Acts. And in later years, when both Mill and Henry Fawcett were dead, she became vigorously active in such campaigns, making up for her early neglect of Josephine Butler by her fulsome praise and by doing all she could to aid Butler's campaigns, especially that against the Contagious Diseases Acts in India.

Having made her decision, Fawcett did not make any comments on the Contagious Diseases Acts or on the agitation led by Josephine Butler. She did not, however, cease to be interested in questions about sexual politics, or more particularly about the question of the relationship between marriage and prostitution. This can be seen by looking at her novel *Janet Doncaster*. Janet Doncaster is an unusual Victorian heroine, not only in her inordinate strength of will, but also in being fatherless—rather than motherless. There are clear autobiographical overtones in the difficulties Janet experiences with her rigidly Evangelical mother.

[68] J. S. Mill to George Croom Robertson, 6 Nov. 1871, *The Later Letters of John Stuart Mill*, ed. F. Mineka and D. Lindley, London, 1972, iv. 1850.
[69] Caine, 'John Stuart Mill', 66.

The novel is didactic and unimaginative, but it does seem to offer a space for the working out of some of Fawcett's ideas which could not be dealt with simply in lectures or in essays on political economy. The central issue in the novel is Janet's marriage, a union with a wealthy young man which she is persuaded to accept, in order to grant her mother's dying wish. Unbeknown to Janet, the young man in question is a hereditary drunkard—hence his relative's acceptance of his marrying a woman of considerably lower social rank. Janet's firmness suggests to them that she will have the capacity to control a very weak young man. On their honeymoon, Janet finds out about her husband's vicious propensities and promptly leaves him. She is shocked to discover that she has no legal right to do this, but insists that she will only return if forced to do so by the courts, and will make sure that the reasons for her unwillingness are widely publicized. Threatened with such scandal, her husband's relatives leave her alone and she makes a living translating French theology, with an occasional work of fiction as a reward.

The central issue for Janet, and the reason why she will not return to her husband, is explained when friends tell her that they disapprove of her course of action. She was persuaded by her mother to accept this marriage because of its promise of material comfort. But she had believed herself beloved and able to love in return. Once this spiritual and emotional bond was removed, the marriage was simply, in her eyes, an exchange of her body for her keep. As she explained to her friends, if she went back to her husband, 'I should be selling myself body and soul. I should be no better than those poor creatures in the streets. I should be much worse.'[70] Fawcett's extreme severity in dealing with the drunken husband has been commented on—and the novel certainly does show an uncompromising spirit and a very considerable harshness of judgement. At the same time, it enabled Fawcett to explore in some detail the radical argument that marriage is often inseparable from prostitution and that both the laws and the expectations surrounding marriage involve the subjection and even the enslavement of women.

During the years of her own marriage, Fawcett dealt with sexual and marital questions only in this indirect way. But, as we have

[70] Millicent Garrett Fawcett, *Janet Doncaster*, London, 1875, 296.

seen, immediately after being widowed she took them up in a more direct way when she became involved with W. T. Stead's campaign in the mid-1880s. Stead had been asked by Josephine Butler and her colleagues to investigate and to write about the white slave trade and especially about the sexual traffic in female children. Their lack of success in gaining any support in Parliament for a Criminal Law Amendment Act, which would raise the age of consent for girls from 12 to 16, led them to seek publicity and support elsewhere. Stead, who had already demonstrated his abilities as an emotive popular journalist, provided an electrifying series of articles, which described the nature and the extent of prostitution and of the traffic in girls from England to European cities. He demonstrated the ease with which this could be done by describing the way in which he had bought a 13-year-old girl for the sum of £5 and transported her across the Channel.[71]

Although Fawcett believed strongly in reticence and decorum in sexual matters, and could not, for example, condone the widespread dissemination of birth-control material, she insisted that on this question, silence was neither acceptable nor desirable. In a short article, significantly entitled 'Speech or Silence', she stated her conviction that speech was now imperative. Stead's articles in the *Pall Mall Gazette* exposed a

hideously perverted state of morals running through, so far as one sex is concerned, the whole of Society from the highest to the lowest; while so far as the other sex is concerned, it condemns the poorest, most ignorant and most helpless to a living death of unspeakable degradation, and drags down certain others, through appeals to their cupidity to a much lower depth of infamy and shame, that of living in luxury on the trade of decoying and selling children and their fellow women.[72]

Fawcett rejected totally the idea that Stead was revealing matters that had not been known in polite society. He had 'not so much told us what we did not know before as whipped and lashed us to a sense of our dastardly cowardice in knowing these things and making no effort to stop them'.[73]

[71] See James E. Mennell, 'The Politics of Frustration: "The Maiden Tribute of Modern Babylon" and the Morality Movement of 1885', *North Dakota Quarterly*, 49, (1981), 68–80.

[72] Millicent Garrett Fawcett, 'Speech or Silence', *Contemporary Review*, 48 (1885), 327.

[73] Ibid.

As we have seen, Fawcett acted upon these convictions through her involvement in the Preventive and Rescue Subcommittee of the National Vigilance Association. This committee engaged in a number of different campaigns. Much of its energy was directed towards children, especially those employed in areas which brought them into moral danger. Fawcett led a particular battle against the employment of children in theatres, publicizing the dangers and the fate of many of these children and seeking to force the London School Board to use its powers to compel the children to attend school and to prosecute those who employed them in contravention of the provisions of the 1876 Education Act. The National Vigilance Association established Homes for Fallen Children and Fawcett often expressed her own horror at the number of girls who entered these homes, already worn out after years of prostitution by the age of 12. Her committee attempted to offer shelters for such girls while seeking amendments to the law which would make it possible to prosecute those who had abducted, seduced, or enticed them into sexual service.

Fawcett led the National Vigilance Association campaign to bring further changes to the 1885 Criminal Law Amendment Act in order to increase beyond three months the time available to girls to bring an action against a man for rape or seduction, to bring incest within the provisions of this Act and hence to make it a criminal offence, and to increase the severity of the punishment meted out to men who sexually abused children under their authority. She also campaigned for changes in the administration of prisons, to ensure female warders for women prisoners, and she engaged in a campaign of letter-writing to the press aimed at bringing changes in the court procedures which would allow the presence of women in court where sexual crimes were dealt with. As Butler was haunted by the vision of prostitutes being first seduced and then arrested, tried, judged, convicted, and imprisoned by men, Fawcett was positively haunted by the horror involved in cases such as one at Middlesex Sessions in 1893 where an 8-year-old girl who had been sexually assaulted was denied the presence of her mother in court, and was thus forced to give evidence and undergo cross-examination about her own sexual trauma in a court filled entirely with men.[74]

[74] Strachey, *Millicent Garrett Fawcett*, 164–5.

As we have seen, Fawcett's involvement with the National Vigilance Association and her concern about the sexual exploitation of young women generally forms the necessary backdrop to her curious campaign to impose a single moral standard on men in public life. This attempt was made in Fawcett's single-handed battle to prevent Harry Cust from becoming the Conservative and Unionist Candidate for North Manchester in 1895. Cust was personally unknown to Fawcett, but his private life was apparently the subject of some discussion in the political and social circles in which Fawcett moved—and what she heard about him made her feel that he was not fit for parliamentary office. With her customary energy, Mrs Fawcett made her views clear, writing first to women's groups and local clergymen in Cust's electorate, then to parliamentary agents, and finally to party leaders. The story, as she understood it, was as follows:

Some time in the Summer of 1893, Mr Cust, M.P. for the Stamford Division of Lincolnshire, seduced Miss Welby, a young girl of good Lincolnshire family ... She became enceinte and he deserted her, and offered marriage to another girl, daughter of a well-known Conservative M.P. Miss Welby wrote Cust a despairing, imploring letter ... the thing was made known to the father and family of the girl to whom Cust had engaged himself. There was a great dispute and finally a sort of family council, with which Lord Brownlow, to whom Cust is heir, acted.... The result ... was that Cust was told that unless he married Miss Welby at once (whom he said he particularly disliked) the whole thing would be made public. He did marry her, and she almost immediately after, in France, had a miscarriage.[75]

This campaign took up a great deal of Fawcett's time, not only in a voluminous correspondence, but also in a series of uncomfortable meetings with Cust's friends and even with his wife. Fawcett kept detailed notes of all that was said in these meetings. Although many attempts were made to get her to drop her attacks on Cust, she was adamant in her refusal to do so. She was asked to desist by her friend and colleague in the suffrage movement, Lady Frances Balfour and even by A. J. Balfour. Cust himself threatened to sue Fawcett, but almost to her regret, did not carry this out. She brushed aside any

[75] Millicent Garrett Fawcett, Copy of Statement sent by Mrs Fawcett to the Rt. Hon. A. J. Balfour, MP, 19 Mar. 1894, Fawcett Papers, 90A, fos. 14–25.

suggestion that her pursuit of Cust would harm the suffrage cause. When Lady Frances Balfour wrote to her that her pursuit of Cust 'must mean the loss of front bench support. I have found it hard eno' [sic] to keep off direct going in to opposition on the part of some of our important friends since this business,'[76] Fawcett sent a rather scathing reply, arguing that Lady Frances was offering her a bribe which she would not accept.[77] She continued her campaign until Cust withdrew his candidature.

This campaign has been extremely problematical for those seeking to understand Fawcett. Why would she, who was always so careful to show her political acumen and her understanding of political matters, and who had worked so long for women's suffrage, threaten that cause by engaging in a curious vendetta—in opposition to the advice of many trusted advisers? In one of her letters to Balfour, Fawcett offers part of the answer. Balfour had written to her, requesting as politely as he could that she end her campaign against Cust. In his letter, Balfour focused on the fact that Fawcett had 'made public, through the length and breadth of Manchester, the unhappy story of a most unhappy woman. Her shame has become the common topic of political gossip.' Fawcett refused to be cowed by Balfour's claim that she was harming Mrs Cust. By focusing concern on the female victim in the case, rather than the male perpetrator, Balfour was himself appealing to a double standard in sexual morality.

Up to our own generation the whole of the social punishment in these cases has fallen on the woman, and none, or next to none, on the man. But now whether we like it or not, a movement is making itself felt towards equality. If we don't level up we shall have to level down. I want to level up; not I hope with Pharisaic harshness as if we were of another and superior creation to the man or woman who has broken the social or moral law; but with sufficient severity to minimise as far as possible the temptation to lapses of this kind. If for the last four or five generations the H. Custs of the world had been disciplined by a healthy 'coercion' of law and public opinion, the whole of this pitiable business might

---

[76] Lady Frances Balfour to Millicent Garrett Fawcett, 19 Mar. 1895, Fawcett Papers, 90A/114.

[77] Millicent Garrett Fawcett to Lady Frances Balfour, 22 Mar. 1895, copy in Fawcett Papers, 90A/116.

have been prevented and two lives at least saved from going to ship-wreck.[78]

Fawcett's attitude in all of this is rather more complex than appears at first sight. She rejected Balfour's argument that once the couple had married, there was nothing more to be said. She was appalled by the fact that the Custs had married: such a union lacked any of the emotional or spiritual bonds which she saw as necessary to a true marriage and she saw it as likely to be disastrous for both parties. In Fawcett's view, Nina Welby should have refused to marry a man who had behaved as Harry had, coping with her situation as best she could and drawing on the support of other women. Where Balfour saw the problem as one centring on Nina Welby, Fawcett saw it as having a much wider application. It was the general assumption that men could engage in whatever sexual behaviour they chose, with impunity, which she was attacking.

Frances Cobbe had long urged women to take a stand and to reject any association with men whose lives were scandalous.[79] Fawcett went further than this, by insisting that women take a part in ensuring that the sexual transgressions of a man standing for office be made known to all his potential electors. In her intransigence and refusal, under any circumstances, to end her campaign against Cust, Fawcett showed something amounting to fanaticism, a quality which is very hard to reconcile with her general mode of public activity. It is hard not to see this as a spontaneous outpouring of anger in which Cust came to symbolize generations of 'gentlemen', who took their sexual pleasure when and where they chose, regardless of the feelings of women and confident that no sexual misdemeanour on their part would affect their careers.

Although Fawcett was filled with admiration for Josephine Butler, as the Cust affair shows, her approach was very different from the approach which Butler advocated. She lacked Butler's sympathy and compassion for individual sinners, and was disposed to censure and even to punish rather than to offer her help or support. Hence unlike Butler, Fawcett was fully in sympathy with the public campaigns which ensured the downfall of Dilke and Parnell. Prior to these events, Fawcett had taken steps to ensure that the women's movement itself was not contaminated by associ-

[78] Millicent Garrett Fawcett to A. J. Balfour, 26 Mar. 1894, copy in Fawcett Papers, 90A.   [79] Cobbe, *The Duties of Women*, 156–8.

ation with individuals whose personal conduct was in any way questionable. Thus in the mid-1870s, she wrote to Elizabeth Wolstenholme Elmy, seeking her resignation as secretary of the Married Women's Property Committee because she believed that the 'circumstances connected with your marriage, and what took place previous to it' meant that her continued presence as secretary would gravely harm not only the work of that committee, but the whole women's movement.[80] Her approach was unquestionably very harsh, but it did not simply entail an acceptance of conventional views. Although very critical of existing attitudes towards marriage, and of the way in which marriage itself often involved effectively a sale of sexual services by a woman in exchange for her keep, Fawcett did not believe that women had anything to gain from an easing of existing moral restrictions. Anything which loosened the bonds of marriage and the family would, in her view, 'mean the immeasurable degradation of women'.[81] She believed that women were innately more pure and self-controlled than men and that their role was to raise men to a higher sexual and moral standard.

Fawcett welcomed the upsurge in morality which she saw developing in the 1880s—and she added a feminist edge to this by directing her attention towards limiting the behaviour of men in the belief that this was the only way to protect women. For Fawcett, the horrors of child abuse and child prostitution revealed by Stead demonstrated yet again the need for women's suffrage. She was convinced, and not without reason, that once women had some say in Parliament, legislation dealing with their protection would be handled in an altogether more adequate and expeditious manner.[82] At the same time, she was aware of the limits of legislative reform and saw economic, social, and moral change as necessary to supplement it. Like Butler she saw the economic and social subjection of women as the root cause of their engaging in prostitution and she followed Butler in her insistence that what was needed was jobs for women and the moral transformation of both women and men.

[80] Millicent Garrett Fawcett to Elizabeth Wolstenholme Elmy, 10 Dec. 1875, Fawcett Library, Autograph Collection, vol. 2C.
[81] Millicent Garrett Fawcett, 'The Woman Who Did', *Contemporary Review*, 23 (1898), 630.
[82] Strachey, *Millicent Garrett Fawcett*, 164.

Deep down at the bottom of the questions that have been raised by the recent agitation is the economical and political subjection of women; their miserably low wages in the poorest classes, wages on which life can hardly be supported unless recourse is had to the better paid trade of sin. If a real remedy is to be found it must be sought in two ways, both full of difficulties and needing patience, enthusiasm, courage and faith. The demand for victims must be diminished by a growth of unselfishness and of purity of heart among men; the supply of victims must be diminished by giving the poorest women more opportunities of fairly remunerative employment, by insisting on an extension to women of the trades-union doctrine of a fair day's pay for a fair day's work, by improvement in the dwellings of the poorest classes, and by endeavouring to form in every girl's mind a worthy ideal of womanhood.[83]

Questions about the sexual exploitation of girls and about prostitution came to occupy more and more of Fawcett's time in the late 1880s and 1890s. She did not let up on her suffrage activity: indeed it was during this time that she became president of the National Union of Women's Suffrage Societies and was constantly exercised by the need to steer the suffrage movement away from the direct party affiliation which was sought by many of her colleagues. At the same time, she was active in the National Vigilance Association and increasingly both active and recognized within the overall abolitionist campaigns. In 1896 Butler recommended her as a speaker to the Westminster Committee of the Abolitionist Federation. Fawcett was superior to any of the other suggested speakers. 'She lacks warmth rather, but she is clear and deeply convinced of the vital character of the abolitionist movement.'[84] The following year, Fawcett made a powerful speech to the National Union of Women Workers, condemning the plan to expand the provision and the regulation of prostitutes for the army in India. This speech, like Fawcett's strong support for the overall programme of the National Vigilance Association, demonstrates the very pronounced differences between her and Josephine Butler. Fawcett opposed any regulation of prostitution, but she sought police action to remove prostitutes from the streets and punitive measures to prevent soldiers from resorting to them. 'Bad women ought to be kept out of the Cantonments; bad houses ought to be

[83] Millicent Garrett Fawcett, 'Speech or Silence', 331.
[84] Josephine Butler to the Misses Priestman, 4 Nov. 1896, Butler Papers.

out of bounds. It ought to be the study of the military authorities to make the practice of vice physically difficult as well as morally repulsive.'[85]

In the first decade of the twentieth century, both Fawcett's national political activity and her involvement with the National Vigilance Association and with morality campaigns lessened. It is unclear whether her interest in questions about sexual morality declined, or rather, as Strachey suggests, that she came to believe more and more strongly that the criminal law and the whole judicial system could only be made to protect women once they were enfranchised and able directly to influence it.[86] If this was Fawcett's position, she was not alone in holding it. The question of the sexual exploitation and victimization of women was widely discussed amongst feminists belonging to all the suffrage societies in the early twentieth century. Indeed concern about male sexual brutality and violence was a significant, perhaps the most significant, issue in the suffrage campaigns.[87] But the strategy for dealing with this problem had increasingly moved away from vigilance activity and towards campaigning for the suffrage.

Fawcett's remaining papers about the suffrage movement make it very hard for one to ascertain how concerned she was about issues of sexual morality in the early twentieth century. She dedicated herself almost entirely to the suffrage campaign, attempting constantly to organize it as a political one which would simultaneously train women in political activity and demonstrate their readiness for political rights. Her whole approach was characterized by pragmatism and by conformity to the accepted practices of national political parties. As we have seen, her pragmatism even extended to her acceptance of an electoral alliance with the Labour Party, the only one which had openly declared its support for women's suffrage.

Throughout the early twentieth century, Fawcett campaigned for the suffrage as a necessary right for women while denying that it would in itself radically transform either women or the society in which they lived. She rejected entirely the millennial visions

---

[85] Millicent Garret Fawcett, speech made at the Croydon Meeting of the National Union of Women Workers, Oct. 1897, on 'The New Rules for Dealing with the Sanitary Condition of the British Army', Proceedings, 1898.

[86] Strachey, *Millicent Garrett Fawcett*, 164–6.

[87] See Kent, *Sex and Suffrage, passim.*

of Emmeline Pankhurst, arguing in contrast that the granting of women's suffrage would be 'a political change, the reverse of revolutionary in its nature; because it simply gives political expression, as it were, to a social change which has already taken place'.[88] She argued constantly in an essentially Burkean vein, attempting to demonstrate that women's suffrage was a measure at once democratic, 'because democracy is based on the faith that liberty is good and that the people may be trusted', and conservative 'because of that preservative, non-destructuve characteristic of women which physiologists tell us is of the essence of the female sex'.[89] The echoes of Burke which can be found in Fawcett's comments were by no means accidental. She quoted him directly when arguing that the time was ripe for women's suffrage. In one of his writings about the French Revolution, Burke 'indicated to us the signs by which we may know when a society is ripe for an important change in its political machinery'. Because 'the minds of men will be fitted to it, the general opinions and feeling will draw that way'.[90] This, in her view, was very much the case as regards women's suffrage at the present time.

In all her speeches and in her whole approach to women's suffrage, Fawcett's demeanour was that of the experienced politician, acting for the good of women and in the interests of a national and a consitutional system in which she firmly believed. All of it, too, can be seen as showing her growing conservatism, and especially her desertion of an earlier political radicalism. In terms of national political affiliation, this reading of Fawcett has some merit—although she was unusual amongst conservatives in her preparedness and ability to work with the Labour Party. But what is even more striking when one is looking at Fawcett in relation to her feminism is her constant concern about Butler, her concerted effort to ensure that Butler was seen as the foremost Victorian feminist, and her insistence that Butler's fight against the sexual double standard be recognized as central to the whole

[88] See e.g. Millicent Garrett Fawcett, 'Women's Suffrage', speech made at the Annual Conference of National Union of Women Workers, Oct. 1896, Proceedings, 79.
[89] Ibid.
[90] Ibid. 82.

women's movement.[91] Moreover, while her own statements about the suffrage contained little about sexual exploitation, Fawcett continued throughout these years to be involved in social purity issues. Hence the view of her which is derived from her suffrage letters and from her speeches and her history of the suffrage movement is one which is qualified considerably if one reads the references to her in Butler's correspondence, in the *Vigilance Record*, and in her biography of Josephine Butler.

What emerges from all of this seems again and again to illustrate the impossibility for Fawcett of connecting her national political activities, including her campaign to have women included within the state, with her whole analysis of sexual politics. Experienced as she was at dealing with the world of national politics, she could not make comprehensible within the framework of that world her concern about the oppression and exploitation of women. As a pragmatist, she worked for each of her aims within what seemed to her the appropriate arena. But for all this, she can only be understood in her entirety by seeing these different arenas in connection with each other—and by recognizing the disjunctions and the tensions which were central to her world.

[91] Millicent Garrett Fawcett and E. M. Turner, *Josephine Butler: Her Work and Principles, and their Meaning for the Twentieth Century*, London, 1927, 1–2.

7

Victorian Feminism and After: The 1890s and Beyond

THE last decade of the ninetenth century was for many years seen as something of a blank in the history of English feminism. This was so largely because the suffrage campaign, the last remaining campaign from the agenda of the nineteenth-century women's movement, was unquestionably in the doldrums, only to be revived by the advent of the Women's Social and Political Union and the start of the militant campaign in the early years of the twentieth century. But recent work on literary and cultural developments and on the overall situation of women during this decade has dramatically altered this view. In view of women's expanding employment opportunities, the growing numbers of women at universities, and the marked expansion in women's public role in terms of local government and education, it is hard to see this period as one in which no significant feminist developments took place. At the same time, the whole 'new woman' debate, in all its various forms in fiction, drama, and in the popular press, dem- onstrate the enormous interest in questions about the changing role and situation of women. Feminist ideas, too, developed, sometimes in new literary forms and organized around questions of women's sexuality and their autonomy rather than around the need for specific reforms. Overall, the 1890s now seem more like a watershed than a dead period.[1]

[1] See e.g. Lucy Bland, 'The Married Woman, the "New Woman" and the

This period was also one of change and even of conflict for the four women in this study as their outlook and approach was questioned and even rejected by some of their late Victorian and Edwardian counterparts. Their liberal economic and political assumptions, their concept of womanhood, and their whole approach to feminist campaigns were subject to challenge by a new generation with new ideas and plans, new strategies, and some new objectives.[2] All of the women in this study were involved to a greater or lesser extent in the generational conflicts and in the whole question of defining feminist ideas and approaches. For some it established the context in which they withdrew from active feminist activity; for others, it required both adaptation and change, if they were to remain central to an organized women's movement.

Looking at this period and at its conflicts from the perspective of this group of feminists does not give a complete or comprehensive picture of the 1890s, nor would it be possible to do so in one chapter. But a discussion of the ways in which their views were criticized and of their participation in particular debates serves to show just how much the world had changed since they first became involved in feminist agitation. Their own views and comments serve also to show their sense of the changes that were occurring.

The differing level of involvement in the changing feminist scene and the different reactions to it of Fawcett as compared with the others, show very clearly their differences in age. Butler and Cobbe were aware of and commented on aspects of the debate over industrial legislation, the rise of social purity in the 1880s, and the 'new woman' debate of the 1890s, but they were both well into their sixties by this time, and feeling increasingly frail and disinclined for public life. Davies by contrast underwent a resurgence of energy and activity at this time, returning to the suffrage campaign in 1888 after an absence of 20 years. She took an active part in suffrage agitation in the early twentieth century—and saw and execrated

Feminist Sexual Politics of the 1890s', in Jane Rendall ed., *Equal or Different: Women's Politics 1800–1914*, Oxford, 1987, 141–64; Carol Dyhouse, *Feminism and the Family in England 1880–1939*, Oxford, 1989; David Rubinstein, *Before the Suffragettes: Women's Emancipation in the 1890s*, Brighton, 1986.

[2] For one analysis couched very much in generational terms, see Martha Vicinus, *Independent Women: Work and Community for Single Women, 1850–1920*, London and Chicago, 1985, *passim*.

the militant campaign. But she spoke as a survivor of a bygone era. It was Fawcett who was just coming to the peak of her importance as a suffrage leader and as a major figure in British politics in the 1880s and early 1890s who was most closely involved in all of these issues. It was she who tried to find a new political framework as the nineteenth-century structure of political parties was replaced by a new one, and she who had to try to negotiate a relationship between the 'constitutionalists' and the 'militants'. It is thus Fawcett who shows most clearly the nature of the transition from mid-Victorian to Edwardian feminism and the conflicts and tensions which accompanied that transition.

This challenge posed to mid-Victorian feminism in the later nineteenth century was not a simple one, nor did it result in any immediate victories or defeats. After all, much of the programme, many of the ideas, and some of the organizations of the nineteenth-century women's movement continued, not only until the War, but through the inter-war period. But during this time, new ideas and new organizations came into existence, offering economic ideas, political orientations, and ways of proceeding which were entirely outside the known boundaries of Victorian feminism. At the same time, new ideas about women, about their nature, their sexuality, and their interests came to the fore and were discussed and espoused by some feminists. Hence the underlying unity of mid-Victorian feminism came to an end.

I

The first significant challenge to the assumptions and the outlook of mid-Victorian feminists came over the question of their relationship to working class women and their ideas about women's work. The mid-Victorian women's movement was predominantly a middle-class one with a membership drawn almost exclusively from the professional and upper-middle classes and from the gentry. It was, however, neither ignorant of nor unconcerned about the needs and the problems faced by working-class women. Several of the first papers given by members of the women's movement at the National Association for the Promotion of Social Science addressed the question of women as industrial workers and as

manual labourers in non-industrial fields.[3] The Society for Promoting the Employment of Women was one of the first organizations to begin working at the Langham Place office and to
establish branches in provincial cities. Emily Davies and Josephine
Butler both belonged to it, undertaking investigations into the
employment of women and attempting to expand their employment
opportunities.

As concerned middle-class women active in philanthropy, many
feminists had become acutely aware of the poverty of working-
class women and of their vulnerability to sexual exploitation and
to marital and domestic violence. This concern was the more easily
expressed because they assumed that working-class and middle-
class women faced the same problems in terms of their subjection
to husbands and masters and to the various legislative restrictions
that reduced their economic freedom. Hence the mid-nineteenth-
century women's movement demanded increased employment
opportunities for working-class women and an end to legislation
which specifically excluded women from certain kinds of work.

During the 1880s, the assumption that middle-class women faced
the same problems as working-class ones was challenged for the
first time by other women. The rise of the Labour movement and
the emergence of groups of feminists affiliated with it meant that
mid-Victorian feminists were now confronted by opposing groups
of women who questioned their right to speak on behalf of all
English women, insisting that it was they, through their connection
with and understanding of the Labour movement, rather than
middle-class feminists who understood the real needs of working-
class women and the best way of alleviating their sufferings.[4] The
major focus of this conflict was the related questions of industrial
legislation and trade union membership for women.

The whole question of industrial legislation for women is a
complex one and it has recently been discussed in considerable

[3] See e.g. Barbara Leigh Smith Bodichon's contribution to the 'Debate on the
Industrial Employment of Women at the first Annual Conference of the NAPSS',
and Bessie Raynor Parkes, 'A Year's Experience in Women's Work' given at the
1859 Conference. *Transactions of the National Association for the Promotion of
Social Science*, London, 1858, 531–44 and 1860, 811–19. See also Philippa Levine,
Victorian Feminism, 1850–1900, London, 1987, 82–104.

[4] See Rosemary Feurer, 'The Meaning of "Sisterhood": The British Women's
Movement and Protective Legislation, 1870–1900', *Victorian Studies*, 31 (1988),
233–60.

detail.[5] It involved a direct conflict of views between the old-style economic liberalism of the women's movement and the much more interventionist ideas of socialists and members of the Labour movement. Members of the women's movement, including Millicent Fawcett and Josephine Butler, continued in the 1880s and 1890s as they had begun in the 1860s and 1870s to oppose any industrial legislation which was applied to women and not to men. Such legislation, in their view, as in the view of political economists such as Henry Fawcett and J. S. Mill, denied that women were rational adults capable of ascertaining or following their own interests. It served also to reduce the employment opportunities and the income-earning capacity of women.

The continued reliance of the women's movement on the economic ideas of the Manchester School was a major target for their opponents. Beatrice Webb and Barbara Hutchins, in particular, bewailed the economic and social ignorance and the outmoded ideas of 'the able and devoted ladies who have usually led the cause of women's enfranchisement' but who lacked any understanding of the problems of industrial labour. In Beatrice Webb's view, members of the women's movement were unable to see the differences between the needs of those women seeking to enter the professions, and those who belonged to the wage-earning classes. Women seeking entry to professions clearly required the abolition of existing restrictions. However, 'when we come to the relations between capital and labour an entirely new set of relations come into play. In the life of the wage-earning class, absence of regulation does not mean personal freedom ... [but] positively increases the personal freedom of those who are subject to it.'[6] In her view, protective legislation was essential for women and would help to provide the basis for organized trade unions amongst women which

[5] Feurer, 'The Meaning of "Sisterhood"'; B. Caine, 'From a "fair field and no favour" to Equal Employment Opportunity', *Refractory Girl*, 30 (1987), 36–40; Levine, *Victorian Feminism*, 105–27; Norbert Soldon, *Women in British Trade Unions*, Dublin, 1978, 23–40; David Rubinstein, *Before the Suffragettes*, 94–134. See also Heidi Hartmann, 'Capitalism, Patriarchy and Job Segregation by Sex', in *Capitalist Patriarchy and the Case for Socialist Feminism*, ed. Zillah Eisenstein, New York, 1979, 130–50, and, for an American discussion, Alice Kessler-Harris, *Out to Work: A History of Wage-Earning Women in the United States*, New York, 1982.

[6] Beatrice Webb, *Women and the Factory Acts* (Fabian Tract No. 67), London, 1895, 5. See also B. L. Hutchins and A. Harrison, *A History of Factory Legislation*, London, 1911, 36–54.

in turn would improve their pay and conditions of work.

Webb's views were accepted by a number of feminists, including other Fabian women and a group sometimes now referred to as 'social feminists',[7] who became involved in organizations such as the Women's Protective and Provident League or the Women's Industrial Council, all of whom came to believe that protective legislation and trade-union organization were essential to improve the lot of working-class women.[8] But they were not accepted by the older generation of the women's movement—nor indeed by large numbers of women workers, desperate to safeguard their livelihoods.[9] Millicent Fawcett and Josephine Butler absolutely rejected Webb's arguments, refusing to see protective legislation for women as having any other purpose than to exclude them from well-paid work. While Beatrice Webb saw the trade-union movement as a necessary ally of women workers, Millicent Fawcett saw it as their positive enemy. In her view, the men's trade unions

exert themselves to keep women out of all except the most unskilled and worst paid trade: they combine to prevent the natural growth of industrial efficiency amongst women, and in so far as they are able to do this, they swell the great army of 'fallen women' whose ranks are so much recruited by industrial inefficiency and want of steady employment.[10]

It is perhaps worth noting that not all of the first generation of the women's movement agreed entirely with Fawcett on this. In the early 1860s Emily Davies had argued that until they were organized and able to take strike action, seamstresses would continue to be exploited: to work excessively long hours while earning below subsistence wages.[11] Forty years later she rejected the idea that enfranchisement would raise the wages of women, arguing

[7] For a discussion of the term, see Naomi Black, *Social Feminism*, Ithaca and London, 1989.

[8] See Ellen Mappen, ed., *Helping Women at Work: The Women's Industrial Council 1889–1914*, London, 1985.

[9] For the views of some of the mid-Victorian feminists who entered into this argument, see Jessie Boucheret, Helen Blackburn, *et al.*, *The Condition of Women and the Factory Acts*, London, 1886; and Helen Blackburn and Nora Vigne, *Women Under the Factory Acts*, London, 1903.

[10] Millicent Garrett Fawcett, 'Home and Politics: An Address delivered at Toynbee Hall and Elsewhere', Central and East of England Society for Women's Suffrage, n.d. 8.

[11] Emily Davies, 'Needleworkers v. Society', *Victoria Magazine*, 1 (1863), 348–60.

that it was combination rather than enfranchisement which had raised the wages of men—and implying that this would be the same for women.[12]

But Fawcett's was the more common view within the mid-nineteenth-century women's movement as a whole. Josephine Butler, in particular, shared her hostility to trade unions and her belief that the exclusive access to trades demanded by male unionists contributed greatly to the economic hardship and to the overall sufferings of women.[13]

Fawcett's hostility both to protective legislation and to the role of trade unions in regard to women's work remained implacable and there was unquestionably much truth in Beatrice Webb's continued insistence that this opposition derived from her mid-nineteenth-century economic ideas and her inability to see that these views were outdated and that there were now new theories and new approaches which had to be applied to women.[14] But for all this, Fawcett was quite correct in her view that much protective legislation was devised in order to exclude women from certain categories of highly paid work—and that it was supported by many trade unionists precisely because they did believe that women had no real place in the paid workforce.[15] Moreover, as Butler argued, women's paid work was by no means their heaviest labour—and every hour of paid work which was taken from them meant another hour during which they could do unpaid work as the servants of their husbands or in the home![16]

The many pamphlets and articles on this subject make it clear that the women who opposed protective legislation differed from those who supported it, not only in terms of their approach to economic questions and to the role of the state, but also in terms of the group for whose interests they spoke. Fawcett and her colleagues took as their object the needs of women—as individuals, as workers, and all too often as the sole support of families. Other

[12] Emily Davies, 'The Women's Suffrage Movement', Central Society for Women's Suffrage, London, 1906, 6.

[13] See Josephine Butler to Albert Rutson, 19 June 1886, Butler Papers.

[14] Beatrice Webb, *Women and the Factory Acts*, 4–6.

[15] For recent work which supports Fawcett's views, see Hartmann, 'Capitalism, Patriarchy and Job Segregation by Sex'; and Solden, *Women in British Trade Unions, passim*.

[16] See e.g. Butler *et al.*, *Legislative Restrictions on the Industry of Women, Considered from the Women's Point of View*, London, n.d. 8.

questions, including the best framework for industrial labour or the needs of the Labour movement, were of no interest to them. By contrast, for Webb, Hutchins, and the Fabian women, as for some of the women involved in the Women's Protective and Provident League or the Women's Industrial Council, the primary concern was the health and well-being of the working class and of the Labour movement. They were all too willing to ignore or to disregard the specific needs of women as workers in their overall concern with working-class family and community life or to accept that the primary role of women was that of wife and mother.[17] Thus Beatrice Webb, in rejecting Fawcett's argument that it was male unionists who excluded women from the profitable branches of work and thus kept down their wages, argued that women themselves were responsible for this.

The real enemy which working women faced, in Webb's view, was the female 'amateur' who was concerned only to make a little money on the side and hence was not a full-time worker. She wished to see legislation laying down working hours which would exclude these amateurs, 'who simultaneously blackleg both the workshop and the home' and would establish a body of self-respecting full-time workers who would then embark on trade union organization.[18] Webb was clearly targeting working mothers who, in her view, carried out their duties neither in the home nor in the workplace.

The amateur worker, about whom Webb was so scathing, was for Fawcett and her colleagues the woman who needed to supplement a family income or to work as best she could in order to combine her familial responsibilities with providing some familial income.[19] She was deserving of all support and help. Fawcett did accept that women's wages were and would continue to be lower than men's for the foreseeable future and, like Webb, she accepted the lack of skill amongst women workers as one reason for this. But instead of seeing women as responsible for their own low pay, she argued that it resulted from their overall social position—and from

[17] For the inconsistencies on this point evident in the Women's Industrial Council, see Mappen, *Helping Women at Work*, 22–6.

[18] Beatrice Webb, *Women and the Factory Acts*, 15.

[19] Boucheret and Blackburn, *The Condition of Working Women*, 29.

their exclusion by male workers from apprenticeships or training.[20]

What is clear from all of this is not that mid-Victorian feminists had a better or clearer understanding of the plight of working class women than did those who took up the woman question from within the Labour movement. On the contrary, their opposition to any form of protective legislation or to any form of trade-union activity unquestionably limited their capacity to understand or to assist the plight of working-class women. At the same time, the very individualism of their approach and its central concern with women as individuals made them able to see the hostility to working women and to any attempt to change the sexual order which was so prevalent in the Labour movement. Their liberalism was outdated, and it lacked any analysis of class or the importance of class in determining the actual nature of women's oppression. None the less, it allowed them to see sex and sexual difference as a cross-class issue and to question the extent to which the needs of women were actually addressed in class-based organizations.

Although mid-Victorian feminists were often intensely class conscious, at a theoretical level they believed that all women made up a single category and that they were oppressed on the basis of their sex. They fought to remove this form of oppression. They may have lacked understanding of industrial questions, but they certainly had a clear sense of the nature and the extent of sexual ones. Their concern with sexual oppression and with sexual issues, such as the sexual double standard, was not shared by many of their socialist critics.

As Olive Banks has pointed out, the decline in the number of feminists with a predominantly liberal national political orientation and the rise in the number of feminists who were also socialists at the end of the nineteenth century was accompanied by a shift away from concern with issues centring on the autonomy of women, the importance of choice and dignity for single women, and the sexual double standard. These issues remained alive in the suffrage movement and in the sexual campaigns of the women's movement which accompanied it. But the interest in regulating the lives of women both as industrial workers and as wives and mothers which was expressed by socialist women became a major strand within femin-

[20] Millicent Garrett Fawcett , 'Mr Sidney Webb's Article on Women's Wages', *Economic Journal*, 2 (1892), 173–6.

ism, and one which was rather more in accord with prevailing social policies and with medical and scientific ideas than was the individualist approach.[21]

The different views as to whether it was women as a group who needed rights, or rather working-class women as members of the working class, reflected fundamental differences amongst feminists which were greater than any differences of opinion about strategy, tactics, and aims within the nineteenth century. They led not only to disagreement about economic questions, but to different approaches to the suffrage question as many Labour women supported adult suffrage rather than women's suffrage.[22] That there should have been division amongst feminists even on the suffrage, the one issue which all recognized as central, is an indication of the fundamental division, even fragmentation, which developed within English feminism at the turn of the century. Because the suffrage campaign was so dramatic, the extent of this fragmentation did not become evident until after the War. But the seeds were already sown long before, as one can see in the increasing differences of opinion as to the very aims and objectives of different feminists.

II

It was not only the economic ideas of mid-Victorian feminism which were attacked in the last decades of the nineteenth century, but also some aspects of the concept of womanhood around which it had been organized. As we have seen, mid-Victorian feminists held to a particular notion of femininity. Women, in their view, were morally distinguishable from men through being more law-abiding, conscientious, temperate, religious, and tender-hearted.[23] Even those feminists who, like Emily Davies, questioned the extent of women's innate nurturance accepted this moral profile.

In the later part of the nineteenth century, this ideal of femininity was challenged in a number of different ways. The assumption

[21] Olive Banks, *Becoming a Feminist: The Social Origins of 'First Wave' Feminism*, Brighton, 1986, 80–4.

[22] For a discussion of the division amongst women in the Labour movement on this issue, see Jill Liddington and Jill Norris, *One Hand Tied Behind Us: The Rise of the Women's Suffrage Movement*, London, 1978, 178–86.

[23] Frances Power Cobbe, *Life of Frances Power Cobbe*, London, 1894, ii. 211.

about women's greater chastity, which was fundamental to it, was undermined by the assertion within both psychoanalysis and sexology of a distinctive form of female sexuality. Indeed, the whole emphasis on women's moral qualities which had been so central to early Victorian discussions of femininity and womanhood was lost. Hence while there was some continuity in the concern with women's bodies, their sexuality, their reproductive capacities, and their whole physical constitution across the nineteenth century, in the last decades of the century questions about women's sexual needs and pleasure and about the need to control their reproduction were introduced into the woman question in a quite new way. At the same time, the emergence of a 'new woman' in literature, complex and contradictory as the various constructions of the 'new woman' were, none the less gave increased currency to a notional woman who displayed few of the feminine qualities or the values and codes of conduct adhered to by mid-Victorian feminists.

The complexity and diversity of constructions of femininity throughout the nineteenth century are increasingly being recognized by historians. Indeed it is becoming evident that what needs to be understood is the existence of a number of ideas about women at any one time, rather than a coherent and specific set. The final years of the nineteenth century saw a shift in this range as more and more interest was taken in women's sexuality and in the physical aspects of their maternal role on the one hand, while women were demanding ever greater degrees of autonomy and of freedom from marital and familial ties on the other.

Many of the changes in the range of ideas which constituted late nineteenth-century constructions of femininity were the result of changes in the social situation of women. The improvements in women's education and the increasing choice of occupations open to them led to the possibility that middle-class women might choose a career and an independent life rather than marriage and a family. The introduction of sport and gymnastics for women, the advent of the bicycle, and hence of the woman cyclist, the whole discussion of dress reform, while all small changes in themselves, had the cumulative effect of suggesting a new mobility and freedom for women, and hence of contributing to an image of a late nineteenth-century woman which was very different from that of her mid-Victorian counterpart.

While the range of activities for women was changing, so too was the locus of concern about women's familial and social role. In the early part of the nineteenth century, industrialization and urbanization led to a widespread concern about changing the social, sexual, and moral order. It was the possibilities women offered as home-makers and as centres of moral and religious values which became the focal point of many works setting out women's role and responsibilities. Later in the nineteenth century, however, concern about the declining birth-rate fuelled concern about Britain's imperial role, about the health and capacity of the British population, and about the state of British national efficiency. Concern now shifted away from the moral function of women as wives and mothers, and towards questions about their physical and intellectual fitness. Motherhood was discussed less in terms of the creation of a safe and protective home, than in terms of the importance of producing large numbers of healthy and efficient citizens. At the same time, sexology and psychoanalysis contributed to this new stress on the physical side of womanhood by stressing the existence of a distinctive female sexuality—but of one which was very problematical and threatened to effect women's mental and emotional balance. Hence in many different quarters, women's ability and preparedness to marry, to produce children and to become competent mothers became matters of pre-eminent concern.

From one perspective then, one can see the whole discussion of the 'new woman' of the 1890s as the reformulation of the early and mid-Victorian 'woman question' in accordance with the broad economic, social, political, and intellectual changes in society at large and with the changes in the legal and social role of women which had occurred in the second half of the nineteenth century. These changes necessarily meant that even when discussing questions which had long been before the public or when putting forward views which resembled those of their mid-Victorian forebears, late nineteenth-century women discussed these questions and put forward their views in new and different terms. Hence the cast of feminist thought and discussion was very different at the turn of the century from what it had been in the 1860s and 1870s, even though many underlying issues continued to be addressed.

Perhaps the change in the cast of feminist thought between the mid- and the late nineteenth century is most evident in terms of changing ideals of womanhood. Mid-Victorian feminists had always assumed that the reforms for which they fought would bring not only a wider sphere of action for women, but also certain changes and reforms in women themselves and in constructions and ideals of femininity. They had sought particularly an end to the idea that womanliness or femininity necessarily involved physical and moral weakness, cowardice, and incompetence. But they saw all of these changes as enhancing women's moral status, not as involving any rejection of Victorian moral values.

Hence when mid-Victorian feminists actually began to see a new generation develop and emerge, some of them saw changes which were not at all the ones they had hoped for—and which seemed to them quite abhorrent. There was no complete uniformity amongst mid-Victorian feminists on this question of the younger generation or of changes in womanhood. Thus Millicent Fawcett, as befitted the mother of an outstanding student, welcomed the new generation of college-educated young women with great enthusiasm, delighted to see a group of women able to assert their independence, to have careers, and to participate in many aspects of public life. Despite her difficulties with some of the young women at Girton, Emily Davies, too, was happy with the advent of women graduates. Her one great regret was that Girton students were inadequately committed to the suffrage cause and she admonished them about this, pointing out that it was their duty to join the struggle for women's emancipation.[24]

But not all of their colleagues shared in this pleasure. Josephine Butler, by contrast, was decidedly unenthusiastic about the new kind of woman who emerged from the universities. She commiserated over the 'unattractive dryness' which her son Stanley complained of in the women students at St Andrews where he taught. 'How is it that learned girls are generally so unattractive?' she wrote, 'I find them so. There is certainly a loss of womanliness or something together with the gain of well-furnished brains. The word which sums up what they are wanting is "grace".' It was perhaps significant that Butler, who was accustomed to her own

---

[24] See Emily Davies, 'The Women's Suffrage Movement'.

pre-eminence felt 'quite stupid and ill-informed often among those learned girls and women'![25]

Although Fawcett and Davies welcomed a more educated group of young women, they were not immune to anxiety about the whole tenor of discussion about the 'woman question' in the last decade of the nineteenth century. Fawcett's concern centred on the advent of the 'new woman' in literature and in a whole range of social discourses. Her response was more temperate than that of Josephine Butler, for whom the very mention of the 'new woman' was apparently enough to make her lose her temper![26] None the less she certainly had some acid things to say.

In one sense, the 'new woman' burst on to the English literary and journalistic scene in 1894, after the term was coined by Sarah Grand. Grand herself sought to differentiate between a new intellectual woman and an older physical, domestic, and ill-treated woman to whom she referred contemptuously as 'the cow woman'.[27] But the very need to find a term was the result of a growing sense that there were changes in the behaviour, the activities, even the nature of women which needed to be articulated. These changes and the women who embodied them had been being discussed since the 1860s—and usually in terms which emphasized a growing concern within society for the ways in which the new generation of women was deserting the standards, values and duties of their mothers. Eliza Lyn Linton's 'Girl of the Period' articles were the first to take up this theme in the 1860s. But it was in the 1880s that the discussion really expanded with debates in periodicals such as the *Nineteenth Century* about the 'revolt of the daughters', the modern girl, and finally the 'new woman'. The 'new woman' theme, along with the criticism of marriage which almost invariably accompanied it, was also widely discussed in fiction in this decade.[28]

Despite the extensive discussion of the 'new woman' in periodicals and in fiction during the 1890s and the early decades of

[25] Josephine Butler to Stanley Butler, 17 June 1895, Butler Papers.

[26] A. S. G. Butler, *Portrait of Josephine Butler*, London, 1954, 211.

[27] For the term and some of the debates incorporated in it, see Ellen Jordan, 'The Christening of the New Woman', *Victorian Newsletter*, 63 (1983), 19–20; and David Rubinstein, *Before the Suffragettes*, 12–37.

[28] See Patricia Stubbs, *Women and Fiction: Feminism and the Novel 1880–1920*, Brighton, 1979.

the twentieth century, there was neither a common idea nor an agreed picture of what exactly the 'new woman' was. This lack of a unified conception of the 'new woman' was particularly evident in fiction. In some novels, such as Gissing's *The Odd Women* or Hardy's *Jude the Obscure*, it was women's rejection of marriage, motherhood, and indeed of their own sexuality which was the central concern.[29] In others, for example Grant Allen's notorious *The Woman Who Did*, the rejection of marriage went along with an endorsement of free love.[30] In yet others, mostly the novels written by women, including Sarah Grand's two novels, *The Beth Book* and *The Heavenly Twins*, and Emma Brooke's *A Superfluous Woman*, the central subject was not so much women's demand for a new freedom as their recognition of the evil consequences which they suffered as a result of male sexual promiscuity and brutality.[31] Grand in particular emphasized women's purity, even their passionlessness, in a way which had a marked similarity to earlier Victorian ideas about women—although she was more outspoken than earlier writers in her discussion of the licentiousness of men and of the exposure of women to venereal disease in marriage.[32] The new women in Grand's fiction, as in that of several other women writers, did not reject marriage entirely, but they showed what women suffered in marriage, and demanded a recognition of their need for personal and sexual autonomy within it.[33]

The prominence of the 'new woman' fiction made it inevitable that fictional ideas and characters would be included alongside actual individuals and events in the broad-ranging debate about the 'new woman' which occurred at the turn of the century. In the whole discussion about women which occurred in periodicals and

[29] George Gissing, *The Odd Women*, London, 1893; Thomas Hardy, *Jude the Obscure*, London, 1896.

[30] Grant Allen, *The Woman Who Did*, London 1898.

[31] Sarah Grand, *The Beth Book*, London, 1897 (repr. London, 1980); *The Heavenly Twins*, London, 1893; Emma Brooke, *The Superfluous Woman*, London, 1894. For an interesting discussion of the women writers who dealt with this question, see Stubbs, *Women and Fiction*, 109–22.

[32] At least a decade before Christabel Pankhurst wrote 'The great Scourge', the threat posed to women by male promiscuity—their infection by venereal disease and their likelihood of giving birth to a child with congenital syphilis—had been extensively canvassed in imaginative literature.

[33] Bland, 'The Married Woman', 141–64.

pamphlets at this time, the term 'new woman' was used to refer simultaneously to a group of fictional characters or novels, to particular women, especially those who took up new activities like cycling or archery, or who entered into new professions, and to a series of new ideas about the role and the nature of women.

The women's movement as a whole had a complex relationship to this 'new woman' debate. It is an area where the extent of generational conflict within the movement can be very clearly seen. But it is also one which shows the ever-increasing diversification and proliferation of feminist ideas and positions in the late nineteenth century. The generational issue is evident in the participation of feminists in the fictional creation of new women and in the outspoken attack on Victorian ideals of marriage and womanliness. Cicely Hamilton, Mona Caird, Sarah Grand and Olive Schreiner were just four of the prominent supporters of the women's movement who attacked Victorian feminine ideals, insisted on a recognition of the servitude women endured in marriage, and demanded a new approach to women's lives, work, and relationships.[34] Although they espoused different ideas about women's needs and women's nature, all of them wrote about this explicitly in terms of a 'new woman' who rejected outmoded ideals and sought a new life.

There was little enthusiasm at all for the 'new woman' amongst the remaining mid-Victorian feminists. But this did not, of course, mean that they automatically espoused an idealized 'old woman' or an 'older' ideal of womanhood. Indeed, the whole debate about the 'new woman' was a particularly troublesome one for mid-Victorian feminists because of their complex attitude to earlier Victorian ideals of womanhood. As we have seen, Davies, Butler, Cobbe, and Fawcett all made explicit their rejection of the idea that all women should marry, that the home was the only sphere for women, that women should be financially dependent, that chastity should be imposed on women but not men, or that women existed primarily to serve the family. At the same time, they all upheld the ideals of chastity, womanly decorum, and of familial and social service, which were part of this ideal—and they had

[34] Cicely Hamilton, *Marriage as a Trade*, London, 1909; Mona Caird, *The Morality of Marriage*, London, 1897; Olive Schreiner, *Woman and Labour*, London, 1911, and *Story of an African Farm*, London, 1893.

spent decades refuting the idea that those women who sought political and social reform also sought to end the family and to assert women's freedom to reject existing moral standards. Hence while unhappy about many aspects of the so-called 'new woman', and fearful of the damage which any association with this creature would do to the suffrage movement, they could not attack it simply in terms of a pre-existing ideal. They needed always to differentiate themselves both from the sexual radicals of the young generation and from the sexual conservatives of their own.

Millicent Fawcett addressed this question explicitly in a lecture entitled 'Old Ideals of Woman'. In this, she rejected unequivocally the old ideal of womanhood, typified for her by Milton's Eve, whose chief characteristics were her 'softness and sweet attractive grace' and her 'submission'. Such a woman did not meet Fawcett's ideal. For her, 'what is best in the best of women [was] industry, thrift, love of order, love of beauty, power of organisation, helpfulness to the poor, fidelity, strength, kindliness, and the capacity of thinking and speaking wisely.' But she went on to insist that her ideal woman was not 'new': examples of this kind of woman could be found in Shakespeare—in Rosalind or Portia or Cordelia—or even further back in the virtuous woman described in the last chapter of the Book of Proverbs. Thus what Fawcett sought to show was that competing ideals of womanhood had always existed and that the ideal espoused by the mainstream of the women's movement had a long and admirable tradition.[35] As we have seen, she added to this tradition by setting up Joan of Arc as one of her heroines.

While she was careful to disassociate herself from certain 'old ideals' of womanhood, Fawcett could not and did not embrace the dominant fictional 'new woman'. Indeed she attacked this ideal with enormous vehemence. Fawcett's attack on 'new woman' fiction was contained in her well-known review of Grant Allen. In Allen's *The Woman Who Did*, involvement in the suffrage struggle was directly connected to the rejection of marriage and the endorsement of free sexual union. For Fawcett, such a connection was nonsense. She regarded Allen as a writer of great pretensions and little ability, addressing herself to his work only because he 'purports to be writing in support of the enfranchisement of

---

[35] 'Old Ideals of Woman' from a Lecture by Mrs Fawcett, *Woman's Signal*, 7 May 1896, 295.

women'. But she hastened to inform her readers that Grant Allen 'has never given any help by tongue or pen to any practical effort to improve the legal or social status of women. He is not a friend but an enemy, and it is as an enemy that he claims to link together the claim of women to citizenship and social and industrial independence, with attacks upon marriage and the family.'[36]

Fawcett would not countenance any suggestion that marriage in and of itself involved a form of slavery for women—or, more particularly, that sexual union without marriage offered women any advantages or any improvement in status. The revolution in relationships described in *The Woman Who Did* 'would amount in its practical result to libertinage, not to liberty; it would mean the immeasurable degradation of women; it would reduce to anarchy the most momentous of human relationships—the relation between husband and wife and parents and children.'[37] Fawcett believed not only that it was necessary to regulate sexual relationships, but that the demands of women were bringing a better and a higher state in marriage. It was in this higher moral state, with its single moral standard and its new ideal of marriage that Fawcett saw the hope for women.

But the very vehemence of Fawcett's position and the fact that she had to take a stand against sexual licence points to the growing diversity of opinion about sexual questions and especially about women's sexuality evident amongst feminists and feminist sympathizers in the 1890s. As we have seen, there was a growing interest in and support for social purity in the 1880s and 1890s. It was in this decade that Fawcett became active in the National Vigilance Association. This enthusiasm for the social purity movement was a very common phenomenon within the women's movement. Butler had reservations about the punitive approach adopted by social purity activists in this decade, but she, of course, had long been involved with social purity as an issue. Davies, who always refused to discuss sexual questions of any kind, refrained from any involvement or any comment. But she stood virtually alone in this stance. Frances Cobbe attended 'At Homes' held by leading members of the National Vigilance Association, and expressed her

[36] Millicent Garrett Fawcett, 'The Woman Who Did', *Contemporary Review*, 23 (1898), 630.
[37] Ibid.

support for the Association and 'her warm sympathy with what was being done'.[38] She was accompanied on one occasion by Lydia Becker.

Indeed, in its first decade, the National Vigilance Association gained the support of the great majority of women who had been active in the women's movement since the 1850s and 1860s. The enthusiasm of mid-Victorian feminists for the whole social purity movement requires far more attention than it has been given. But what is of particular importance here is the virtual unanimity of mid-Victorian feminists in favour of social purity and the contrast which this offers with the very diverse range of ideas about women's sexuality evident amongst turn-of-the-century feminists.

It is of course clear that social purity, celibacy, and the whole idea of women's need for sexual autonomy were central issues for many late Victorian and Edwardian feminists. Lucy Bland, Sheila Jeffries, and Susan Kingsley Kent have all shown the extent of the concern about women's sexual autonomy amongst feminist novelists and within feminist campaigns.[39] The violation of women, especially in marriage, where they were expected always to meet a husband's sexual demands, was a particular cause of concern. It is interesting to see how the whole focus of feminist concern about venereal diseases shifted at this time away from prostitutes—who were the target of feminist concern in the 1860s and 1870s—and towards wives who were now seen as the innocent victims of diseases given to them by profligate husbands. The risk marriage posed to women's health was an issue taken up by some members of the medical profession and not just by the women's movement, but it certainly occupied an important place within that movement.

But while the treatment of sexual purity and the issue of women's sexual freedom were put forward in a more militant way in the 1890s than ever before, it is also clear that the ideal of women's sexual purity had ceased by the 1890s to be a defining idea of feminism. On the contrary, the whole discussion of women's sexual purity took place alongside a series of feminist demands for women's sexual autonomy, which were anathema to mid-Victorian

[38] Report in *Vigilance Record*, 2, July 1888, 70.
[39] Bland, 'The Married Woman'; Sheila Jeffries, *The Spinster and her Enemies*; and Susan Kingsley Kent, *Sex and Suffrage in Britain, 1860–1914*, Princeton, NJ, 1987.

feminists. It is immediately evident that the whole discussion of sexual relations within marriage was undertaken more openly in the 1890s than before: mid-Victorian feminists had rarely discussed it at all. They had complained about the subordination of women within marriage and hinted at the problems posed to married women by male sexual demands. But they had rarely addressed the question of a wife's sexual autonomy, assuming rather that in allowing women a choice between celibacy and marriage, those women to whom marital ties were repugnant would be able to avoid them. Once excessive male power within marriage was brought to an end, and marriage became genuinely companionate, there was little thought about residual sexual questions.

In the 1890s, by contrast, the very fact of male sexual expectation became an issue for discussion. The need for women to have control of their bodies, to be autonomous, and able to reject even the sexual demands of husbands was an issue explored extensively in feminist fiction. The extent to which marriage involved the giving of women into sexual bondage was another literary theme of the 1890s, taken up by feminist writers who stressed women's right to reject male sexual advances and to retain their bodily integrity. But the other side of this discussion involved women's own sexual desires and the possibility that they might find particular men, even their husbands, sexually unattractive, while desiring others.

Hence the militant demand for sexual autonomy and for an end to women's sexual subjection within marriage came alongside, and indeed as the counterpart to, the assertion from feminists themselves of the need for women to be able to develop their own sexuality and to establish sexual relationships which met their needs.[40] Feminists such as Rebecca West and Olive Schreiner stressed the centrality for women of their sexuality and demanded the kind of freedom for women which would allow them to explore it in different ways and outside the boundaries of marriage. For the first time, birth control and the right of women to separate sexual activity from procreation was asserted as a feminist demand.

These sexual demands were absolutely unacceptable, even unthinkable, for mid-Victorian feminists. They are yet another sign not only of the growing diversity of feminism at this time, but of the assertion by some feminists of views which others would

[40] See Bland, 'The Married Woman', 158–63.

not only reject, but would see as coming from viewpoints totally opposed to their own.

Fawcett herself was very aware that the debate about a 'new woman' who demanded sexual freedom undermined the moral basis of Victorian feminism —and did her best to dissociate feminism from it. But here again, her approach belonged to a bygone era. She managed to demonstrate the enmity to the women's movement of authors such as Grant Allen himself. But she could no more remove the issue of women's sexuality from feminist debate than she could the interests of the Labour movement, and while she remained a pre-eminent figure in the women's movement, her version of feminism was moving further and further away from the centre of intellectual debate and becoming increasingly the basis only for a specific political programme.

III

The late nineteenth century and particularly the first decade of the twentieth brought changes and challenges right into the very centre of the women's movement. Like so many other reform movements, the nineteenth-century English women's movement had worked through private member's bills, petitions, and careful lobbying combined with 'At Homes', drawing-room discussions, and occasional public meetings. This discreet but limited form of campaigning was dramatically altered in the early twentieth century with the start of a militant campaign by the Women's Social and Political Union. Even the 'defensive' militancy of its early years, which Millicent Fawcett often defended, was very different in tenor to the conduct of the nineteenth-century women's suffrage campaign—or to that of the National Union of Women's Suffrage Societies up to that time. The first militant action of Christabel Pankhurst and Annie Kenny, their interruption of a Liberal Party election meeting to ask Sir Edward Grey if he would support a bill to enfranchise women, was a very small act by later standards. But it signalled the start of direct and public feminist intervention in, even confrontation with, the male political sphere. This public intervention in political campaigns had been tried by Josephine Butler in the Contagious Diseases agitation—and sparked a degree of violence similar to that visited on the Women's Social and Political Union. But it had not been a form of activity in which the suffragists engaged, and it was deeply worrying to many of them.

The advent of the militant campaign was the prelude to a whole new way of campaigning through spectacles involving banners, pageants, marches, giant public meetings, massed demonstrations outside Parliament, dramatic symbolic protests such as the chaining of women to the railings outside Westminster, and attacks on property. This new form of campaigning also drew on the earlier model offered by the Contagious Diseases agitation and the American temperance movement by focusing public attention on women's femininity at the very moment that they were emerging into the public world and demanding change. Josephine Butler had been very taken by the power which women could gain from emphasizing their purity and their domestic concerns in public. The spectacle of the silent female vigil outside a brothel, undertaken by women wearing white, was one she saw as guaranteed to gain attention to their message. It was not just chastity and purity which were emphasized in suffrage demonstrations: the Pankhursts always insisted that women be smartly dressed and not dowdy, that their clothes be fashionable and well cared for. But here, as in the pageants or marches in which women wore national costume, it was still their femininity which was being stressed.

The new kind of suffrage campaign drew on large-scale organizations, requiring unprecedented amounts of money and careful planning. It produced a whole range of new art works and artefacts and was accompanied by the production of suffrage plays, novels, and songs. It resulted in massive publicity, making the whole women's movement newsworthy as it had never been before. The agitation against the Contagious Diseases Acts had been talked about, but it was nowhere near as prominent in the public mind as was the revived suffrage campaign, especially after 1905.

As the militant campaign and the revival in the constitutionalist campaign did not occur until the early twentieth century, there were fewer survivors of the mid-Victorian women's movement to witness it than had been the case in regard to the 'new woman' debate. Butler and Cobbe both lived to see the emergence of the Women's Social and Political Union in 1903, but they died before the militant campaign was really under way. It was Davies and

Fawcett who had to find some way of accommodating the campaigns of a new generation.

For Emily Davies, there was no real possibility of accepting or coming to terms with the new suffrage campaign. Not only was Davies unable to condone the militants, she was unhappy even with the moderate campaign run by Millicent Fawcett and the National Union of Women's Suffrage Societies. As we have seen, Davies withdrew from the suffrage movement in the 1860s and did not resume her activity within it until 1888, by which time Girton College was established and hence could not be harmed by her being associated with the suffrage. In that year, she joined the London National Society for Women's Suffrage. Within a few years, she had become a member of its executive committee and was a prominent figure in its activities.

Davies's age and renown ensured that she would immediately assume a prominent place in the suffrage movement. She was an ideal person to lead deputations to Members of Parliament—and of course this kind of campaigning was the sort of which she most approved. Davies led several suffrage deputations to the Prime Minister through the late 1890s and the early years of the twentieth century. In addition, she addressed public and private meetings, wrote constant letters to newspapers, and published brief articles explaining to Girton students why they should become involved in the suffrage struggle. Their education, in Davies's view, made them precisely the people who should speak and write on behalf of the movement.

But while very happy to add her name and prestige to the suffrage movement, Davies was increasingly unhappy about various developments within it. Her ideas on what women's suffrage meant and on how suffrage campaigns should be undertaken had not changed at all since the 1860s. She circulated petitions amongst her women friends and colleagues, again trying to get the names of influential and respected men and women who supported the cause. She also sent a constant stream of letters seeking the active help of prominent Members of Parliament. Davies was quite prepared to write to Liberal MPs, but as ever her heart lay with the Conservative Party. In her spare time, she took steps to establish a Conservative suffrage tradition—beginning with Disraeli and showing him as the first Member of Parliament publicly to suggest that there should be women's suffrage.[41] Unfortunately for Davies, this endeavour was not entirely welcomed by the Tories, many of whom had little sympathy with women's suffrage.

Davies's approach had little impact at a time when the whole suffrage movement was being transformed by the establishment of large organizations using novel tactics to maximize their public exposure and she did recognize that this was so. Although she opposed the formation of the National Union of Women's Suffrage Societies in 1897, preferring, as she had in the 1860s, to work on a smaller scale and through a committee she knew and trusted, she did her best to work with it, once it was formed. Thus she appeared at the monster demonstration of June 1908, marching from the embankment to the Albert Hall in the cap and gown she was entitled to as the holder of an honorary LL.D. from Glasgow. At the Albert Hall, she sat on the platform in full public gaze.

But while she could countenance some expansion of the suffrage campaign, the advent of the militant Women's Social and Political Union filled Davies with horror. When Millicent Fawcett, who supported the militants in what she saw as the defensive part of their campaign, arranged a banquet to celebrate the release of the first group of militants who were imprisoned, Davies wrote to rebuke her, insisting that Fawcett was both wrong and misguided. She did her best to ensure that meetings of the London Society avoided any expression of sympathy or support for the imprisoned militants and wrote letters and pamphlets attempting to dissociate 'the great body of Suffragists' from the unworthy actions of a small but noisy minority. While she supported some of the actions of the National Union of Women's Suffrage Societies, she objected to it becoming involved with other sections of the suffrage movement. She expressed strong opposition to the participation of the National Union in the giant Women's Coronation Procession planned by the Women's Social and Political Union for June 1911 and tried, unsuccessfully, to dissuade the executive of the National Union from joining it.[42]

---

[41] See Davies Papers, ED XXI/24a.

[42] For a fascinating discussion of this procession, see Lisa Tickner, *The Spectacle of Women: Imagery of the Suffrage Campaign, 1907–1914*, London, 1987, 122–31. See also Emily Davies to Edith Palisser, 29 Oct. 1900, Fawcett Library Autograph Collection.

But it was not only the militants who were engaging in activities of which Davies strongly disapproved. Many of the suffragists held political and social beliefs by which she was appalled. While Davies was trying to strengthen the ties between suffragists and the Conservative Party, some of her younger colleagues were working to establish a connection between the National Union and the Labour Party. When their work was finally successful, through the setting up of the Electoral Fighting Fund in 1911, Davies felt unable to continue her membership of the London Society for Women's Suffrage. She resigned—and found a place more to her taste in the Conservative and Unionist Women's Franchise Association.

Where Davies found herself quite unable to cope either with the new national political framework for women's suffrage or with the new methods of large-scale demonstrations, Fawcett showed to the full her great capacity as a leader by her ability to adapt to and work with these new developments.[43] Although many of Fawcett's friends and colleagues were apprehensive about the formation of the Women's Social and Political Union, she made very clear her own awareness that the start of the militant campaign was very beneficial for the constitutionalists. From the moment that the first arrests of members of the WSPU occurred, there was a boom in women's suffrage. 'New members are pouring into the societies, demands for literature come by every post and cheques and banknotes flow into the treasury.'[44] Fawcett indicated her sense of obligation and her endorsement of the WSPU by holding a banquet to greet some of the militants when they were released from prison.

Sylvia Pankhurst noted somewhat acidly that Fawcett did not ever give a banquet for Emmeline or Christabel Pankhurst, choosing instead to fête lesser lights in the WSPU, including her close friend Annie Cobden Sanderson.[45] But for all this, it is clear that Fawcett made far more effort to work with the Pankhursts than they did to work with her. She learnt from and applied some of their tactics, encouraging the organization of huge demonstrations accompanied by pageantry and spectacle within the National

[43] This view of Fawcett is endorsed in a number of recent studies. See e.g. Liddington and Norris, *One Hand Tied Behind Us*, 13; Sandra Holton, *Feminism and Democracy: Women's Suffrage and Reform Politics in Britain, 1900–1918*, Cambridge, 1986, 32.

[44] Quoted in Holton, *Feminism and Democracy*, 38.

[45] Sylvia Pankhurst, *The Suffragette Movement*, London, 1931 (repr. 1977), 27.

Union. She attempted to organize joint demonstrations with the militants, defended their activities, and attacked their treatment by the Government until the militants began seriously to threaten public order by advocating violence and by attacking property in 1909.[46] Fawcett did not go as far as her sister Elizabeth in participating in militant demonstrations, but she certainly recognized their power and their public appeal. She could not and did not condone their acts of arson or of violence, criticizing them strongly for lawlessness and deploring their outlook as well as their tactics—but she rarely omitted to state her belief that it was the Government and not the militants which was really at fault.

Fawcett welcomed many of the new developments in the suffrage campaign, even if they were attached to political groups with whom she did not sympathize. Hence she championed the radical suffragists and helped them to survive. In the early years of the twentieth century, a group of radical suffragists in the Lancashire Women's Textile Workers Representative Committee attempted to organize their own suffrage campaign in which they emphasized the importance of the suffrage for working women. One of their persistent problems was lack of funds. They split both from the North of England Society for Women's Suffrage and from the Women's Social and Political Union and hence were dependent on the very small amounts which their working-class supporters could give them. At a point where it seemed questionable as to whether or not they could continue, Fawcett came to their aid donating £20 to them personally. At the same time, the National Union donated more than £100 as well as offering employment to several of the leading members of the Lancashire Representation Committee as paid organizers.[47]

This was not Fawcett's only entry into the world of Labour politics. A few years after their involvement with the Lancashire women began, the National Union formally entered into its electoral alliance with the Labour Party by setting up the Electoral Fighting Fund of which Fawcett was the president. But as her followers soon came to realize, her preparedness to work with the Labour Party or with the Labour movement were indications of

---

[46] For an excellent discussion of the relationship between the militants and the constitutionalists, see Holton, *Feminism and Democracy*, 29–52.

[47] Liddington and Norris, *One Hand Tied Behind Us*, 212.

her extreme pragmatism and not a sign that she was changing her own political framework and outlook. Fawcett always insisted on the non-party basis of the suffrage movement—and managed at the same time to provide different arguments as to why it should be supported, depending on whether her audience was Liberal, Conservative, or Labour. Hence she accepted what she saw as a temporary alliance with the Labour Party because it was the only one which had formally committed itself to the support of women's suffrage.

Her pragmatism and her political skills enabled Fawcett to adapt to the changes of the early twentieth century and to supervise monumental changes within the National Union as it was transformed from a small group of suffrage societies into a genuinely national body with well over two hundred local branches organized into a number of local federations. Her success and her stature as a leader was accepted by all her followers. But even she could not entirely cope with the growing diversity of outlook and approach evident within her own suffrage organization. One of her great skills as a leader was her capacity to delegate to trusted lieutenants and to follow their suggestions where appropriate. Hence, as Sandra Holton has shown, while Fawcett was not whole-heartedly in favour of an electoral alliance with the Labour Party, she saw the need for such an alliance if the National Union was to continue to have an effective voice in the political arena. But she left the negotiation of this alliance to the younger women who were most deeply committed to it: Catherine Marshall, Margaret Robertson and Kathleen Courtney. These women did not share Fawcett's nineteenth-century liberal outlook. They were leaders amongst the 'democratic suffragists' for whom the question of women's suffrage was necessarily tied to a demand for universal suffrage and for proper representation for workers.

The federated structure of the National Union of Women's Suffrage Societies allowed for considerable autonomy of local branches and hence for considerable diversity. It enabled Fawcett to hold together a diverse movement until the outbreak of the First World War. At that point, the differences in overall political outlook within the movement and the divergences between her views and those of a powerful group of the younger women on her national executive became too great to be contained.

When war began, Fawcett's pragmatism and her political skills were very evident. The National Union agreed to suspend suffrage agitation during the War and to devote itself instead to relief work. In this way, it was able simultaneously to support the war effort—and to keep its organization intact. It suspended direct suffrage campaigning but continued to keep a close watch both on the economic situation of women and on political developments which affected them. But while Fawcett's strategy was very effective, it failed to do one thing which she had attempted, namely to hold the National Union together. Fawcett herself was an ardent patriot for whom the rightness of the British cause was self-evident. In the First World War, as in the Boer War, she had no patience with those who questioned the Government or its policies. But there were several women who were members of the national executive who did just that. There was a substantial group within the executive of the National Union who were pronounced pacifists and who rejected the idea of giving any support to the war effort.[48] Many of them had moreover regarded the alliance between the National Union of Women's Suffrage Societies and the Labour Party not as a temporary expedient, but as a statement of the fundamental political sympathies of the National Union. Fawcett pressed her views and kept the National Union on her chosen course. But as a consequence several leading figures resigned from the executive and left the National Union of Women's Suffrage Societies altogether. Amongst them were Kathleen Courtney, the secretary of the National Union of Women's Suffrage Societies, Catherine Marshall, then secretary of the Electoral Fighting Fund and Helena Swanwick, long-time editor of the *Common Cause*.

This split with many of her closest lieutenants showed very clearly how distant Fawcett's broad political assumptions were from the new generation of leaders of the women's movement. This distance was shown even more clearly after the war when, in 1925, under the leadership of Eleanor Rathbone, the National Union of Societies for Equal Citizenship, the successor to the National Union of Women's Suffrage Societies,[49] formally gave its support to family allowances. Fawcett spoke against the endorse-

[48] Jo Vellacot Newbury, 'Anti-War Suffragists', *History*, 62 (1977), 411–25.

[49] In 1919, the National Union of Suffrage Societies changed its name to the National Union of Societies for Equal Citizenship.

ment of family allowances at the Annual Council of the National
Union, explaining her fears that 'a system of Family Allowances
would undermine the sense of parental responsibility', but to no
avail.[50] As a result, Fawcett resigned her position as Chairman (*sic*)
of the Board of Directors of the *Woman's Leader*, the weekly paper
attached to the National Union of Societies for Equal Citizenship.
She did so with deep regret, but in the belief that she could not
'continue to be in any degree responsible for a paper which is now
bound to advocate an economic change of great importance of
which I entirely disapprove'.[51] Fawcett herself had long recognized
this growing distance. She had worked throughout the War,
helping to ensure that the question of women's suffrage was not
entirely forgotten and that the victorious end of the War was
accompanied by 'the great victory also for the cause of women's
freedom'. But once that was achieved, she had resigned her presi-
dency, explaining that 'the time has come when younger women
should lead the National Union'. Her resignation signalled finally
the end of Victorian feminism.

[50] 'Women in Council', *Woman's Leader*, 20 Mar. 1925, 61.
[51] 'Dame Millicent', *Woman's Leader*, 10 Apr. 1925, 84.

Bibliography

UNPUBLISHED PAPERS

The Butler Papers, Fawcett Library, City of London Polytechnic, London.
The Bodichon Papers, Girton College Archives, Cambridge.
The Davies Papers, Girton College Archives, Cambridge.
The Fawcett Papers, Fawcett Library, City of London Polytechnic, London.
The Cobbe Papers, Huntington Library, Los Angeles.
Papers of the National Union of Women's Suffrage Societies, Manchester Public Library [NUWSS].
Autograph Collection of Letters, Fawcett Library, City of London Polytechnic, London.
Somerville Papers, Bodleian Library, Oxford.

JOURNALS

Englishwoman's Journal.
Journal of the Vigilance Association for the Defence of Personal Rights.
Shield.
Woman's Signal.
Women's Suffrage Journal.

BOOKS AND ARTICLES

ABRAY, JANE, 'Feminism in the French Revolution', in *American Historical Review*, 80 (1975), 43–62.
ANNAS, JULIA, 'Mill and the Subjection of Women', *Philosophy*, 5 (1977), 179–94.
Anon, *Woman as She is, and as She Should Be*, London, 1835.
Anon, 'The New Woman', 29 Nov. 1894, *Woman's Signal*, 345.
Anon, 'More New Women', *Woman's Signal*, 25 Feb. 1897, 118.
ARMSTRONG, ISOBEL, ed., *The Major Victorian Poets: Reconsiderations*, London, 1969.

AUERBACH, NINA, *Woman and the Demon: The Life of a Victorian Myth*, Cambridge, Mass., and London, 1982.

BANKS, J. A. and OLIVE, *Feminism and Family Planning*, Liverpool, 1964.

BANKS, OLIVE, *Becoming a Feminist: The Social Origins of 'First Wave' Feminism*, Brighton, 1986.

——*Faces of Feminism: A Study of Feminism as a Social Movement*, Oxford, 1986.

BARRY, WILLIAM, 'The Strike of a Sex', *Quarterly Review*, 179 (1894), 289–318.

BASCH, FRANCOISE, *Relative Creatures: Victorian Women in Society and the Novel*, New York, 1984.

BAUER, CAROL, and LAWRENCE RITT, '"A Husband is a Beating Animal"—Frances Power Cobbe Confronts the Wife-Abuse Problem in Victorian England', *International Journal of Women's Studies*, 6 (1983), 99–118.

BENNETT, DAPHNE, *Emily Davies and the Liberation of Women*, London, 1989.

BLACK, NAOMI, *Social Feminism*, Ithaca, NY, and London, 1989.

BLACKBURN, HELEN, *Women's Suffrage*, London, 1902.

——and NORA VIGNE, *Women Under the Factory Acts*, London, 1903.

BLEASE, W. LYON, *Emancipation of English Women*, London, 1910.

BOUCHERET, JESSIE, HELEN BLACKBURN *et al.*, *The Condition of Women and the Factory Acts*, London, 1886.

BRADBROOK, MURIEL, *'That Infidel Place': A Short History of Girton College*, London, 1969.

BRENNAN, T., and C. PATEMAN, '"Mere Auxiliaires to the Commonwealth": Women and the Origins of Liberalism', *Political Studies*, 27 (1979), 183–200.

BRIDENTHAL, RENATA, and CLAUDIA KOONZ, eds., *Becoming Visible: Women in European History*, Boston, 1977.

BRISTOW, EDWARD J., *Vice and Vigilance: Social Purity Campaigns in England, 1700–1900*, Dublin, 1977.

BROWN, L. W., 'Jane Austen and the Feminist Tradition', *Nineteenth Century Fiction*, 28 (1973), 321–8.

BURGON, J. W., BD, *A Sermon Preached before the University of Oxford, June 8, 1884*, London, 1884.

BURMAN, SANDRA, ed., *Fit Work for Women*, London and Canberra, 1979.

BURTON, EMILY, 'The New Woman: Ideal and Reality', *Woman's Signal*, 30 Apr. 1896, 296.

BURTON, HESTER, *Barbara Bodichon*, London, 1949.

BUTLER, A. S. G., *Portrait of Josephine Butler*, London, 1954.

BUTLER, JOSEPHINE E., *The Education and Employment of Women*, London, 1868.

—— ed., *Woman's Work and Woman's Culture*, London, 1869.

—— *Memoir of John Grey of Dilston*, Edinburgh, 1869.

—— *Some Thoughts on the Present Aspect of the Crusade against the State Regulation of Vice*, Liverpool, 1874.

—— *Government by Police*, London, 1879.

—— *Our Christianity Tested by the Irish Question*, London, 1887.

—— *Sursum Corda: Annual Address to the Ladies' National Association*, Liverpool, 1891.

—— *Recollections of George Butler*, Bristol, 1892.

—— *Personal Reminiscences of A Great Crusade*, London, 1896.

—— *The Native Races and the War*, London, 1900.

—— *In Memoriam: Harriet Meuricoffre*, London, 1901.

—— *An Autobiographical Memoir*, ed. George and Lucy Johnson, Bristol, 1909.

—— *et al.*, *Legislative Restrictions on the Industry of Women, Considered from the Women's Point of View*, London, n.d.

CAINE, BARBARA, 'John Stuart Mill and the English Women's Movement', *Historical Studies* (1978), 52–67.

—— 'Feminism, Suffrage and the Nineteenth-Century English Women's Movement', *Women's Studies International Forum*, 5 (1982), 537–50.

—— 'From a "fair field and no favour" to Equal Employment Opportunity', *Refractory Girl*, 30 (1987), 36–40.

—— E. A. Grosz, Marie de Lepervanche, *Crossing Boundaries: Feminisms and the Critique of Knowledges*, Sydney, 1988.

CARR, CORNELIA, ed., *Harriet Hosmer: Letters and Memories*, London, 1913.

COBBE, FRANCES POWER, *Theory of Intuitive Morals*, London, 1858.

—— 'Celibacy v. Marriage', *Fraser's Magazine*, 65 (1862), 228–35.

—— *Friendless Girls and How to Help Them. Being an Account of the Preventive Mission at Bristol*, Paper read at the NAPSS Congress in 1861, London, 1862.

—— 'Female Charity—Lay and Monastic', *Fraser's Magazine*, 66 (1862), 774–88.

—— 'What Shall We Do with our Old Maids?', *Fraser's Magazine*, 65 (1862), 594–606.

—— *Essays on the Pursuits of Women*, London, 1863.

—— ed., *The Collected Works of Theodore Parker*, London, 1863.

—— 'Self-Development and Self-Abnegation', in *Studies New and Old of Ethical and Social Subjects*, London, 1865, 65–85.

—— 'Woman's Work in the Church', *Theological Review*, 2 (1865), 505–21.

—— 'The Final Cause of Woman', in *Woman's Work and Woman's Culture*, ed. Josephine Butler, London, 1869, 1–26.

—— *Darwinism in Morals and Other Essays*, London, 1872.

—— 'The Fitness of Women for the Ministry', *Theological Review*, 13 (1876), 239–73.

—— *Re-echoes*, London, 1876.

—— 'Wife Torture in England', *Contemporary Review*, 23 (1878), 56–87.

—— 'The Little Health of Ladies', *Contemporary Review*, 31 (1878), 276–96.

—— 'The Medical Profession and its Morality', *Modern Review*, 2 (1881), 630–50.

—— *The Duties of Women*, London, 1881.

—— *The Life of Frances Power Cobbe*, 2 vols., London, 1894.

COTT, NANCY, *The Grounding of Modern Feminism*, New Haven, Conn., and London, 1987.

DAVIDOFF LEONORE, and CATHERINE HALL, *Family Fortunes: Men and Women of the English Middle Class 1780–1850*, London, 1987.

DAVIES, EMILY, *The Higher Education of Women*, London, 1866 (repr. London, 1988).

—— 'The Women's Suffrage Movement', Central Society for Women's Suffrage, 1906, reprinted from *Girton Review*, 1905.

—— *Thoughts on Some Questions Relating to Women*, London, 1910.

DAVIN, ANNA, 'Imperialism and Motherhood', *History Workshop*, 5 (1978).

DAVIS, T., *et al.*, 'The Public Face of Feminism: Early Twentieth Century Writing on Women's Suffrage', in *Making Histories: Studies in History Writing and Politics*, ed. R. Johnson *et al.*, Birmingham, 1983.

DELAMONT, SARA and LORNA DUFFIN, eds., *The Nineteenth Century Woman: Her Cultural and Physical World*, London, 1978.

DYHOUSE, CAROLE, *Girls Growing up in Late Victorian and Edwardian England*, London, 1981.

EISENSTEIN, ZILLAH, *The Radical Future of Liberal Feminism*, New York, 1981.

ELLIS, SARAH, *The Wives of England: Their Relative Duties, Domestic Influence and Social Obligations*, London, 1844.

—— *The Daughters of England*, London, 1845.

EVANS, RICHARD, *The Feminists: Women's Emancipation Movements in Europe*, London, 1978.

FADERMAN, LILIAN, *Surpassing Love of Men*, London, 1980.

FAWCETT, MILLICENT GARRETT, 'The Uses of Higher Education to Women', *Contemporary Review*, 50 (1866), 719–27.

—— 'The Medical and General Education of Women', *Fortnightly Review*, 4 (1868), 554–71.

—— *Janet Doncaster*, London, 1875.

—— 'The Future of English Women: A Reply', *Nineteenth Century*, 4 (1878), 347–57.

—— 'Speech or Silence', *Contemporary Review*, 48 (1885), 326–31.

—— 'The Emancipation of Women', *Fortnightly Review*, NS 50 (1891), 672–85.

—— *The New Rules for Dealing with the Sanitary Condition of the British Army*, Speech made at the Croydon Meeting of the National Union of Women Workers, Oct. 1897, London, 1898.

—— 'The Women's Suffrage Movement', in *The Woman Question in Europe*, ed. T. Stanton, London, 1888, 1–6.

—— 'The Appeal against Female Suffrage: A Reply', *Nineteenth Century*, (1889), 86–96.

—— 'Women's Suffrage', speech made at the Annual Conference of National Union of Women Workers, Oct. 1896, *National Union of Women Workers Annual Report for 1896*, London, 1897.

—— ed., *A Vindication of the Rights of Woman* by Mary Wollstonecraft, new edn., London, 1891.

—— 'Mr Sidney Webb's Article on Women's Wages', *Economic Journal*, 2 (1892).

—— 'Old Ideals of Woman', *Woman's Signal*, 7 May 1896.

—— 'The Woman Who Did', *Contemporary Review*, 23 (1898).

—— *Five Famous French Women*, London, 1908.

—— *Joan of Arc*, NUWSS, London, 1912.

—— 'Home and Politics, An Address delivered at Toynbee Hall and Elsewhere', Central and East of England Society for Women's Suffrage, n.d.

—— *What I Remember*, London, 1925.

—— and E. M. TURNER, *Josephine Butler: Her Work and Principles, and their Meaning for the Twentieth Century*, London, 1927.

FERGUSON, MOIRA, *First Feminists: British Women Writers, 1578–1799*, Bloomington, Ind., 1975.

FEURER, ROSEMARY, 'The Meaning of "Sisterhood": The British Women's Movement and Protective Legislation, 1870–1900', *Victorian Studies*, 31 (1988), 233–60.

FLETCHER, SHEILA, *Feminists and Bureaucrats: A Study in the Development of Girls' Education in the Nineteenth Century*, Cambridge, 1980.

—— *Maude Royden*, Oxford, 1989.

FORSTER, MARGARET, *Significant Sisters: The Grassroots of Active Feminism 1839–1939*, Harmondsworth, Middx., 1986.

FRAISSE, GENEVIEVE, 'The Form of Historical Feminism', *m/f*, 10 (1985), 6–11.

FRENCH, RICHARD D., *Antivivisection and Medical Science in Victorian Society*, Princeton, NJ, 1975.

GASKELL, ELIZABETH, *Ruth*, London, 1852 (repr. London, 1978).

GATES, M. LE, 'The Cult of Womanhood in Eighteenth Century Thought', *Eighteenth Century Studies*, 10 (1976), 21–3.

GERARD, JESSICA, 'Lady Bountiful: Women of the Landed Class and Rural Philanthropy', *Victorian Studies*, 30 (1987), 183–211.

GISSING, GEORGE, *The Odd Women*, London, 1893.

GORHAM, DEBORAH, 'The "Maiden Tribute of Modern Babylon" Reexamined: Child Prostitution and the Idea of Childhood in Late Victorian England', *Victorian Studies*, 21 (1978), 353–79.

HALL, CATHERINE, 'The Early Formation of Victorian Domestic Ideology', in Sandra Burman (ed.), *Fit Work for Women*, London and Canberra, 1979.

HAMILTON, CICELY, *Marriage as a Trade*, London, 1909 (repr. London, 1981).

HAMMERTON, J. A., *Emigrant Gentlewomen: Genteel Poverty and Female Emigration, 1830–1919*, London, 1978.

HARDY, THOMAS, *Jude the Obscure*, London, 1895.

HARRISON, BRIAN, *Separate Spheres: The Opposition to Women's Suffrage in Britain*, London, 1978.

HARRISON, FREDERICK, 'The Emancipation of Women', *Fortnightly Review*, NS, 50 (1891), 437–51.

HARTMANN, HEIDI, 'Capitalism, Patriarchy and Job Segregation by Sex', in *Capitalist Patriarchy and the Case for Socialist Feminism*, ed. Zillah Eisenstein, New York, 1981.

HELPS, ARTHUR, *Friends in Council: A Series of Readings and Discourses Thereon*, London, 1854, 2 vols.

HERSTEIN, SHEILA R., *A Mid-Victorian Feminist: Barbara Leigh Smith Bodichon*, New Haven, Conn., 1986.

HILL, BRIDGET, ed., *The First English Feminist: The Writings of Mary Astell*, London, 1987.

HOLLIS, PATRICIA, *Women in Public. The English Women's Movement, 1850–1900*, London, 1979.

——*Ladies Elect. Women in English Local Government 1865–1914*, Oxford, 1987.

HOLTON, SANDRA, *Feminism and Democracy: Women's Suffrage and Reform Politics in Britain, 1900–1918*, Cambridge, 1986.

HOUGHTON, WALTER, *The Victorian Frame of Mind*, New Haven, Conn., 1957.

HUDSON, GERTRUDE REESE, ed., *Browning to His American Friends: Letters between the Brownings, the Storys and James Russell Lowell*, London, 1965.

HUME, LESLIE PARKER, *The National Union of Women's Suffrage Societies*, New York, 1982.

HUNT, FELICITY, ed., *Lessons for Life: the Schooling of Girls and Women, 1850–1950*, Oxford, 1987.

HUTCHINS, B. L., and A. HARRISON, *A History of Factory Legislation*, London, 1911.

HUXLEY, LEONARD, ed., *Elizabeth Barrett Browning: Letters to her Sisters, 1846–59*, London, 1932.

JAMES, R. M., 'On the Reception of Mary Wollstonecraft's *A Vindication of the Rights of Woman*', *Journal of the History of Ideas*, 39 (1978), 293–302.

JEFFRIES, SHEILA, *The Spinster and her Enemies: Feminism and Sexuality 1880–1930*, London, 1985.

JORDAN, ELLEN, 'The Christening of the New Woman', *Victorian Newsletter*, 63 (1983), 19–20.

JORDANOVA, LUDMILLA, *Sexual Visions*, London, 1990.

KAMM, JOSEPHINE, *Hope Deferred: Girls' Education in English History*, London, 1965.

——*Rapiers and Battleaxes: The Women's Movement and its Aftermath*, London, 1966.

KAPLAN, CORA, *Sea Changes: Essays on Culture and Feminism*, London, 1986.

KENT, SUSAN KINGSLEY, *Sex and Suffrage in Britain, 1860–1914*, Princeton, NJ, 1987.

KESSLER-HARRIS, ALICE, *Out to Work: A History of Wage-Earning Women in the United States*, New York, 1982.

KILHAM, JOHN, *Tennyson and The Princess: Reflections of an Age*, London, 1958.

KINNAIRD, JOAN, 'Mary Astell and the Conservative Contribution to English Feminism', *Journal of British Studies*, 19 (1979), 53–75.

KINZER, BRUCE, ed., *The Gladstonian Turn of Mind: Essays Presented to J. B. Conacher*, Toronto, 1985.

KIRKHAM, MARGARET, *Jane Austen: Feminism and Fiction*, Brighton and Princeton, NJ, 1983.

LACEY, CANDIDA, ed., *Barbara Leigh Smith Bodichon and the Langham Place Group*, London and New York, 1987.

LANSBURY, CORAL, 'Gynaecology, Pornography and the Anti-vivisection Movement', *Victorian Studies*, 28 (1985), 413–38.

LANTA, M., 'Jane Austen's Feminism. An Original Response to Convention', *Critical Quarterly*, 23 (1981), 27–36.

LEVENTHAL, F. M., *The Last Dissenter: H. N. Brailsford and His World*, Oxford, 1985.

LEVINE, PHILIPPA, *Victorian Feminism, 1850–1900*, London, 1987.

LEWIS, JANE, *The Politics of Motherhood*, London, 1980.

——ed., *Before the Vote was Won: Arguments For and Against Women's Suffrage*, London, 1987.

LIDDINGTON, JILL, *The Life and Times of a Respectable Rebel: Selina Cooper*, London, 1984.

——and JILL NORRIS, *One Hand Tied Behind Us: The Rise of the Women's Suffrage Movement*, London, 1978.

LLOYD, GENEVIEVE, *The Man of Reason*, Sydney and London, 1986.

LURIA, GINA, ed., *The Feminist Controversy in England, 1788–1810*, New York, 1974.

MANTON, JO., *Elizabeth Garrett Anderson*, London, 1965.

MAPPEN, ELLEN, ed., *Helping Women at Work: The Women's Industrial Council 1889–1914*, London, 1985.

MCWILLIAMS-TULLBERG, RITA, *Women at Cambridge: A Men's University—Though of a Mixed Type*, London, 1975.

MENNELL, JAMES E., 'The Politics of Frustration: "The Maiden Tribute of Modern Babylon" and the Morality Movement of 1885', *North Dakota Quarterly*, 49 (1981), 68–80.

MILL, JOHN STUART, *The Subjection of Women*, London, 1869, repr. in John Stuart Mill and Harriet Taylor Mill, *Essays on Sex Equality*, ed. Alice S. Rossi, Chicago, 1970.

MINEKA, FRANCES, and DWIGHT LINDLEY, eds., *The Later Letters of John Stuart Mill, 1849–1873*, London, 1972.

MITCHELL, JULIET, and ANN OAKLEY, eds., *What is Feminism?*, Oxford, 1986.

MOERS, ELLEN, *Literary Women*, New York, 1976.

MORLEY, ANN, and LIZ STANLEY, *The Life and Death of Emily Wilding Davison*, London, 1989.

MOYNIHAM, R. D., 'Clarissa and the Enlightened Woman as Literary Heroine', *Journal of the History of Ideas*, 36 (1975), 159–66.

OAKLEY, ANN, 'Millicent Garrett Fawcett: Duty and Determination', in *Feminist Theorists: Three Centuries of Women's Intellectual Traditions*, ed. Dale Spender, London, 1983.

OFFEN, KAREN, 'Defining Feminism: A Comparative Historical Approach', *Signs*, 14 (1988), 119–57.

OKIN, SUSAN MOLLER, *Women in Western Political Thought*, London, 1980.

PARKES, BESSIE RAYNOR, 'A Year's Experience in Women's Work', *Transactions of the National Association for the Promotion of Social Science*, London, 1858.

PATEMAN, CAROLE, *The Sexual Contract*, Oxford, 1988.

PEDERSON, JOYCE SENDERS, 'Some Victorian Headmistresses: A Conservative Tradition of Social Reform', *Victorian Studies*, 24 (1981), 463–88.

PERRY, RUTH, *The Celebrated Mary Astell. An Early English Feminist*, Chicago and London, 1986.

PETRIE, GLEN, *A Singular Iniquity. The Campaigns of Josephine Butler*, London, 1971.

POOVEY, MARY, *Uneven Developments. The Ideology of Gender in Mid-Victorian England*, Chicago, 1988.

PROCHASKA, F. K., *Women and Philanthropy in Nineteenth Century England*, Oxford, 1980.

PUGH, EVELYN L., 'John Stuart Mill and the Women's Question in Parliament, 1865–1868', *Historian*, 42 (1980), 399–418.

RAMELSON, MIRIAM, *The Petticoat Rebellion*, London, 1967.

RENDALL, JANE, *The Origins of Modern Feminism: Women in Britain, France and the United States*, Basingstoke, 1985.

—— *Equal or Different: Women's Politics 1800–1914*, Oxford, 1987.

Report of the Conference of the Association for the Defence of Personal Rights, 14 Nov. 1871, Manchester, 1871.

Report of the Married Women's Property Committee. Presented at the Final Meeting of their Friends and Subscribers, Nov. 1882, Manchester, 1882.

Report on the Concentration Camps in South Africa by the Committee of Ladies appointed by the Secretary of State for War containing Reports on the Camps in Natal, the Orange River Colony and the Transvaal, London, 1902.

ROSEN, ANDREW, *Rise Up Women*, London, 1974.

ROVER, CONSTANCE, *Women's Suffrage and Party Politics in Britain, 1866–1914*, London, 1967.

RUBINSTEIN, DAVID, *Before the Suffragettes: Women's Emancipation in the 1890s*, Brighton, 1986.

RUSKIN, JOHN, *Sesame and Lilies*, London, 1891.

SANDFORD, JOHN, Mrs., *Woman in Her Social and Domestic Character*, London, 1831.

SCHEIBINGER, LONDA, 'Skeletons in the Closet: The First Illustrations of the Female Skeleton in Eighteenth Century Anatomy', in *Representations*, 14 (1986), 42–82.

SCOTT, JOAN, 'Deconstructing Equality-versus-Difference: Or the Uses of Poststructuralist Theory for Feminism', *Feminist Studies*, 14 (1988).

SHOWALTER, ELAINE, *A Literature of Their Own: British Women Novelists from Brontë to Lessing*, Princeton, NJ, 1977.

SKLAR, KATHRYN KISH, *Catherine Beecher: A Study in American Domesticity*, New Haven, Conn., 1974.

SMITH-ROSENBERG, CAROLL, 'The Female World of Love and Ritual: Relations Between Women in Nineteenth-Century America', *Signs*, 1 (1973), 58–72.

SOLDON, NORBERT, *Women in British Trade Unions*, Dublin, 1978.

SOMERSET, ISOBEL, 'The Woman Who—Didn't', *Woman's Signal*, 28 Mar. 1895.

SPENCER, SAMIA, ed., *French Women and the Age of Enlightenment*, Bloomington, Ind., 1984.

SPENDER, DALE, *Women of Ideas and What Men Have Done to Them From Aphra Behn to Adrienne Rich*, London, 1983.

——ed., *Feminist Theorists: Three Centuries of Women's Intellectual Traditions*, London, 1983.

SPIES, S. B., *Methods of Barbarism: Robertson and Kitchener and Civilians in the Boer Republic, January 1900–May 1902*, Cape Town, 1976.

ST JOHN PACKE, MICHAEL, *The Life of John Stuart Mill*, London, 1954.

STANTON, THEODORE, ed., *The Woman Question in Europe*, London, 1884.

——*Reminiscences of Rosa Bonheur*, New York, 1910.

STEBBINS, EMMA, ed., *Charlotte Cushman: Her Letters and Memories of Her Life*, Boston, 1912.

STEPHEN, BARBARA, *Emily Davies and Girton College*, London, 1927.

STRACHEY, RAY, *The Cause: A Short History of the Women's Movement in Great Britain*, London, 1928 (repr. London, 1978).

——*Millicent Garrett Fawcett*, London, 1931.

STUBBS, PATRICIA, *Women and Fiction: Feminism and the Novel 1880–1920*, Brighton, 1979.

SUMMERS, ANNE, 'A Home from Home—Women's Philanthropic Work in the Nineteenth Century', in Sandra Burman, ed., *Fit Work for Women*, London and Canberra, 1979.

TAYLOR, BARBARA, *Eve and the New Jerusalem: Socialism and Feminism in the Nineteenth Century*, London, 1983.

TICKNER, LISA, *The Spectacle of Women: Imagery of the Suffrage Campaign, 1907–1914*, London, 1987.

UGLOW, JENNIE, 'Josephine Butler: From Sympathy to Theory', in

Dale Spender, ed., *Feminist Theorists: Three Centuries of Women's Intellectual Traditions*, London, 1983.

VALENZE, DEBORAH M., *Prophetic Sons and Daughters: Female Preaching and Popular Religion in Industrial England*, Princeton, NJ, 1985.

VELLACOT NEWBURY, JO, 'Anti-War Suffragists', *History*, 62 (1977), 411–425.

VICINUS, MARTHA, ed., *A Widening Sphere: Changing Roles of Victorian Women*, Bloomington, Ind., 1977.

—— *Independent Women: Work and Community for Single Women, 1850–1920*, London and Chicago, 1985.

VINCENT, JOHN, *The Formation of the British Liberal Party, 1857–68*, Harmondsworth, Middx., 1972.

VOGLER, MARTHA S., *Frederick Harrison: The Vocations of a Positivist*, Oxford, 1984.

WALKOWITZ, JUDITH R., *Prostitution and Victorian Society: Women, Class and the State*, Cambridge, 1980.

WARD, MAISIE, *Robert Browning and His World: The Private Face (1812–1861)*, London, 1968.

WEBB, BEATRICE, *My Apprenticeship*, London, 1926.

—— 'Women and the Factory Acts' (Fabian Tract No. 67), London, 1895.

Index